EUROPEAN AVANT-GARDE : NEW PERSPECTIVES

AVANT GARDE

CRITICAL STUDIES

15

EUROPEAN AVANT-GARDE : NEW PERSPECTIVES

Avantgarde – Avantgardekritik – Avantgardeforschung

Edited by

Dietrich Scheunemann

Amsterdam - Atlanta, GA 2000

All titles in the Avant Garde Critical Studies (from 1999 onwards)
are available to download and read from the CatchWord website:
http://www.catchword.co.uk

The paper on which this book is printed meets the requirements of "ISO 9706:1994, Information and documentation - Paper for documents - Requirements for permanence".

ISBN: 90-420-1204-8 (bound)

Printed in The Netherlands

CONTENTS

III. Avant-Garde in Context

PREFACE

This volume is designed to lay the foundations for a comprehensive reassessment of the European avant-garde movements of the 1910s and 1920s which have created such a wealth of new artistic techniques and new art forms in painting and literature, cabaret, theatre and film. For 25 years Peter Bürger's *Theory of the Avant-Garde* has shaped our understanding of these movements and has provided the frame for the discussion of its innovations and manifestations. It is to Bürger's credit that an integrating platform for the study of the avant-garde and a set of categories for the analysis of its artistic production has been established.

However, a quarter of a century on there is clearly a need to take the discussion further, to revise some of its co-ordinates and explore new approaches which might remedy shortfalls and replace the highly problematic basic assumption of Bürger's theory. This volume is intended to provide a fresh impetus in these directions. The reader might therefore find some prior indication helpful how the general approach towards the avant-garde in this volume differs from the set-up of Bürger's theory and which alternative avenues it intends to pursue.

A major problem in presenting a comprehensive discussion of the historical avant-garde movements arises in Bürger's theory from its restricted field of observation. The basic assumptions about the avant-garde are derived from an analysis of dadaist and early surrealist manifestations and of works of the "Russian avant-garde after the October revolution". The theory remains largely uninformed and at times helpless vis-à-vis those movements which have actually established the avant-garde as a vital force in the European art world, i.e. French cubism, Italian futurism, German expressionism and a variety of Russian movements before the revolution.

A theory of the avant-garde that deserves its name will have to integrate these early avant-garde movements into its frame of reference and may well derive the most important insights into historical, cultural and artistic factors determining the formation of the avant-garde from a thorough study of these movements. The construction of an alternative theory of the avant-garde, beginning with an exploration of cubist, futurist and expressionist art, will also illuminate the pioneering role which the new developments in painting played for the emergence of artistic innovations in other arts and for the dynamic advance of avant-garde movements throughout Europe.

Confining the field of observation to particular movements has enabled Bürger to construct a relatively homogenous discussion frame for his theory ascribing a single universal intention to the avant-garde, namely the intention of reintegrating art into the practice of life. "That art becomes practical once again", becomes the emphatically exposed outlook of the *Theory of the Avant-Garde*. Not surprisingly, such a formula is of little help in trying to understand the significance of the cubists' abandonment of spatial illusionism in painting or the expressionists' experiments with non-representational colour. And it is also difficult to see how this formula can be related to various forms of abstract painting in the early avant-garde movements.

Yet even when exploring the heartland of Bürger's theory, dadaist and surrealist works of painting and writing, or the work of Marcel Duchamp, the most distinctive representative of avant-gardist intentions, Bürger's general characterisation of the avant-garde remains highly questionable. Already the observation made by Duchamp in his discussion with Pierre Cabanne, namely that "African wooden spoons were nothing at the time when they were made, they were simply functional; later they became beautiful things, 'works of art'", suggests precisely the opposite of Bürger's speculative assumption, pointing to a transformation of practical objects into works of art rather than art becoming practical again. The issue is clearly more ambiguous and more complex than Bürger's formula indicates.

The contributors to this volume share the view that the formulaic characterisation of the avant-garde's intention based on a reversal of the aestheticists' call for separating the spheres of "art" and "life" rather than on a comprehensive analysis of the manifestos and activities of the great variety of the historical avant-garde movements, requires careful dismantling. The formula is all too coarse, the categories of "art" and "life" are in urgent need of differentiation, and the basic assumption of a unified intention of the avant-garde, i.e. the intention of reintegrating art into the life process, is far too simplistic to serve as a guide to the exciting diversity and complex nature of the manifestations of the avant-garde. It is also inadequate in terms of the historiographic armature of the theory. Describing whole epochs or movements in cultural history in terms of a single, unified style, philosophical outlook or intention was a favourite exercise of our critical ancestors, but can hardly be considered an enlightened method of contemporary historiography or criticism of art and literature.

A new approach towards a comprehensive assessment of the avant-garde will need to overcome the confinements and constrictions of its current theory. It will need to establish a wider discussion frame by integrating early avant-garde movements in its theoretical construction. It will have to confront more clearly the complex and often contradictory nature of the avant-garde's manifestations and its theoretical discourses. And it will have to open up the discussion to include neo-avant-gardist manifestations emerging since the 1960s, dismissed by Bürger as "inauthentic" gestures of protest and surprisingly marginalised in recent discussions of modernism and postmodernism. An exploration of the neo-avant-garde will, however, require the story of the avant-garde to be rewritten, taking into consideration the fact that it was not a self-inflicted "failure of sublating art into the practice of life", but the political forces of European Fascism and Stalinist cultural politics which strangled the avant-garde and its further development in the 1930s. Little insight has so far been provided into the significance of the reappropriation of avant-garde principles and artistic practices which have been gaining momentum since the 1960s.

Extending the frame of discussion is one of the changes, replacing the simplistic formulaic approach by an exploration of the multifaceted, complex and often contradictory nature of the great variety of avant-gardist innovations is another urgent undertaking proposed by the contributions to this volume for the future orientation of avant-garde studies. Both these shifts by necessity imply the development of new categories of description and assessment of avant-garde manifestations as well as a redefinition and refinement of existing parameters. A revised theoretical framework will also have to include art forms which have often been discussed in their own right, but only rarely in terms of their significance for, and their contribution to, the development of the avant-garde. This applies to cabaret and other forms of performance as well as to avant-garde cinema.

In order to prepare the ground for a revised picture of the avant-garde, a more circumspect contextualisation of its formation and development will also be required. This will involve investigations into dominant cultural technologies of the period concerned as well as a variety of scientific parameters. It is one of the contentions pursued in this volume that the advance of new technical media of reproduction provided vital momentum for the emergence of new art forms and new artistic techniques, and that the interaction between traditional art forms and the new technical possibilities was one of the major driving forces behind the creation of the great wealth of innovations in avant-garde art. New questions will also be raised concerning the institutional framework for the production, communication and reception of art and literature. The immaterial nature of "art as an institution" as presented in Bürger's theory certainly calls for investigations which try to put the category of "institution" on its feet.

In trying to lay new foundations for the study of such a wide-ranging field of artistic activity as represented by the avant-garde, a single volume can only attempt to provide initial outlines of alternative approaches and put forward first proposals of a revised practice of interpretation. The present volume starts with three contributions which present the avant-garde, its formation and further development from a perspective which emphasises the role which the advance of new cultural technologies played for the radical changes in artistic technique and the understanding of art's nature and function. Not surprisingly, Walter Benjamin's seminal essay on "The Work of Art in the Age of Mechanical Reproduction", criticised by Bürger in its materialistic approach, acts here as an important guide to new discoveries.

In the following chapters the book presents a range of essays on avant-gardist and neo-avant-gardist concepts, productions and trends, which aim to give as wide and varied a picture of avant-gardist innovations as possible ranging from cubist painting and the screeching voices of futurism to dadaist photomontage and film, surrealist photographs and sculptures and an illuminating episode of the Russian avant-garde. Investigations also include neo-avant-gardist theory and practice as developed by the French avant-garde group OuLiPo. The fact that Gertrude Stein appears in one of the first and the last of these essays is a *chance event*, underlining, though, the importance of Stein's explorations into the properties of her artistic material for the development of avant-gardist writing. The volume concludes with three articles which derive new insights from placing the avant-garde in the broader contexts of literary institutions and of psychoanalytical and sociological concepts and methods of thought.

The main body of the present volume is based on presentations and discussions from a three-day research seminar held as part of the annual meeting of the American Comparative Literature Association at Yale University, New Haven, in February 2000. I would like to thank Catherine Labio for her excellent support in organising the seminar. The research group formed on this occasion intends to continue with its efforts to elaborate a new theory of the avant-garde in the coming years, starting with a symposium to be held at the University of Edinburgh in September 2001.

Edinburgh, September 2000

D.S.

I.

REWRITING THE THEORY OF THE AVANT-GARDE

ON PHOTOGRAPHY AND PAINTING. PROLEGOMENA TO A NEW THEORY OF THE AVANT-GARDE.

DIETRICH SCHEUNEMANN

I.

In his introduction to an exhibition of paintings by Max Ernst, André Breton maintained that "the invention of photography has dealt a mortal blow to the old modes of expression, in painting as well as in poetry" (Breton 1948: 177). Breton's statement is of particular value for the development of a new approach to the study of the avant-garde for several reasons. It highlights the significant role which the advent of photography and more generally of technical reproduction played for the radical changes in artistic techniques and the development of new art forms in the first decades of the last century. By so doing, it draws attention to the fact that material pressures emanating from technological advances and not a common ideological orientation or unified intention of the various art movements provided the main impetus for the development of the new modes of expression. In addition, the statement lends support and authority to the assumption that the impact of technological changes reached beyond the sphere of the visual arts, affecting literary production as well.

In following up Breton's observation this essay aims to establish a new approach to the avant-garde, to the wealth of its innovations and its relevance for the present. The essay takes as its basic assumption that not one common intention, i.e. the intention of reintegrating art into the practice of life, but a common challenge caused the avant-gardist storm in the arts world, the challenge which the advances of new technical media, in particular photography and film, posed to traditional art forms and the traditional understanding of art. The immense wealth, diversity and often provocative nature of the artistic innovations developed by the avant-garde represent nothing other than the range of responses to this challenge and various modes of reflecting upon the place which artistic production can hold in an age in which industrialisation and technological processes rapidly gained ground in all other realms of life.

To approach the avant-garde this way means that the formulaic description of the avant-garde's assumed intention which Peter Bürger imposed on some of the movements, whilst excluding others from closer investigation because they did not fit the formula, will be abandoned altogether. It simply does not make sense to squeeze the great variety and wealth of innovations produced by the avant-garde under different paroles and with different aims in view into the confines of a single formula. Starting with a consideration of the material conditions and challenges of artistic work will instead encourage a theoretical framework that pays attention to the gradual formation of a growing variety of artistic practice in the avant-garde movements and takes into account differences as well as convergences in their development. Such an approach will also need to take on board the fact that it was painting, not literature nor aesthetic theory, which provided the first, igniting sparks for the revolutions in all the arts. It is the abandonment of the age-old spatial conception of the Renaissance in cubist painting, not the literary celebration of roaring racing cars in the futurist manifesto, nor any ideological project resembling the proposed intention of sublating art into the practice of life, that marked the beginning and served as a constant reference point of the avant-garde's epochal innovations.

The idea of taking the impact of technological innovation as a starting point for an alternative approach to the avant-garde, does of course not come out of the blue. Along with Breton's statement Walter Benjamin's essay on "The Work of Art in the Age of Mechanical Reproduction" has acted as an important stimulus for the formulation of this approach. It is the general focus which the essay places on the repercussions of technological reproduction for the understanding of art, and the particular question "whether the very invention of photography had not transformed the entire nature of art" (Benjamin 1973: 229), that have encouraged the present attempt to rewrite the theory of the avant-garde. The present essay will not take up Benjamin's melancholic and ambiguous concept of the *loss of the aura*, and will not take on board some of the conclusions at which Benjamin arrived in his time, but will try to make the *questions* which Benjamin raised fruitful for a reassessment of the avant-garde.

Benjamin's deliberations were of course familiar to Bürger, but he rejects them on several grounds. Particularly relevant in this context is the last point which Bürger brings up in his critique. Although conceding that he does not wish to "deny the importance the development of techniques of reproduction has [...] for the evolution of the fine arts", he keeps any consideration of the impact of technological developments on the arts at arm's length because of what he considers the limitations of Benjamin's "materialist explanatory scheme":

> Because the advent of photography makes possible the precise mechanical reproduction of reality, the mimetic function of the fine arts withers. But the limits of this explanatory model become clear when one calls to mind that it cannot be transferred to literature. For in literature, there is no technical innovation that could have produced an effect comparable to that of photography in the fine arts. (Bürger 1984: 32)

The first of these assumptions highlighting the fading away of the mimetic function in the fine arts is a statement of great importance, providing a platform for the discussion of a range of significant changes in all the arts. Unfortunately, Bürger does not pursue this point any further. Concerning his attempt to confine the explanatory model to the fine arts, however, Bürger overlooks the fact that significant changes in one art will normally also affect others, the more so if the changes are of such a fundamental nature that they affect the principle task of all arts, the task of *imitatio naturae*.

Not only Breton, but other contemporary authors too have reflected on this issue in similar terms. Bertolt Brecht, who serves as a reference point and authority for Bürger in relation to other aspects of his critique, has provided a very different prospect in this question. In his essay on the *Threepenny Lawsuit* he maintained that

> the old forms of communication are not unaffected by the development of new ones, nor do they survive alongside them. The filmgoer develops a different way of reading stories. But the man who writes the stories is a filmgoer too. The mechanisation of literary production cannot be thrown into reverse. Once instruments are used even the novelist who makes no use of them is led to wish that he could do what the instruments can; to include what they show [...] as part of that reality which constitutes his subject-matter; and, above all, when he writes, to assume the attitude of somebody using an instrument. (Brecht 1978: 47)

Other contemporary comments, including Paul Valéry's farsighted prediction of profound changes to the "physical component" in all the arts, which affects "artistic invention itself" and "our very notion of art", likewise showed a greater sensitivity for the relevance of the technological innovations for all branches of the "ancient craft of the beautiful" than Bürger is prepared to allow (cf. Benjamin 1973: 219). Even the concept of a *pure novel* which André Gide developed in his novel *Les Faux-Monnayeurs* drew its legitimacy from a reflection of the technological inventions affecting the visual arts as well as literature:

> Just as photography [...] freed painting from its concern for a certain sort of accuracy, so the phonograph will eventually no doubt rid the novel of the kind of dialogue which is drawn from the life and which realists take so much pride in. Outward events, accidents, traumatisms belong to the cinema. The novel should leave them to it. (Gide 1966: 70-71)

Strangely enough, all these observations of contemporary writers were not taken on board by Bürger. Neither *photography* nor the *phonograph* nor *cinema* found their way into the fabric of his theory. A discussion of the role which cinema played for the development of the most important new artistic technique in avant-garde art, the technique of montage, is even explicitly excluded — with the short-sighted argument that *montage* in cinema is merely a "technical procedure", not a "specifically artistic technique" (Bürger

1984: 73). The very existence of an avant-garde cinema is not even noted.

The present essay must leave the discussion of some of the issues raised to other contributions and to further explorations of the avant-garde on other occasions. What it aims to present, however, is an outline of the lively interaction between photography and painting in the formative years of the avant-garde, the variety of repercussions provoked by the advance of photography and the relevance which these developments had for other art forms, in particular for the literary production of the avant-garde. It will hardly come as a surprise to find that painters as well as writers showed little concern for the idiosyncrasies of aestheticism and the question of the autonomous status of bourgeois art in their comments. In trying to find a place and legitimate task for painting in an age in which the techniques of technological reproduction were rapidly advancing, they were instead fully engaged in projecting and testing radical departures from photographic imagery and alternatives to imitative functions of their art. It was indeed the age-old mimetic function of all the arts that came under attack at this point. In terms of the artistic style of historical periods it meant that any realist, naturalist or impressionist conception of art and artistic production was consigned to the past.

II.

In a compilation of statements by cubist and futurist, expressionist, dadaist and surrealist painters Aaron Scharf has provided impressive evidence of the painters' great concern about the advances of the rival medium of photography and the need they felt to respond to photography's triumphs by searching for new modes of expression in their own métier. These should, as the cubist painter Albert Gleizes believed, "perforce be antagonistic to the photographic image" (cf. Scharf 1983: 252). Pablo Picasso rarely commented on his work. Fernande Olivier, however, has handed down a statement by Picasso which is of great significance in this context. "I have discovered photography", he is claimed to have said, "now I can kill myself" (Baldassari 1997:17). In an article of 1913 Fernand Léger, hinting at a correspondence between the revolution accomplished by

"Gutenberg's invention in the field of human expression" and the changes resulting from more recent inventions such as colour photography and the cinematograph, emphasises the antiquated nature of "representational subjects" and "visual realism" in painting in the light of these "modern mechanical achievements". How can all those historical or dramatic pictures shown at the French Salons, he asks, "hope to compete with what is shown on the screen of any cinema in the world" (Fry 1966: 125).

Critics were quick to support the cubist project of leaving behind the academic task of imitating nature. "Imitation may be an art", Maurice Raynal pointed out, "but one that photography may easily bring to perfection" (Fry 1966: 91). Guillaume Apollinaire, a long-standing friend of Picasso's who had been instrumental in establishing the close cooperation between Picasso and Georges Braque, echoed Raynal's sentiment in his famous celebration of the cubist painters. "Photographers manufacture duplicates of nature", he maintained, not without a hint of derogation. The cubist painters, however, while still looking at nature, "no longer imitate it". Their art, Apollinaire pronounces enthusiastically, is an "art of conception", rising to the "height of creation" (Apollinaire 1962: 11 and 17).

Although cubist, futurist and expressionist painters developed different styles and pursued different goals in their artistic practice, including such traditional aims as "glorifying all forms of originality" (Boccioni 1973b: 30), or observing the artist's "inner necessities" (Kandinsky 1968: 158), the project of departing from imitative modes of representing nature was common to all movements — and also the reason referred to as to why this age-old artistic task had become superfluous and outmoded. "Given the existence of photography and of the cinema", the Italian futurist painter Giacomo Balla remarked, "the pictorial representation of the truth does not and cannot any longer interest anyone". Ernst Ludwig Kirchner, the leading artist of the German expressionist group "Die Brücke", maintains in similar terms that "today photography takes over exact representation. Thus painting, relieved from this task, gains its former freedom of action" (cf. Scharf 1983: 253). Scharf regrets the "negative character" of many of the contemporary references to photography and cinema, and feels that the modern techniques of reproduction are rather unreasonably turned into scapegoats to conceal a multitude of sins on the side of the artists. However, the negative accent is merely an expression of the partisan approach which painters and critics took in this matter. What they essentially suggest, however, is a distribution of labour between photography and painting, reserving the traditional mimetic function of the arts to photography while opening up new domains for the art of painting.

The search for new tasks and new techniques of painting is ex negativo determined by the fact that it must lead to modes of production and perception that differ from those of the photographic camera. This applies indeed in a rather conspicuous way to all the major new stylistic features of painting in all avant-garde movements. The series of innovations conceived by the cubist painters was the most convincing overture to it. As Edward Fry emphasised in his excellent introduction to a collection of critical articles on cubist painting, it was the particular treatment of space, the abandonment of the "spatial illusionism of the one-point perspective", which along with the reduction of the human figure to geometrical shapes was the extraordinary starting point for the range of radical aesthetic innovations in cubist painting (Fry 1966: 13). Replacing the one-point perspective, a traditional feature of European painting since the Renaissance, with a combination of multiple view-points in one and the same image undermined the traditional coherence and uniformity in the organisation of the pictorial space. At the same time, the introduction of multi-perspective composition set off a range of further related devices such as the fragmentation and faceting of depicted objects, or the use of letters and figures in painting, also unseen in European painting since the Middle Ages.

How closely the introduction of letters and figures was related to the cubist painters' central concern with the pictorial treatment of space and the related mode of perception of the viewer is made clear by Braque, who maintained that letters and figures

> being themselves flat were not in space and thus, by contrast, their presence in the picture made it possible to distinguish between objects situated in space and those which were not. (Cooper 1983: 64)

However, it is not only the insertion of "flat" letters and figures, but also the invention of collage which springs from the same source.

Still Life with Chair Caning, the first collage in modern art, made by Picasso in May 1912, offers the strongest, though frequently overlooked indication of it.

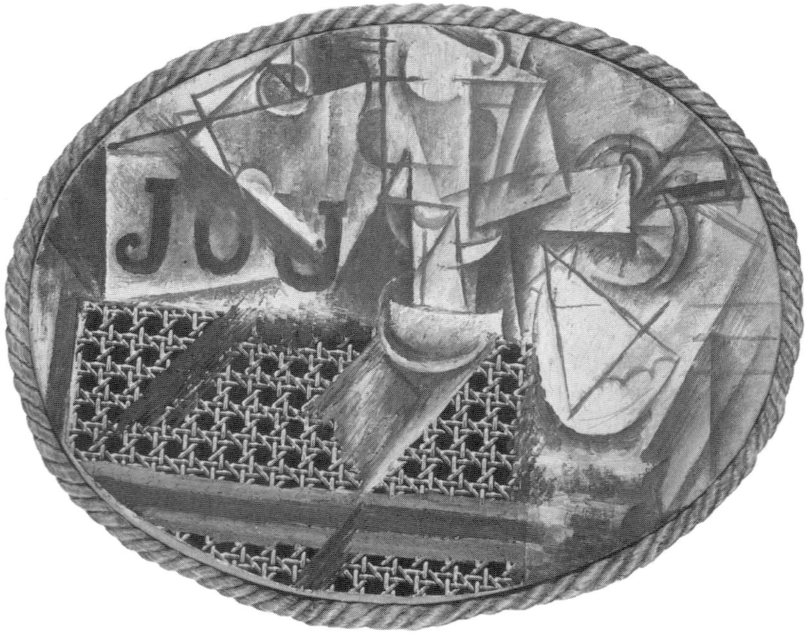

1 Pablo Picasso: *Still Life with Chair Caning*. 1912

The still life consists of a range of characteristic cubist notations of a newspaper, a glass, a pipe, a sliced lemon and a scallop shell painted in oil on an oval canvas. The fragmented notation of the title of a journal is inserted in black letters. The canvas is framed by a piece of rope. The remarkable feature of the picture, which transcends previous cubist innovations, however, is a piece of oil-cloth stuck onto the canvas. The oil-cloth bears the pattern of chair caning imprinted on its fabric. It is not uncommon to find *Still Life with Chair Caning* discussed as an encounter between illusion and reality, art and real objects, or in terms of an insertion of "reality fragments" into the art work (cf. Bernadac 1991: 44). Bürger's *Theory of the Avant-Garde* extends these questionable distinctions even further by confusing the oil-cloth with a real "piece of woven basket" (Bürger 1984: 77-78). William Rubin counters such readings, "which abound in discussions of collage", with the simple remark that Picasso "could have acquired and affixed to his canvas a piece of chair caning" had he wished (Rubin 1989: 37). However, what he inserted was neither a piece of chair caning, nor a piece of woven basket, but a piece of oil-cloth "*picturing* chair caning". With good reason Pierre Daix highlights the fact that the insertion of the imprinted piece of oil-cloth was the "inroad of an industrial sign into painting" (Daix 1982: 99). To be even more precise: it is the inroad of the industrial technique of photographic reproduction into the realm of the fine arts. The rival of painting, photographic reproduction, and the alternative developed by the cubist painters, the faceted, multi-perspective notation of objects, are brought together and confront each other on the same canvas. *Still Life with Chair Caning* thus tells the story of the formation of the avant-garde and encapsulates the nucleus of its theory.

While the cubist painters relentlessly explored the properties of artistic materials and techniques, both futurist and expressionist painters began with rather decisive views concerning the subject matter of their pictures. They also concentrated on different core innovations in developing their specific pictorial styles and techniques. Celebrating the "frenetic life of our great cities", the "whirling life of steel, of pride, of fever and of speed", the futurist painters declared the inscription of "universal dynamism" into their pictures through "movement and light" to be their primary goal (Boccioni 1973a: 25; 1973b: 30). In order to depict motion, energy and the dynamism of contemporary life, the futurist painters developed pictorial strategies designed to transcend the genuinely static nature of the medium. The cubist painters had preserved, even emphasised this quality by advancing their radical innovations within the framework of the traditional genre of still life. Although the futurist painters adopted some of the stylistic features of cubism, above all the practice of fragmentation and the multi-perspective organisation of the painting, they put these devices to different use in the context of their particular aims. Through superimposing successive phases of motion and inscribing rays of energy into their pictures the futurist painters developed an explosive style of painting leaving behind the contemplative mode of reception normally associated with still lives, portraits and landscapes. The exhibition of futurist paintings touring the capitals of Europe made the Italian brand of "anti-traditionalist" innovations known in all quarters of the European art world in the first months of 1912.

Expressionist painters emphasised throughout that not the visual world with its discernible contours, but inner urges of the artist and the "inner side of nature" determined their approach to the pictorial organisation of their pictures. "We no longer cling to the reproduction of nature", Franz Marc states, but reveal instead "the mighty laws which hold sway behind the beautiful exterior" (cf. Dube 1972: 132). Similarly, Ernst Ludwig Kirchner and Wassily Kandinsky having renounced photographic imagery emphasise that the creative process is determined not by the detailed depiction of "material objects", but by "sensual experience" and "inner necessity" (cf. Buchheim 1956:174; Kandinsky 1968: 158). The main pictorial strategy which the expressionist painters developed to achieve this aim was, along with the reduction of natural forms, the non-representational use of colour. Just as the exploration into perspective marked the beginning of a new era of painting in France, it was the use of colour as an emotional and mental indicator, rather than a means of rendering objects recognisable, that signalled the beginning of a new era in Germany. In Kirchner's oscillating street scenes, dominated by a confined, yet powerful scale of colours, and Kandinsky's abstract compositions with their remote ciphers of objects and freely floating colours, expressionist painting soon attained its ultimate forms.

Abolishing the traditional spatial illusionism of painting, overcoming its traditional static nature and making use of the expressive power of colour represent a variety of strategies by which the first movements of the avant-garde fundamentally changed the art of painting. Although the strategies of the various movements differ, and each developed its own, unmistakable profile in terms of general aims and specific styles and techniques, they all have one moment in common: their aesthetic innovations emerged as a response to the advances of photography. They counter photographic imagery, the precise depiction of material objects, the illusionism of forms of representation striving for imitative functions. In their place they offer pictorial forms, functions and effects which not even the "most perfect camera" can attain(Matisse, in Scharf 1983: 253).

III.

However, the formation of the avant-garde follows neither a single, uniform intention, nor does it advance in a one-dimensional fashion. Through her intensive research Anne Baldassari, the curator of the Musée Picasso, has recently brought to light the fact that Picasso's interest in photography was not at all limited to the use of photographs as source material for paintings or the insertion of the piece of photographic reproduction in the first collage in modern art. Picasso experimented widely with "photographic compositions" and with a variety of transformations of such compositions into graphic drawings, constructions with wood and other materials and also etchings (cf. Baldassari 1997: 106-124).

Of even greater importance was the application of photographic technique in futurist painting. Although futurist artists fiercely "rejected with disgust and contempt even the most distant relationship" of their works with photography, let alone any relationship with the experiments in chronophotography which Eadweard Muybridge and Etienne-Lules Marey had carried out since the late 1870s, it is generally accepted that not only the famous statement in the *Technical Manifesto of Futurist Painting*, "thus a running horse has not four legs, but twenty", but also the way in which motion was depicted by the futurist painters are clearly indebted to the chronophotographic studies of motion. Thus critics had every good reason to relate the paintings to "instantaneous photographs" and highlight their "cinematographic tendency" (cf. Scharf 1983:258). However, the fact that they presented such characterisations as a critique and denunciation of the new school of painting, rather than as a discovery of an exciting novelty, seems to have hindered the futurists from openly promoting the shift of the boundaries of art which they had undertaken in their artistic practice. The fact that in commenting on their own creative practice the futurist painters kept the worlds of art and technology strictly and categorically apart is particularly surprising, as the celebration of modern technology is otherwise at the heart of the futurist movement. Nowhere else does the dilemma in which painting finds itself entangled vis-à-vis the advance of means and modes of technical reproduction emerge with greater clarity than in the contradictory stance of the futurist painters. It was Marcel Duchamp who did not hesitate to identify the chronophotographic source of the pictorial strategies employed. Commenting on his own experiment in the "static representation of movement" in *Nude Descending a Stair-Case*, which adopts the same technique of depicting motion through the superimposition of successive images, Duchamp explained the technique as a

> convergence of various interests, among them the cinema, still in its infancy, and the separation of static positions in the photo-chronographs of Marey in France, Eakins and Muybridge in America. (Rowell 1994: 45)

Duchamp thus removed the spell, paving the way for a concept of art which ultimately accommodates technical reproduction as an integral part of artistic production.

The invention of photomontage by the Berlin dadaists makes it entirely clear that the response to the advance of photography was not a one-dimensional departure from photographic imagery and technique, but a dialectical process in which the avant-garde initially developed a range of radically new, non-mimetic techniques and styles, but eventually integrated photographic material and technical processes into its newly furnished arsenal of artistic possibilities. While cubist and futurist experiments had already prepared for the full orchestration of this double-sided process, and Duchamp had mapped out the terrain, it was the emergence of dadaist photomontage through which the encounter between traditional art forms and new forms of technological reproduction reached a new quality. Mass-produced photographic material formed the basis of the new art form, calling into question the validity of a number of traditional artistic concepts such as *originality* and *uniqueness*, the veneration of *handicraft* and *personal style* and above all the demarcation of art and technological reproduction. The dadaist photomontage marks the point where technological reproduction becomes a recognised integral part of artistic production.

The dadaist inventors of photomontage were clearly aware of the fact that the new artistic technique and new art form they had developed implied a far-reaching shift in the idea and the very notion of art. Raoul Hausmann, who according to Hans Richter was the "self-styled inventor of this technique" and its first theorist (Richter 1965: 116), makes the point that the term "photomontage" was chosen for the new technique in order to accentuate the break with traditional notions of art and the artist:

> We called this process photomontage because it embodied our refusal to play the part of the artist. We regarded ourselves as engineers, and our work as construction. (cf. Richter 1965: 118)

Hausmann's description of photomontage is of particular value also for two other reasons. Notwithstanding the reluctance of the dadaists "to play the part of the artist", the definition provides a precise and most convincing account of the *artistic* techniques employed and the *aesthetic* qualities achieved in photomontage:

> Photomontage in its earliest form was an explosive mixture of different points of view and levels, more extreme in its complexity than futuristic painting. [...] With its contrast of structure and dimension, rough against smooth, aerial photograph against close-up, perspective against flat surface, the utmost technical flexibility and the most lucid formal dialectics are equally possible. [...] The formal dialectic qualities which are inherent in photomontage, ensures the medium a long and richly productive span of life. (cf. Richter 1965: 116)

By emphasising the "mixture of different points of view" and the particular effects which photomontage draws from the structural contrasts of its materials, Hausmann confirms that the invention of photo-montage was far removed from any intention to regain exactness in the representation of objects or develop a *new objectivity* in pictorial style. Rather the opposite is the case. Photomontage builds on the advanced artistic techniques which had been developed by the cubist and futurist artists. Although based on photographic material, whose prime property is the authentic reproduction of objects, the application of new artistic devices such as fragmentation, the combination of multiple view-points and cinematic effects not only prevented a recourse to any realist, illusionist mode of artistic production, but actually pushed photomontage to the forefront of the avant-gardist revolution in the arts. Nowhere else was the spatial illusionism of the one-point perspective more radically undermined and replaced by a myriad of visual facets than in the early forms of photomontage. Nowhere else do we encounter a

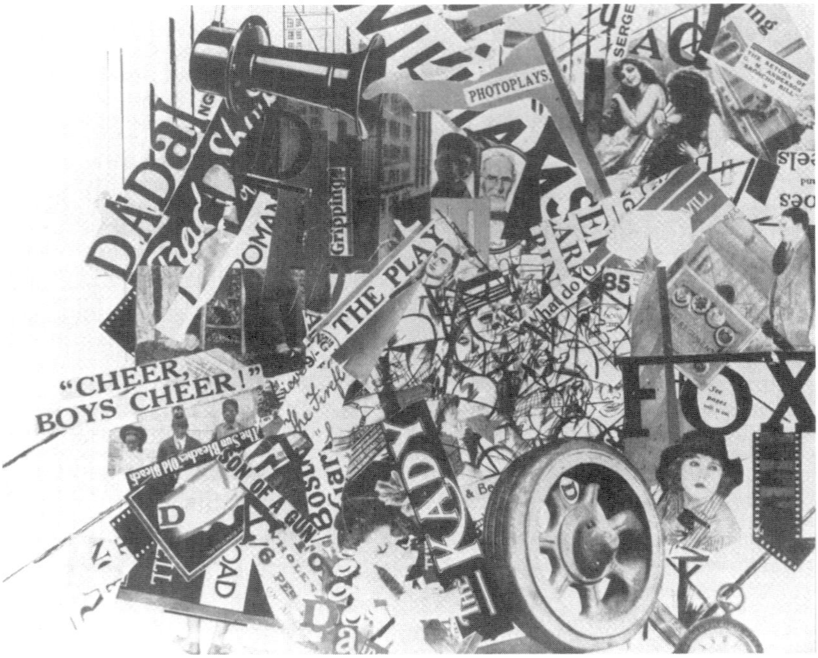

2 George Grosz and John Heartfield: *Life and Activity in Universal City at 12.05 midday*. 1919

visually more explosive combination of interlocking planes, different levels and different angles of perception. And no other art form of the decade showed a greater affinity to cinematic effects than photomontage. In contrast to the futurist painters, Hausmann saw no reason to hide this fact. Quite the opposite. He emphasised the cinematic relationship of the new art form by referring to photomontage as "a kind of motionless moving picture" (cf. Richter 1965: 129).

One of the first photomontages produced by George Grosz and John Heartfield clearly foregrounds this affinity. *Life and Activity in Universal City at 12.05 midday* alludes to a Hollywood studio complex in its title. A range of references to film and "photoplay" are inserted into the picture. Photomontage, emerging from cubist collage and anticipating a new aesthetics of film, moved very much into the centre of the avant-garde transformation of the concept of art. The fact that a transformation, not a destruction or sublation of art was intended, is emphasised by one of the panels at the *First International Dada Fair* in Berlin in 1920. "Art is dead", the panel reads, only to continue: "Long live Tatlin's new machine art". The panel was surrounded by photomontages.

IV.

In his "Foreword" to Bürger's *Theory of the Avant-Garde* Jochen Schulte-Sasse rightly points out that

> the success of any theory of the avant-garde can be measured by how convincingly it can anchor the avant-garde formal principle of the collage and montage. (Bürger 1984: xxxix)

It is here where Bürger fails most spectacularly. This is partly due to a lack of precise observation and categorisation, partly to the overall approach of the theory. In dealing with cubist collage Bürger not only confuses the imprinted oil-cloth, a photographic imitation of chair caning, with a woven basket, a "reality fragment", but also the technique of collage with montage. When discussing montage, he refers positively for once to Benjamin's writings. However, as Ansgar Hillach has already pointed out, the reference is unfortunately not to the essays in which Benjamin actually discusses the new technique (Hillach 1976: 105). Instead, Bürger refers to Benjamin's discussion of Baroque allegory, ultimately likening photomontage to the Baroque emblem. Such analogies do certainly not present the most convincing description of an art form based on modern technology. In addition, Büger's claim to a resemblance between emblem and photomontage can only be made on the basis of a rather questionable selection of works.

Bürger concentrates on photomontages by John Heartfield produced in the early 1930s, when dada was dead and political pressures had brought about a transformation of the genuine form of dadaist photomontage into more easily accessible *reading pictures*. Focusing on these pictures enabled Bürger to avoid any reference to technical reproduction in general, and to those art forms in particular in which montage most spectacularly presented itself as the new dominant principle of aesthetic organisation: in genuine dadaist photo-montage, in the cinema of Sergei Eisenstein and, as illustrated by Benjamin, in literary works by Brecht and Döblin.

Bürger's decision to bar cinema from entering his discussion of montage, is based on a notion of art that does not keep pace with the changes which the avant-garde had inflicted on it. In the chapter of his book entitled "Montage" Bürger explains: "In the film, the montage of images is the basic *technical procedure*. It is not a specifically artistic technique." It is only in painting, he maintains, "in the *papiers collés* of Picasso and Braque", that montage obtains "the status of an artistic principle" (Bürger 1984: 73).

Montage in film may of course be understood as the mere *technical procedure* of cutting and gluing of film strips. Yet cubist collage involves a similar *technical* procedure too. While Bürger is prepared to recognise the artistic status of collage — perhaps because a collage also includes drawing and painting by hand in addition to the procedure of cutting and gluing — he is unable to appreciate cannot make out the working of art in filmic montage. Such an approach not only falls short of recognising the transformation of art that emerged in the pronouncements and practice of the avant-garde; it also falls short in principle of any theory of film, and in particular of the aesthetic idiosyncracies of avant-garde cinema. Standish Lawder points out that

> in its broadest outlines the avant-garde film movement followed a course similar to modern painting [...] from a rigorously geometric and abstract style [...] to the hallucinatory content of Surrealism in the late twenties. (Lawder 1975: 35)

In its abstract beginnings in the work of Walter Ruttmann, Viking Eggeling, Hans Richter and Man Ray, and on a grand scale in the films of Eisenstein and Dziga Vertov, the technique of montage was very much at the centre of avant-garde film aesthetics. Although Eisenstein in his articles on *montage of attractions* from 1923 and 1924 maintained that montage as "a new method of structuring a show" could be applied to various art forms — to theatre, cinema and the music-hall (Eisenstein 1988a: 33 and 35) — he emphasised at the same time the great advantage which accompanied its use in cinema. Only here does the juxtaposition of independent images and sequences at the artistic level meet with the basic technical conditions of the medium (Eisenstein 1988b: 40-41). The development of an aesthetic structure which rests on a corresponding technical procedure and is supported in its effects by the characteristics of cinematic perception has made montage such a powerful concept and the undisputed axiom of Russian avant-garde cinema.

Unfortunately, Bürger excludes the whole area of avant-gardist film aesthetics from his theory. He appears so anxious to avoid a discussion of technological input in the artistic production and aesthetic considerations of the avant-garde that along with the cinema even photomontage is ultimately discarded as a useful reference point for the discussion of montage:

> Within the frame of a theory of the avant-garde, the use to which film puts the concept cannot become relevant because it is part and parcel of the medium. And photomontage will not be made the point of departure for a consideration of the concept for it occupies an intermediate position between montage in films and montage in painting. [...] A theory of the avant-garde must begin with the concept of montage that is suggested by the early cubist collages. What distinguishes them from the techniques of composition developed since the Renaissance is the insertion of reality fragments into the painting. (Bürger 1984: 76-77)

The reference to the "reality fragment" in early cubist collage leads the reader back to the "piece of woven basket" which Picasso is supposed to have glued onto the canvas and to the conclusion which Bürger draws from it, i.e. that parts of the picture are "no longer signs pointing to reality, they *are* reality" (Bürger 1984: 78). Neither the oil-cloth in Picasso's first collage, nor the "imitation wood" in cubist *papiers collés*, nor the photo-bits of dadaist photomontages live up to that expectation. It is not the relationship between art and reality (or the practice of life), but the challenge of technological reproduction to the art of painting which is thematised by collage as well as photomontage. The conceptual framework of Bürger's theory, it seems, affects the precision of his observations and leads to unsound categorisation.

Starting from the alternative observation that an industrially produced photographic imitation of a pattern of chair caning forms part of the first collage, and that mass-produced photographic reproductions provide the material basis for dadaist photomontage, together with the fact that both art forms as well as film employ a technique of cutting and gluing as dominant artistic device in constructing the work of art, other conclusions concerning the significance of montage seem to be called for. The emergence of the technique of montage is an integral part of the process of the adoption of photographic materials and reproduction techniques in the art production of the avant-garde. Its aim is not to exploit the representational properties of technological reproduction, but rather the opposite: to integrate technological reproduction into the highly constructive modes of artistic production developed by the avant-garde in its radical departure from imitative functions in its formative years. The main achievement of the new technique is the juxtaposition of fragmented, faceted materials of different origins, perspectives and proportions, provoking an active contribution from the viewer in establishing relationships between the disparate materials displayed. Through the juxtaposition of disparate materials montage abolishes the homogeneous, continuous shape of traditional art forms. Their surface is split up into heterogeneous elements, their uniformity replaced by the diversity of the material fragments. When applied to cinema, montage as a technique of the avant-garde undermines in principle the *continuity style* which main-stream narrative cinema has made its dominant feature. Interrupting spatial orientation and juxtaposing discontinuous images is consequently the avant-garde cinema's preferred option.

Just as the rules of the traditional one-point perspective had wider implications than merely providing the principles of the formal organisation of an art work, one may be tempted to try to discern the ideological or at least perceptual implications of its replacement. In his essay on "Symbolic Form as a Vivid Cognitive Principle" Klaus Honnef has recently attempted to do precisely that. Beginning with the assumption that "since the pioneering achievements of the Renaissance, the world view of the fine arts has rested in the established structure of the one-point perspective", he observes that this mode of perception "disappeared into the chasms of the interrupted perspectival space of cubist painting" and the "heterogeneous and discontinuous space of montage" which he sees currently taking hold of film and modern theatre, literature and the fine arts (Honnef 1992: 4 and 8). He therefore concludes that

> montage appears not only as a symbolic form of our time but also as a model of a view of the world and its experience, as self-evident [to us] as perspective was to our ancestors. (Honnef 1992: 13)

Montage did indeed become the avant-garde's fully developed alternative concept to the traditional central-perspectival organisation of art works. To what extent the characteristics of its perceptive properties have become self-evident to us, or not obstructed by cultural conventions, may have to remain unresolved.

V.

As an extension of Jochen Schulte-Sasse's proposition one may wish to suggest that a theory of the avant-garde needs to offer not only a convincing description and explanation of the technique of montage, but also of the work of Marcel Duchamp. In particular Duchamp's ready-mades have come to be recognised as epitomising the spirit of the avant-garde. In spite of the myths surrounding his work, and also in spite also of Joseph Beuys' warning that "Marcel Duchamp's silence has been overrated" (cf. Blume 1999:494), a cogent qualification of his manifestations represents the inescapable touchstone for any theory of the avant-garde.

Bürger has rightly placed considerable emphasis on Duchamp's work. He refers at great length in particular to the celebrated case of the *Fountain*, considering it in terms of its provocative effect on the art market where "the signature means more than the quality of the work", and at the same time as a prime example of what Bürger calls the "negation of the category of individual production" (Bürger 1984: 51-52). Concerning the institutional provocation, Bürger quickly comes to the conclusion that once ready-mades have been accepted as objects deserving "a place in a museum, the provocation no longer provokes". Indeed, neither the art market nor institutions of art exhibition will consider Duchamp's work a provocation any longer. However, the *Fountain's* history has probably less been determined by acts of "provocation" and "acceptance" than by the inspiration which it has given to a wide range of artists from John Cage to Jasper Jones and Andy Warhol to Joseph Beuys. Instead of pursuing the creative impact which Duchamp's invention had on the

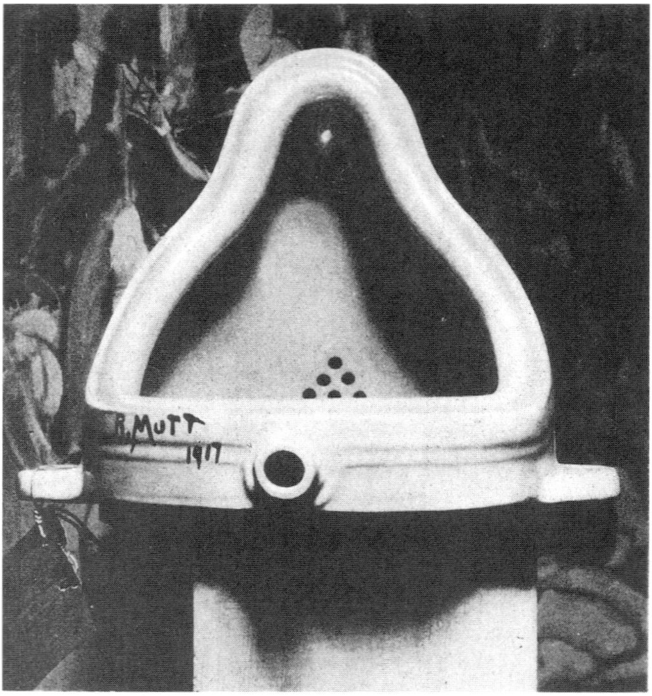

3 Marcel Duchamp: *Fountain*. 1917

further development of major manifestations of 20th century art, Bürger unfortunately dismisses the latter as "inauthentic gestures of protest" (Bürger 1984: 53).

Concerning his diagnosis of a "negation of the category of individual production", this categorisation again lacks precision. The category of *individual production* is introduced in Bürger's theory as the opposite of *collective production* (Bürger 1984: 47-48). Reading the *Fountain* and ready-mades in general as acts of a negation of *individual creation* may in such a context raise false expectations, expectations which are above all not supported by the way in which Duchamp presented himself as a highly individualistic, idiosyncratic artist, shying away from any allegiance to groups and movements, as Breton points out in his article on Duchamp from 1922 (Breton 1989: 209-210). It is not surprising, therefore, to find that Duchamp accentuates the issue slightly differently when commenting on the *Fountain* in his response to the jury's refusal to exhibit the urinal:

> Whether Mr Mutt with his own hands made the fountain or not has no importance. He CHOSE it. He took an ordinary article of life, placed it so that its useful significance disappeared under the new title and point of view — created a new thought for the object. (cf. Dachy 1990: 83)

Not the category of *individual production*, but "whether Mr Mutt *with his own hands*" made the fountain is Duchamp's point of departure. Whether the fountain is handmade or industrially produced, whether it has been shaped by handicraft or by technical procedures, is dismissed by Duchamp as a distinction of any relevance for the *Fountain's* status as work of art. Duchamp anticipates what will eventually become consensus among avant-garde artists with the invention of photomontage: a notion of art that is no longer bound to the imprint of the hand or the brush stroke of the artist, but relies instead on ready-made materials, their selection and placement. The creative process is characterised not by the skill of the hand, but rather the autonomous gesture of the artist, who chooses an object or photo-bits, places them in a new context and thus transforms utilitarian articles into art works, attributing to them a new significance, "a new thought".

It was once again André Breton who noticed the nuance in Duchamp's statement with utmost precision. "The practice of drawing and painting", Breton writes,

> appeared to him as a kind of trickery that tended towards the senseless glorification of the *hand* and of nothing else. The hand is the great culprit, so how can one consent to be the slave of one's own hand? *It is inacceptable that drawing and painting should today still stand where writing stood before Gutenberg* —

at the point of handicraft (Breton 1959: 90). So, it is not Mr. Mutt's or Marcel Duchamp's individuality or individual creativity that is provocatively called into question by the submission of the urinal to the Salon's jury. It is the question of whether art should continue to be based on handicraft in an age where other spheres of life are determined by mechanical production and industrial reproduction processes, which is raised by the *Fountain*.

Duchamp's own comments on his ready-mades support both aspects of this interpretation. His comments start with a rather pronounced self-reference to his own inventiveness when creating the first ready-made: "As early as 1913 I had the happy idea to fasten a bicycle wheel to a kitchen stool and watch it turn" (cf. Richter 1965: 89). The comments end with explanations of two related properties of ready-mades, their "lack of uniqueness" and the fact that they are "manufactured". In a capricious leap Duchamp even declared all paintings in the world "ready-mades" and gave an interesting reason for this proposition:

> Since the tubes of paint used by an artist are manufactured and ready-made products we must conclude that all paintings in the world are *ready-mades*. (Richter 1965: 90)

In characterising Duchamp's work Octavio Paz struck a cord which also ties in with the reading of the ready-mades presented here. Emphasising the importance of Picasso and Duchamp as "the two painters who have had the greatest influence on our century", he distinguishes the pictures of the former, in which the *image* is still the dominant aspect, with the work of the latter which he calls "meditations on the image" (cf. Waldman 1992: 135-136). Although Robert Motherwell and also Robert Melville have discovered a surprising beauty in the *Bottlerack* and the *Fountain* (cf. Camfield 1989: 47 and 95), I tend to share Paz' view that in his work art has been transformed into a medium of meditation, of reflection on the status of art in an age of technical reproduction. This characteristic applies to the early, scandalous *Nude Descending a Stair-Case* as well as the manufactured ready-mades and last not least to *Anémic Cinéma*.

VI.

Valéry's prediction that profound changes to "the physical component" are pending in the "ancient craft of the beautiful" and that great innovations will transform "the entire technique of the arts" and "our very notion of art" also extend to poetic production (cf.

Benjamin 1973: 219). The "physical component" of literature, however, has had its own history of revolutions in the past dating from the transition of oral poetry to manuscript culture and further on to book printing, the "mechanical reproduction of writing". Not by chance do Apollinaire and Tzara, Duchamp and Breton and also Benjamin refer to Gutenberg's invention of the printing press while reflecting on the changes in the visual arts, but more timely also to the "daily newspaper".

Apollinaire discovers a particular quality in the daily press which he wishes might also be available to writers. "On a single sheet", he notices, the daily paper is able to "touch on the most diverse subjects" (Apollinaire 1963: 335). His wish to obtain a similar degree of freedom in the choice and composition of poetic subjects shows great affinity with the principles of collage, and clearly anticipates the juxtaposition of heterogeneous materials, which was to become so characteristic of photomontage. Tzara and Breton took up the idea and carried it a few steps further. In his famous recipe of "how to make a dadaist poem" Tzara proposed to use newspaper articles as material for poetic production (Tzara 1989: 92). Breton made a similar suggestion in the first manifest of surrealism and included an example of such a poem in the manifest (Breton 1972: 41-43). The correspondence of these proposals with Duchamp's exhibits and dadaist photomontage in the choice of *ready-made* materials is again very obvious. For Benjamin the role of the press was above all instrumental in gradually removing the distinction between author and reader with the consequence that readers become potential authors. This aspect is again normally associated with the practice of both collage and photomontage. Thus, although not achieving the same impact, literature responded to the advance of the press as a modern, mass-circulated medium of communication in a similar fashion as can be observed in the interaction between painting and photography, with the rather surprising result that the use of ready-made materials and the process of putting it together show a great affinity between the art forms.

Apollinaire, Gide and Benjamin also draw attention to the challenge which the advance of cinema posed to theatre, affecting not only the production modes of theatrical presentation, but also the conventions of playwriting. In rejecting any kind of "historical reconstruction" and any "psychological photography" in drama, the first manifest of futurist playwrights makes it clear even in its choice of terminology, that they resent — as strongly as the painters did — any encroachment of technical apparati into their domain (cf. Asholt/Fähnders 1995: 19). A radical separation between cinema and theatre and the conventions of their modes of production was also the first response of expressionist theorists and writers to the challenge of cinema. "The borderline between cinema and theatre needs to be emphasised most strongly", Kurt Pinthus maintained in the introduction to his famous *Kinobuch* from 1913 (Pinthus 1983: 19). Pinthus' categorical distinction aimed at both, a return of drama to its genuine means of expression, the word, and a concentration of cinema on milieu and action expressed by motion and gesture.

To Georg Kaiser, however, it was a foregone conclusion that cinema showed the same lack of artistic sensibility as the whole period of "naturalism". While expressing his contempt for both "naturalism" and kinoism", he praised the eternal power of expressionist drama, based also on the power of the word (Kaiser 1971: 572). In a dialectic leap, however, Kaiser developed in his play *From Morning to Midnight* a new dramatic structure which was to become a model for other expressionist writers, and which was immediately identified by contemporary critics as *cinematic*. It is the structure of *Stationendrama*, an episodic structure in which the dramatic action unfolds in a series of self-contained scenes. "That is indeed cinema", Yvan Goll wrote in a commentary on the play (cf Schürer 1971: 43). "Can you not see the flicker of the film?" an English critic remarked in a review of the London production of *From Morning to Midnight* (MacCarthy 1920: 769). In spite of his "surprising emphasis on the word", Brecht observed, "Kaiser shoots a film" (Brecht 1967: 58). Unintentionally, it seems, and contrary to his aesthetic convictions Kaiser paved the way for the integration of filmic technique and eventually film itself in plays by other expressionist writers, among them Goll and Ernst Toller.

Apart from direct forms of interaction between literature and modern media of technical reproduction such as the press and cinema, one can observe mediated effects which the radical innovations in the visual arts had on literary concepts and literary production. The Russian cubofuturists made it clear in their first manifesto, *A Slap in the Face of Public Taste*, that not the father-figures of literature, but the *new painting* offered the decisive impetus for innovations in all the arts. "The word", the manifesto demands, should "audaciously and courageously follow painting" (Chlebnikov 1972: 105). The manifesto was signed by the poets Vladimir Majakovskij and Viktor Clebnikov as well as the painters David Burljuk and Alexander Kruchonykh. Apollinaire's visual poems in *Calligrammes* and the futurist and dadaist use of typography as an expressive means are early attempts even to achieve a material status for poetic production comparable to painting by introducing visual effects to the presentation of literary texts. Expressionist writers emphasised their departure from photographic modes of perception as strongly as the expressionist painters, and shaped their literary programmes in correspondence to the painters' new orientation. "The artists of the new movement", Kasimir Edschmid proclaimed in his seminal essay on "Expressionism in Literature" from 1917, "do not take a photograph, they have a vision". In the same way, he maintained, the expressionist writer "would not represent" what he sees, but provide "a vision" (Edschmid 1965: 95-96).

Although in a different camp, Tzara and Breton likewise refer to the authority of the painters when presenting a new literary concept or genre. In his "Note pour les Bourgeoís" in the first dadaist journal Tzara justifies the application of the principle of *simultaneity* to poetic production by referring to the faceting of the images by Picasso and Braque, Picabia, Duchamp-Villon and Delaunay (Tzara 1916: 6). Whilst here it is the new dadaist genre of the *poème simultan* as presented in the *Cabaret Voltaire* that develops compositional features comparable to the experiments of the cubist painters, Breton's proposal to use newspaper clips for the composition of a surrealist poem seems to have been encouraged by the same source:

> The pieces of paper that Picasso and Braque insert into their work have the same value as the introduction of a platitude into a literary analysis of the most rigorous sort. It is even permissible to entitle POEM what we get from the most random assemblage possible (observe, if you will, the syntax) of headlines and scraps of headlines cut out of the newspaper. (Breton 1972:41)

In the case of Kurt Schwitters' poems and sonata a reference to any other painter would have been inappropriate. Schwitters preferred to transpose his own method of creating MERZ assemblages to his poetic production. While the assemblages are made out of scraps of diverse, discarded materials including pram wheels, toy engines, wooden strips, a kitchen funnel, cotton wool and chicken wire, the poems consist of "letters, syllables, words, sentences" from a wide range of sources such as graffiti, grammar books, nonsense verses and magazines (cf. Schwitters 1989: 59). By assembling the linguistic material in such a way that its sounds, shapes and semantics engage in a lively interaction, Schwitters created one of the most enchanting love poems that has emerged from the avant-garde, the poem on "Anna Blume".

A particularly illustrious example of the mediated impact of the innovations in the visual arts on literary production is the genesis of the style of one of the outstanding novels of the 1920s, Alfred Döblin's *Berlin Alexanderplatz*. It is so illustrious because it combines the literary response to the advances in painting with a response to the new technical medium of film. Döblin apparently acquired the first impetus for the development of a new style of writing apparently from the famous exhibition of futurist paintings touring the European capitals in 1912. Döblin saw the exhibition in the *Sturm Galerie* in Berlin and wrote an enthusiastic review. "Futurism", he proclaimed, "is a great step forward", referring to it as "an act of liberation." In a conversation with Marinetti, "at Dalbelli's", he added to his praise of the pictures his wish to see literature progress in a similar vein: "If we only had something like this in literature!" (Döblin 1963a: 9) The radical innovations in painting obviously evoked the desire to achieve comparable effects and a comparable advance in literature. In the following year Döblin published his "Berlin Programme", an outline of a new concept of novel writing which was clearly designed to fulfil the expectations expressed at Dalbelli's. In this programme Döblin called for a "cinema style" in epic composition (Döblin 1963b: 17). In 1929 he published his novel *Berlin Alexanderplatz* which tells the story of Franze Biberkopf and simultaneously the story of the city Berlin in the most vibrant montage style, combining radio reports, newspaper clippings, children's songs, bible verses, advertisements, public announcements and innumerable stories to create a panorama of life in the big city.

Not surprisingly, Walter Benjamin was the critic to notice the particular qualities of the new style. In a review of Döblin's novel, which was one of the most important contributions to novel theory in its time, Benjamin gave a portrayal of the stylistic principle of montage, its origin in dada, its striking use in film "in its best moments" and its particular effect in Döblin's *Berlin Alexanderplatz*:

> The stylistic principle governing this book is that of montage. Petty-bourgeois printed matter, scandalmongering, stories of accidents, the sensational incidents of 1928, folk songs, and advertisements rain down in this text. The montage explodes the framework of the novel, bursts its limits both stylistically and structurally, and clears the way for new, epic possibilities. (Benjamin 1999a: 301)

The "new epic possibilities" depend on the use of material that is not invented by the author, but collected from everyday life, that is not unique and original, but has passed through many hands and is consequently soaked with collective experience. To turn the form of the novel from an individual confession into a document of collective experience, the experience of life in the big city of Berlin, was the project which Benjamin discovered in Döblin's novel and which he wholeheartedly supported. Such a project differs from the one presented by Bürger in the name of the avant-garde in that respect that instead of projecting the sublation of art into life it tries to promote the advance of literary technique, with a view to strengthening literature's capability to penetrate contemporary life and make contemporary experience discernible to the reader.

VII.

Approaching the avant-garde by pursuing the challenge which the advances of technological reproduction posed to traditional art forms and the traditional notion of art means abandoning the illusion that a single, unifying formula can provide a reliable guide to the variety of avant-gardist concepts and productions. Following the range of diverse responses to this challenge, however, not only allows for a precise and substantive qualification of the very formation of the avant-garde, but also for exploring the complexities and contradictions of its further development and the variety and heterogeneity of its manifestations. It is easy to see how further developments such as Max Ernst's discovery of the *automatism* of *frottage* and *collage* or Man Ray's inventions of the *photogram* and *rayograph*, the constructivist projects of Tatlin and Rodchenko, but also Dali's "hand-done colour photographs" or Magritte's intelligent play with "painted reproductions", including the painting *Not to be reproduced*, fit into such theoretical scheme and contribute additional facets to it.

In her article on "Photography in the Service of Surrealism", Rosalind Krauss calls surrealist photography a "paradox". "It would seem", she remarks, "that there cannot be surrealism *and* photography". Whilst she concedes that painting might hope to chart the surrealists' "pure creations of the mind" erupting in dreams, free association or hypnotic states, she feels that "photography would seem most unlikely as a medium" (Krauss 1986: 15). A similar paradox can be observed with regard to expressionist film. An art movement that had proclaimed "inner visions" and the "inner necessities" of the artist as the creative forces behind its artistic production, eventually manifests itself in film, a medium based on photography. This contradiction in terms, however, only supports the crucial argument in the construction of the present theoretical framework, the argument that a dialectical process of demarcation from technological reproduction and its eventual integration into the practice and the concept of art characterises the avant-gardist responses to the technological advances.

Such a framework also provides appropriate, and indeed indispensable access to the artistic production of the neo-avant-garde. Shunned by Bürger and widely marginalised in the context of the debates on Modernism and Postmodernism, major manifestations of the neo-avant-garde have indeed been locked into their existence as museum pieces. A fresh confrontation with them in the light of a revised understanding of the historical avant-garde appears to be overdue. The new techniques and new art forms of the historical avant-garde have clearly acted as an important stimulus for artists associated with abstract expressionism or pop art, minimalism or conceptual art. Specific forms of their artistic production such as *mixed media* and the *multiple*, the wide-spread use of the *grid* and the attention paid to the surface of the canvas, or new combinations of photography and oil-painting in a multi-stage production process, as well as the use of dot patterns of technical reproduction in imitations of cartoon strips, show the ongoing reflection of the basic questions which the historical avant-garde had raised. While the integration of technical reproduction into artistic production has become irre-versible, the encounter of heterogeneous and disparate materials, means and methods not only remains worthy of reflection, it is also the source of the most creative impulses in neo-avant-garde art production.

Although the visual arts undoubtedly provided the terrain on which the most notable changes in perception and modes of artistic production took place, literature could not remain unaffected by these developments. The radical devaluation of the imitation of nature as the basic premise of painting necessarily called into question literary concepts which continued pursuing representational functions. This explains not only the drive towards new concepts of writing, but also why these often showed great affinity with the innovations that emerged in the fine arts. In addition, literature also responded directly to technological changes and challenges in its own domain caused by the daily press and the cinema. All the pictorial and literary developments, however, can hardly be conceived as moments contributing to the sublation of art into the practice of life. This formula, reminiscent of the calls of May 1968 rather than the manifestos of the avant-garde, needs to be laid to rest. What the new art forms of collage, photomontage and simultaneous poetry and fundamentally new artistic techniques, above all the technique of montage, achieved was the formation of modes of perception and construction that are more in tune with processes in other fields of activity and other spheres of life, more appropriate also to establish communication and interaction between the world of arts and other life spheres. As such their very invention has worked towards bridging the gap between art and technology, between handicraft and industrial production, between the culture of taste and the culture of technical skills. "Bringing down one of the barriers, surmounting one of the contradictions which inhibit the productive capacity" of the artist, was in Benjamin's view one of the most important tasks confronting the arts (Benjamin 1999b: 775). The avant-garde movements have not only contributed to this task, they have truly and effectively acted as avant-garde of the bulk of contemporary art production in this respect.

Bibliography

Apollinaire, Guillaume

1962 *The Cubist Painters*. New York: Wittenborn.

1963 "The New Spirit and the Poets". In: Francis Steegmuller. *Apollinaire. Poet among Painters*. London: Rupert Hart-Davis, 333-344.

Apollonio, Umbro (ed.)

1973 *Futurist Manifestos*. London: Thames and Hudson

Asholt, Wolfgang, and Walter Fähnders

1995 *Manifeste und Proklamationen der europäischen Avantgarde*. Stuttgart: Metzler.

Baldassari, Anne

1997 *Picasso und die Photographie*. Munich: Schirmer/Mosel.

Benjamin, Walter

1973 "The Work of Art in the Age of Mechanical Reproduction". In: Benjamin, *Illuminations*. Fontana, 219-253.

1999a "The Crisis of the Novel". In: Benjamin, *Selected Writings*, vol. 2. Cambridge, Mass.: Harvard University Press, 299-304.

1999b "The Author as Producer". In: Benjamin, *Selected Writings*, vol. 2, 768-782.

Bernadac, Marie-Laure

1991 *Picasso Museum Paris. Die Meisterwerke*. Munich: Prestel.

Blume, Eugen

1999 "Das Schweigen von Marcel Duchamp wird überbewertet. Marcel Duchamp, John Cage, Joseph Beuys". In: *Das XX. Jahrhundert*. Berlin: Nationalgalerie, 494-499.

Boccioni, Umberto, et al.

1973a "Manifesto of the Futurist Painters 1910". In: Apollonio 1973: 24-27.

1973b "Futurist Painting: Technical Manifesto 1910". In: Apollonio 1973: 27-31.

Brecht, Bertolt

1967 "Aus den Notizbüchern 1920-1926". In: Brecht, *Schriften zum Theater I. Gesammelte Werke*, vol. 15. Frankfurt am Main: Suhrkamp, 41-70.

1978 "The Film, the Novel and Epic Theatre". In John Willett (ed.), *Brecht on Theatre*. London: Methuen, 47-51.

Breton, André

1948 "Max Ernst". In: Max Ernst, *Beyond Painting*. New York: Wittenborn, 177.

1959 "Lighthouse of the Bride". In: Robert Lebel, *Marcel Duchamp*. London: Trianon Press, 88-94.

1972 *Manifestoes of Surrealism*. Ann Arbor: University of Michigan Press.

1989 "Marcel Duchamp". In Motherwell 1989: 209-211.

Buchheim, Lothar-Günther

1956 *Die Künstlergemeinschaft Brücke*. Feldafing: Buchheim.

Bürger, Peter

1984 *Theory of the Avant-Garde*. Minneapolis: University of Minnesota Press.

Camfield, William A.

1989 *Marcel Duchamp. Fountain*. Houston, Texas: Houston Fine Art Press.

Chlebnikov, Viktor

1972 "Eine Ohrfeige dem öffentlichen Geschmack". In: Chlebnikov, *Werke*, vol. 2. Reinbek: Rowohlt, 103-108.

Cooper, Douglas, and Gary Tinterow

1983 *The Essential Cubism*. London: Tate Gallery.

Dachy, Marc

1990 The Dada Movement 1915-1923. New York: Rizzoli.

Daix, Pierre

1982 *Der Kubismus in Wort und Bild*. Stuttgart: Klett-Cotta.

Döblin, Alfred

1963a "Futuristische Worttechnik. Offener Brief an F.T. Marinetti". In: Döblin, *Aufsätze zur Literatur*. Freiburg: Walter Verlag, 9-15.

1963b "An Romanautoren und ihre Kritiker. Berliner Programm". In: Döblin, *Aufsätze zur Literatur*, 15-19.

Dube, Wolf-Dieter
1972 *The Expressionists*. London: Thames and Hudson.

Edschmid, Kasimir
1965 "Expressionismus in der Dichtung". In: Paul Raabe (ed.), *Expressionismus. Der Kampf um eine literarische Bewegung*. Munich: dtv, 90-108.

Eisenstein, Sergei
1988a "The Montage of Attractions". In: Eisenstein, *Selected Works*. Vol. I: *Writings, 1922-34*. London: British Film Institute, 33-38.

1988b "Montage of Film Attractions". In: Eisenstein, *Selected Works*. Vol. I, 39-58.

Fry, Edward F.
1966 *Cubism*. London: Thames and Hudson.

Gide, André
1966 *The Counterfeiters*. Harmondsworth: Penguin.

Hillach, Ansgar
1976 "Allegorie, Bildraum, Montage". In: W. Martin Lüdke (ed.), *›Theorie der Avantgarde‹. Antworten auf Peter Bürgers Bestimmung von Kunst und Gesellschaft*. Frankfurt am Main: Suhrkamp, 105-142.

Honnef, Klaus
1992 "Symbolic Form as a Vivid Cognitive Principle. An Essay on Montage". In: Peter Pachnicke and Klaus Honnef (eds), *John Heartfield*. New York: Harry N. Abrams, 49-64.

Kaiser, Georg
1971 "Ein neuer Naturalismus?" In: Kaiser, *Werke*, vol. 4. Frankfurt am Main: Propyläen, 571-572.

Kandinsky, Wassily
1968 "On the Problem of Form". In: Herschel B. Chipp (ed.), *Theories of Modern Art*. Berkeley: University of California Press, 155-170.

Krauss, Rosalind
1986 "Photography in the Service of Surrealism". In: R. Krauss and Jane Livingstone (eds), *L'Amour fou. Photography and Surrealism*. London: Hayward Gallery, 13-54.

Lawder, Standish D.
1975 *The Cubist Cinema*. New York: New York University Press.

MacCarthy, Desmond
1920 "A New Dramatic Method". In: *The New Statesman*, April 1920.

Motherwell, Robert (ed.)
1989 *The Dada Painters and Poets*. Cambridge, Mass.: Harvard University Press.

Pinthus, Kurt
1983 *Das Kinobuch*. Frankfurt am Main: Fischer.

Richter, Hans
1965 *Dada. Art and Anti-Art*. London: Thames and Hudson.

Rowell, Margit
1994 "Kupka, Duchamp and Marey". In: Anthony Hill (ed.), *Duchamp: passim*. G + B Arts International, 45-50.

Rubin, William
1989 *Picasso and Braque. Pioneering Cubism*. New York: The Museum of Modern Art.

Scharf, Aaron
1983 *Art and Photography*. Harmondsworth: Penguin.

Schürer, Ernst
1971 Georg Kaiser und Bertolt Brecht. Frankfurt am Main.

Schwitters, Kurt
1989 "Merz". In: Motherwell 1989: 57-65.

Tzara, Tristan
1916 "Note pour les Bourgeois". In: *Cabaret Voltaire*, ed. Hugo Ball. Zurich, 6-7.

1989 "Manifesto on Feeble Love and Bitter Love". In: Motherwell 1989: 86-98.

Waldman, Diane
1992 *Collage, Assemblage and the Found Object*. London: Phaidon.

DADA AND THE CONSTITUTION OF CULTURE: (RE-) CONCEPTUALISING THE AVANT-GARDE

STEPHEN C. FOSTER

This paper seeks to establish a distinction between the creator and the agent of the avant-garde; the theoriser of the avant-garde and the prosecutor of the avant-garde. It assumes that someone theorised it into existence, that there is a history of that kind of theorising of it, and that there are competing theories of it (those derived internally, perhaps being the least important of them). The avant-garde more than submits to theorising; it is the product of theorising, early on as well as more recently. Better yet, it satisfies a theory "function". I would liken theorising the avant-garde to historicising the avant-garde, where one can also productively distinguish between the creator and the agent of the histories. This requires distinguishing the agent of the theorised and/or historical avant-garde from the agency of the theorising and/or historicising of the avant-garde. Interest should be focused on the avant-garde as a thing theorised into existence where theorising is understood as a constituting process and not the medium for producing theoretical "things".

This paper will concentrate on this last, rather little discussed matter, and present it as a critique of the former, rather overly discussed matter; will concentrate on the historical effort to discard the "role" of "agent" of the avant-garde (an avant-gardist) in favour of occupying the place or role in "theorising culture" (the culture of theorising) from where it is constituted theoretically. In a significant sense, I am interested in an "anti-avant-garde" position required for achieving the "stated mission" of the avant-garde or as a means of competing for power with its creators.

Given this as a starting point, I feel obliged to understand current theories of the avant-garde as sentimental reflections on doubtful and historically suspect concepts that the late teens and twenties also found politically and morally suspect some eighty years ago. This paper will concentrate on what I see as the conflict between the culturally "appointed" or named avant-garde (the property of majority culture) and certain individuals' attempts to achieve, in operational fact, what was implied or hidden in larger culture's reigning or ruling concept of the avant-garde. I will conclude that what I describe here as an "authentic" avant-garde (or anti-avant-garde) aspired precisely to the "defining technologies" (not the application technologies) possessed by the majority culture that the avant-garde was cleverly created (by the majority culture) to obscure or defeat (or better, to give the appearance of defeating).

The avant-garde is badly over-realised as a counter-culture reality and equally under-realised as an institutionally based majority culture concept. The appointed or "named" avant-garde typically spoke for majority culture and, with very few exceptions, served, as well as applied, its process of culture-making of which the avant-garde is but a part. And, it is the named avant-garde that has traditionally, and mistakenly from my point of view, served as the object and subject of avant-garde studies. I wish to concentrate precisely on the exceptions, notably the implication of Berlin Dada, where art tried to intercept culture at the horizon of its "defining technologies"; that is, intercept culture at the point of its (the avant-garde's) creation by larger culture. Certain changes in art will be seen as reflections of the authentic or anti-avant-garde's efforts to exceed the mere representation of culture in favour of playing a significant role in the constitution of culture and, consequently, of the avant-garde itself. I will here concentrate on photomontage and its relationship to photography and the text.

Throughout the period under discussion, there were competing concepts of culture which posed questions not only to the particular values embedded in a particular culture and their cultural pro-secution (what the "named avant-garde" usually addressed itself to), but, more importantly, the nature of how, within a culture, values were constituted and structured. What one sees in the development of photomontage is, in part, a recognition that culture involves more than the changing face of a constant value structure but, of much greater significance, the expression of the process by which the value structures are constituted. It is the latter that this essay addresses, since photomontage's critique, the critique of the facts of culture, disclosed not merely the nature of changing German culture, but of a changing concept of culture and "culturing" in general.

Photomontage has always been, and has been understood, as a matter of imaging culture and imaging and critiquing cultural images of culture. In this, it is like all imagining of culture and images of culture. What is forgotten, no matter how contemptible sounding (which of course it really is not) is that it was and is the establishment that provides and provided the spaces within, which these kinds of cultural or mental operations occurred; within which a culture's fictions and myths (abstractions) were produced. The establishment's means were givens of culture making, and its cultural spaces, the medium of their use. The point is this: to critique, restore or rehabilitate culture requires re-evoking these same "productive spaces", or spaces like them, since the artists' tasks are centred upon the problems of culture, per se. Independent of the specific content with which one might want to invest a culture, one must first achieve culture. Insofar as the Berliners' aims entailed the critique of, or provision of alternatives for culture and not for other cultures, they, de facto, observed the "production" prerequisites of all culture. The Berliners' works, put simply, became the abstractions of these abstractions. Photomontage's dis-tinction lay not only in its wish to image culture (its own and others), but in its concern to expose and enlist the constituting and defining technologies of those who wished to disguise their constituting and defining basis and, indeed, that there was such a thing as these constituting and defining bases.

Most attempts to address photomontage, despite their respective merits and despite what they contribute as corridors of access to the works as "art", have, with few exceptions, committed themselves to photomontage as a "thing defined". Although somewhat self-conscious in these endeavours, the field continues to describe photomontage through "exhibited properties" and the affinity of these properties to those of other genre such as painting, collage, photography, etc.

This avoids, I believe, the more central and, to my way of thinking, more interesting problem of how photomontage is, in its essential and defining terms, different from painting, collage, photography etc., and how and why photomontage deliberately defined itself away from these traditional genres, indeed, from the tradition of genre. In the present situation of the literature, one is too often left with contemplating a look-alike body of work within which one then proceed to address questions of specific contexts, specific time and place objectives, and the instrumental value of these works as they are perceived to reflect a variety of cultural landscapes.

The questions might better be redirected to the initial propositions of photomontage, to its first-terms that mandated the appropriation and critique of collage, photography and the media in the first place. This permits rethinking its strategies, strategies that can clearly not be understood, or that could not have been historically satisfied by, or attributed to photomontage's relation-ships to existing and traditional genre including the media with which it bears a much more basic relationship. This, I believe de-feats the idea that the purpose of photomontage involved the mere synthesis of these genre and defeats the historicising of photo-montage as "breaking out" of genre or "breaking into" genre, a situ-ation that continues to describe the relationship between it and the traditional arts through terms dictated by the traditional arts.

One seems on firmer ground if photomontage is addressed in terms of its defining purpose: that is, as something whose major attribute is the unexhibited property of defining something; a culture, ideology, set of social relations, or whatever. Such an approach has produced some of the best discussions in the literature but still fails to account for the character of the thing doing the defining. That is, although the agent of the defining changes, the defining itself continues to proceed on the same grounds as it would through painting, collage, photography or whatever.

I wish to state at the outset that I regard photomontage as the aesthetic emergence of a basically and fundamentally new defining technology, distinct particularly in terms of how photomontage differs from how, and by what means, the visual arts have traditionally been understood to "define" or make culture in the past. In the embrace by photomontage of ideology, technology, social relations etc., the latter should be seen less as the objects/subjects of representation than as the revealment of other modes or inventories of cultural definition. Their use value for photomontage is dis-covered less in their appearance as subjects than in their appro-priation as "social means of definition" and in their existence as reflections of them in social practice. What we witness is the death of realistic concepts of culture where reality resided precisely, and only, in their projection as cultural realities; as results of a culture's means of reality production and reality technology.

That photomontage was as much a reaction against "straight" photography as it was a rethinking of its potential use in representing culture, is typically neglected in the literature. The photograph, for decades committed to verifying the realms of whole world-views, had long recommended itself as a tool for the projection of ideology and the prosecution of politics. As an idea, it had, in fact, displaced the conventional arts, more or less com-pletely, as a means of confirming "realistic" concepts of the cultural world and the kind of cultural space it was thought to inhabit. Part of the history of photomontage involves recognition of the conven-tionality of the photograph, its usefulness in lending truth value and visual veracity to the world-views of the status quo, and the im-possibility of separating these issues from cultural politics in general. For those perpetuating the cultural conventions sub-stantiated by the photograph, its social instrumentality was frequently disguised. By those critiquing the same cultural con-ventions, it was just as frequently exposed. The point is that successful critique of whole-world views understandably would occur most productively where the power of their representation was greatest; the photograph. That is, re-thinking cultural space (views on the world) became primarily a question of rethinking photo-graphic space or rethinking space photographically. The photograph became the touchstone of re-thinking culture whether it was a question of entrenchment, revisionism, or critique.

The significance of these matters far exceeded that of photography itself, and sets the battlegrounds for textual and other representations of culture as well. There is good reason that photomontage is as much, or more, a textual affair than a photographic affair. Although photography was present because of its power in representing culture, and symbolic of the recent "revolutions in representing" culture, it was the representation of culture, and not photography, that was most critically at stake. The power of photomontage rests, finally, in its radical application back into other dimensions of artistic as well as media, advertising and design representations of culture. It is a question of making a culture's visual discourse competitive with culture's other related discourses.

Well understood as a powerful "abstraction of the perception of culture" and fully appreciated for its capacity for manipulation and alteration to achieve specific objectives, photography became the site for performing visual operations on culture. It became the means for visualising the abstraction of cultural space that so powerfully affected not only photography itself, but visual culture, or cultural visualisation in general. Its role was essential to how culture was transmitted; that is, in how it could/would be retrieved, revisited or rehearsed. Photomontage became the impetus for, and not the genre of, the transformation of traditional concepts of space (including photographic space); became reflections of the abstractions we call world-views and the site for the formulation of new cognitive models by which we came to know and transact the cultural world. If this all seems objectionably theoretical, it is because photo-montage itself is highly theoretical. Seeing it any other way devalues and does violence to its revolution and traditionalises its visual work.

It follows that I am interested in this defining moment or technology of photomontage in terms of how it preceded its "application" in different dimensions of culture (advertising, journalism etc.) and different geographical and temporal circumstances: Germany, the Low Countries, Russia etc. This distinction is significant as it permits a separation of photomontage as a defining issue and the means, rarely as revolutionary as photomontage, of its application. That is, the nature of the application of photomontage (the technology of application, if you will), does or does not, is intended or is not intended to, keep pace with photomontage depending on the specific concepts and objectives of the application.

It is worth addressing some of the implications contained in thus separating the questions and interrogating both the effec-tiveness and moral basis of historical applications of photomontage. Although these questions bring one close to the issue of photomontage's complicity with majority culture, the point I wish to make is somewhat different. I am less interested in its complicity with industry, fashion, journalism, or whatever, than I am in concepts of application which these areas share, concepts which, I will maintain, are diametrically opposed to the conceptualisation of photomontage as a defining technology. Put differently, I am inter-ested in the first terms of defining, and only then in their application in different circumstances, a totally different matter since ap-plication already has a different kind of purpose behind it. The first operates on a level of constituting cultural definition; the second with policing it. Application is culture bound and tells us much more about the "culture of application" than it does the facts of defining. Dada's rejection of culture may have rested in part on its perception of a culture as bad culture. More importantly, however, this rejection was prerequisite to recreating defining within a framework that logically disentailed its application, its independence from what I have termed reigning cultures of application.

All this argued for the establishment of a "centre" from which defining purpose could be altered or redirected. Dada was faced with two distinct, but closely related histories; the history of photo-montage and the history of its application, or misapplication. As a revolution in definition, photomontage flourished best in social vacuums where the reconstitution of culture was still a viable concept. I stress its viability as a concept since "its viability as a concept" is what the initial photomonteurs were most committed to securing. Its pragmatic value, understood as dependent or independent of existing cultures of application, was never really the issue, and insistence on photomontage's sources in its pragmatic value only serves to devalue photomontage, if not its subsequent application.

Mapping the long-term development of photomontage, then, seems to be a matter of the created relations between photomontage as a defining technology and various explorations of its usefulness "applied" to other dimensions of culture. Any defining capabilities are sources of empowerment, and it was precisely in these interests that photomontage was conceived. "Application" is also a power structure and it should come as no surprise that the use of photomontage freely crossed political, aesthetic and ideological lines. It could equally serve Dada and the German liberal left, the utopian De Stijl artists, the "scientific communism" of the Russian constructivists, and subsequently, and in a way that entirely severed any relationships between photomontage in its defining purposes and in its application, the German and Italian Fascists.

I have tried to describe photomontage preceding its use, photomontage as an attempt to apply what it promised as a defining technology where the relationship between the defining "centre" and its usefulness was maintained, as opposed to photomontage divorced from its status as a self-reflective technology and its devaluation, or valuation, to the status of a "tool". My concentration on the first of these rests on my conviction that it is here that photomontage best reflects the human actions we call social environment, most significantly participates in the constitution of alternative cognitive structures (and cultures), and most forcibly asserts its definitional revolution (and the existence of all defining structures) as primarily aesthetic affairs.

Art has rarely been responsible for making culture work, to say nothing of making culture. At best, it has taken sides, proselytised or condemned, but rarely taken on the process of "culturing". In this, the Berliners were different, and with this difference came the recognition that providing a transactional basis for culture entailed adopting the strategies of majority culture.

The Weimar Republic's February, 1919 National Assembly provided an unequalled opportunity for Berlin's "Oberdada", Johannes Baader, to perform in precisely such a capacity.[1] Although he did not significantly change the event itself, Baader carefully managed perception of the event in a way that adjusted the designs of this founding celebration to give added point, and significant context, to his own perspective as presented in a little broadside entitled *Grüne Leiche*. Initially quiet, Baader took advantage of a lull in the proceedings to present his own rather eccentric point of view. Before his almost immediate arrest, Baader threw the broadsides into the press boxes directly below him. He was exonerated on grounds of his legal certification as insane and because of evidence of his previous correspondence with the Republican constituents involved. The incident provided Dada with one of its great successes of the season.[2]

The significance of this event relates primarily to Baader's manipulation of the public press, by the agency of his text as given relevance through the event, to assure wide coverage of this programme.[3] Baader had long been a favourite of the newspapers based on his extreme and outrageous actions. For example, Baader's nomination of himself for the Nobel Prize, published in an open

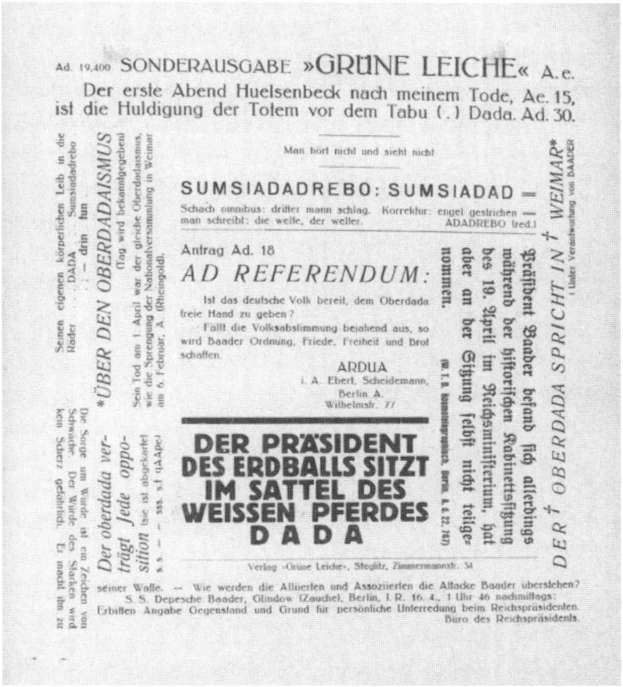

4 Johannes Baader: *Grüne Leiche*. 1919

letter to poet Paul Ernst (*Weltbühne*, July 1918), and which advocated his theories of Monism, was also event based ; the events begin in this case, with the slightly earlier parliamentary debates(!) on the dangers and destructive effects of Monism and the Monistenbund on respectable German intellectual life.[4] In the case of the Weimar National Assembly, we are looking at one of the most newsworthy, media-centred events of the decade. Giving the press a sensational incident to report, strengthened by a short and interesting text to quote, the assembly served beautifully as the context out of which Baader's adversarial position could find a meaningful reception.

Over and above all this, other aspects of Baader's strategies threw the whole affair into a rather odd light. The government was certainly no less aware than Baader of the historical importance of the event and promoted its proceedings in a way that would be perceived, by the public, as an historical event of the kind through which changes in history are made. Conducted in Weimar's *Hof-theater*, an appropriate setting for such a theatrical event, se-renely nested into a venerable seat of old German culture (the city of Goethe and Schiller), and comfortably distanced from the political turmoil of Berlin, the proceeding gave the appearance of sanity and stability. Baader, not unexpectedly, pronounced the event a piece of theatre with little or no consequence for the real dilemmas of mod-ern, post-war Germany. Thus, he asserted his own superior, non-theatrical reality, proclaimed his mock jurisdiction over the Weimar authorities and justly, from his point of view reiterated his claim to being "President of the World".

Roles are typically as useful as they are believable, and they are normally made believable by the authority of the culture as a whole; that is, the culture understood as a whole thing or as the world com-posed of a compatible and stable set of world-views. Whether this compatibility or stability is real or imagined is irrelevant. Indeed, it is probably as real as it is successfully imagined, a fact accounting for Baader's easy adoption of a variety of roles including that of politician. For Baader, then the question of role was inseparable from questions of cultural politics (of which God and the Kaiser are outstanding examples), and their consequences were decipherable through their determination of those politics.[5] Reduced to the level of materials for composing alternative authority and power, the truth value claimed by a specific role was neutralised in favour of its largely structural purposes in the reconfiguration of culture as a whole.

The use value of roles depended precisely on their disembodi-ment of any culturally "real" content; that is, the can-cellation or nullification of content became the necessary condition of "role value" in formulating and transacting concepts of culture. In the course of this, the artist's concepts of truth, power and authority become no more than the cause for identifying and configuring useful concepts of role. In no case was the truth, power or authority derived from the role. New or better truths are not secured through advancement of the content of the roles. Rather, preferred truths are substantiated by means of reconsidering the nature and cultural location of the roles embracing them. Short of this, roles are disempowered as a constitutive basis in structuring culture. What Baader believed was never the issue. The constitution of these beliefs as truths and their cultural empowerment was forever the issue.

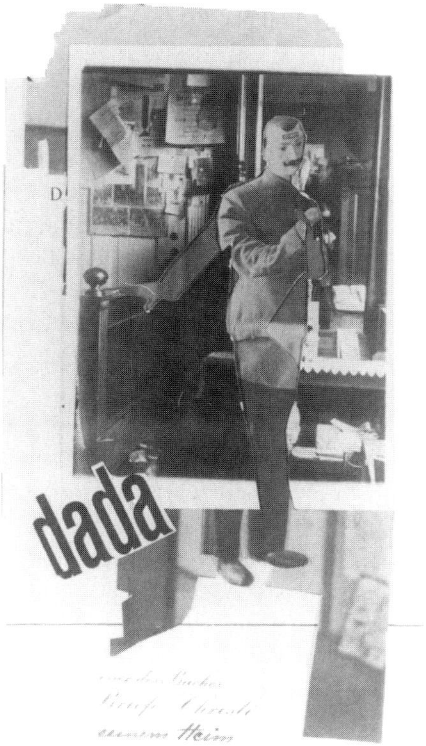

5 Johannes Baader: *The Author in his Home*. 1920

Despite the artist's devaluation of a role's content as truth, power or whatever, he had to be perceived as a truth-teller, power-base, or authority figure-had to be seen as one in whom one believed. Baader's *Der Verfasser des Buches Vierzehn Briefe Christi in seinem Heim* (The Author in his Home) pictures, on one level, the artist in his studio and, on another level, "God in his Heaven" at the moment of the "Creation". The cosmic principles and revisionist platforms of the earlier works are now entirely assimilated into his "role" as artist, the artist as creator and the artist as God. What has occurred is nothing short of the complete asestheticisation of his role, the content it carries, and the means by which it is constituted.[6] The success of this was to rest in the "truth" of the strategy of truth (which may or may not be true) and the "power" of the transaction of power (which may or may not be powerful); where the "role of the authority" is transformed into the "authority of role".

Baader sought nothing short of a new world-view achieved through the aesthetic management of roles. Intersecting at sur-roles, characteristic of "whole" cultures, Baader's alternative was bodied forth and given the appearance of substance through its constant rehearsal in his visual texts and actions where Baader played all the roles. Events became the unfolding of his roles and the exercise of their content, both the "creations" of responses to reconstituted truths. Their authority, won through their interception of, and projection onto conventional events, acted *parallel* to conventional culture but never in its service.

The theory of roles implied in Baader's overall activities were made explicit in many of his pictorial, performatory and textual works. Nowhere in the twentieth century do we get such a clear image of role, or such a compelling image of the artist as role. Neutralised in terms of their conventional content, the specific roles are stated in terms that can best be described as structural, where the structural is made to coincide with the aesthetic, and where both are made to coincide with the political. Ranging from the conservative to the reactionary, these roles nevertheless persuade out *belief*, in the truth of their "strategy of truth", and the power of their "transaction of power". Baader's alternative culture, reflected in such works as *Gutenberggedenkblatt* rests on political fictions (understood broadly), no different in kind than the fictions of all cultures; its wholeness on the creation of high-level abstractions characteristic of all cultures; its *prosecution* in the restructuring of the role patterns by which the new culture is played out.

In no way cumulative, virtually devoid of any comprehensible narrative, and conceived of independently of his beliefs which he frequently parodied as "mere" beliefs, the whole point seems to rest in the establishment of an order, recollaged daily, of which his own actions and deeds, as well as those of others became the source, but

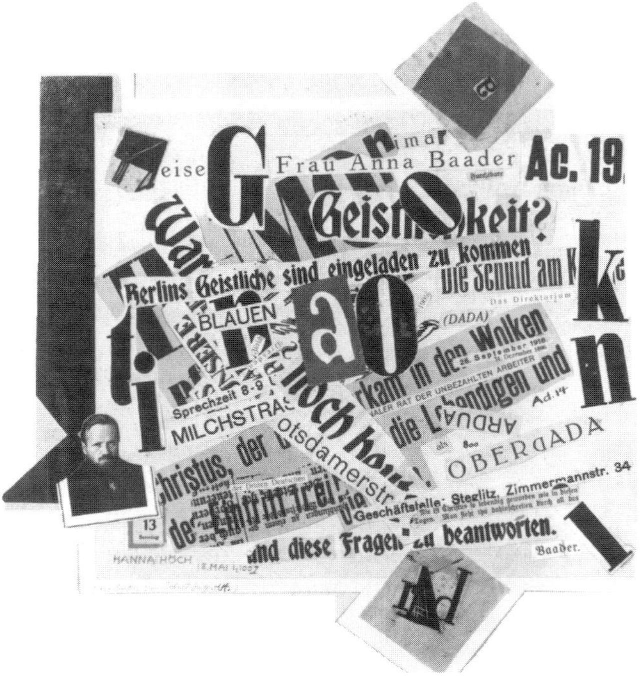

6 Johannes Baader: *Gutenberggedenkblatt*. 1920/22

not the point. Witness to his creations, but not "of" his creations, he gives proof of the mortality of roles and of his own godliness.

Baader's success lay in his identification of a sur-role located outside conventionally scripted human affairs; a role that assiduously avoided the normalcy, advocacy and partisanship that roles, as we typically understand them, involve. *Dada Milchstrasse*, a photocollage dating from 1920, presents Baader's programme, worked out, for the most part, in terms of the roles it configures.[7] His role is evolved from manifestation of world principle to Dadaist (collaborative photomontage with Raoul Hausmann, partner in so many role conceived events) to prophet (indicated by a performance announcement of 1919) and is signed *Architekt* Baader. Baader becomes the principle by which the chaos of war-time Germany is reconstituted into a new order — a new era of world peace which, significantly enough, commenced with the occasion of Baader's death and resurrection on April 1 and April 2, 1919! Historical roles, as they are reflected in the texts and images incorporated into his works, are repositioned, structured according to substantially new terms, and made the "mere" materials of an aesthetically conceived recreation of the world. It is scarcely surprising that the architect of the universe exerted his authority, over human affairs as well, absorbing as his subjects the roles of Weimar's political leaders. Subsumed under the same authority and subjected to the same structure, the society of temporal affairs is cast in the image of universal order, that is, Baader himself.

All this gets us close to a finer distinction between the "named" and the authentic (or anti-) avant-garde. In developing this idea, I would like to distinguish between the fiction writer and the fiction functions which they serve. I would like to maintain that the conventional avant-garde's continued life was ultimately based on its writing of fictions which obeyed the rules, if not the content, of all conventional writing of cultural fictions. The "establishment", although the fiction-making function remained in their hands, was in no position, based on its lack of credibility, to author the fictions. Nor, however, did it want others to write fictions that did not obey the rules, or that would in some way jeopardise the establishment's ownership of fiction-writing functions. The function could be kept in place by the mere writing of alternative fictions. Their believability, as fictions, was not so terribly important. Thus, the avant-garde's authorship of these fictions faithfully served the establishment both in terms of executing the tasks for which it had been conceived in the first place, and in terms of keeping the "technology" of culture-making in the hands of the powers that be. Understandably, it is exactly to this place in culture that the authentic (anti-) avant-garde aspired. It was the technology of culture-making (fiction writing) that it sought to intercept.[8]

Thus, the concept of the named avant-garde must be attributed to the culture that authored its roles and not to the avant-garde itself. What has been described as the avant-garde's internally derived roles and agendas now seem no more than reflections of the source of their production in the culture responsible for its very existence; the avant-garde's theories were ineffective as they failed to achieve a self-reflexive understanding of the cultural theories begetting the avant-garde. Aware of the avant-garde's "designed" function in culture, Berlin Dada critiqued the avant-garde in terms of the theo-

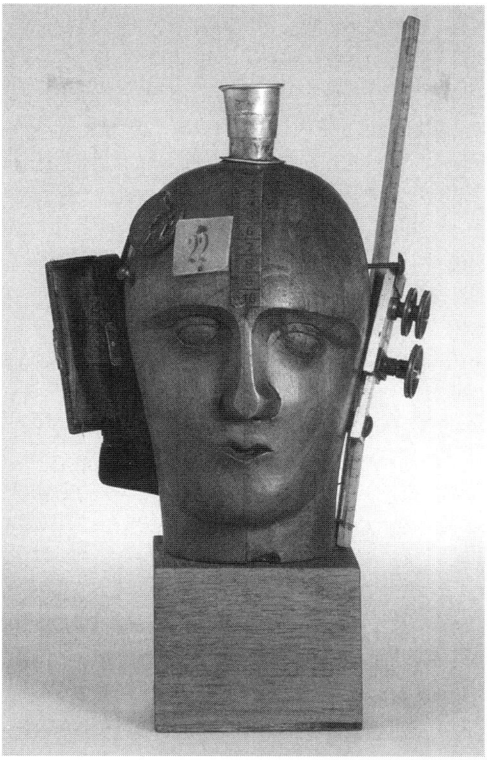

7 Raoul Hausmann: *The Spirit of our Time.* 1919

ries accounting for its existence and not on terms of the internally derived theories (content) that historically sustained it. Largely the result of theory, the avant-garde was perceived by Dada as blinded to its operational purposes and to its status as part of normal cultural production. The critique of the avant-garde by Berlin Dada (by the anti-avant-garde) concentrated itself on intercepting the institutional site responsible for authoring the avant-garde. By occupation of the site responsible for creating the avant-garde, the authentic avant-garde sought to guarantee its own role in the constitutive processes of larger culture, what was perceived as the only way of achieving the avant-garde project rather than the project's inherited and naively "radical" concept of itself. The traditional arts' and avant-garde's failure to compete for influence in the domain of culture-making accounts, in great part, for the Berliners' rejection of art and the avant-garde as inadequate to the tasks of meaningful cultural politics. The only course open for the Berliners was the execution of the avant-garde; putting it to death and prosecuting it. The avant-garde was demythified into something like its real status in culture through a process that was tantamount to the assassination of the avant-garde.

This thesis, tacitly and explicitly, seeks to retire idealistic aesthetics in favour of institutional theory (and theorising) and looks at avant-garde art in terms of its potential cultural and instrumental value. It further dismisses any conventional relationship between art and life in favour of an uncompromisingly transactional approach to social environment (environing). The advantages of such an approach are several-fold. They do not privilege the avant-garde in terms of how we best know it; indeed, it attempts to de-mythify it. They also render less important the distinction between the avant-gardes of the left and the right (different versions of the same thing), make no claim, imagined or otherwise, on the good life, and reduce any aesthetics to their proper status as part of the history of ideas.

Such a theory as this will certainly narrow rather than widen a usable concept of the avant-garde. It reflects on a few years and a few individuals. It will withdraw, however, from serving as a pacifier for current theories of the avant-garde dedicated to mourning the failure of something, as created by its creators, that never existed except in the minds of its enemies. I respectfully submit this thesis as a critique of the existing avant-garde literature and to the unbelievability of what remains its basic assumptions, its romantic ideas concerning art and life, and the passive concepts of humanism that it encourages.

NOTES

[1] For discussions of Baader, see the publications by Stephen C. Foster and Karl Riha as listed in the bibliography.

[2] The following discussion of Baader's actions in the Weimar National Assembly is excerpted with minor modifications from "The Prerequisite Text" (Foster 1988).

[3] It is hard to characterise a programme as eclectic as Baader's. Like Ritschl, he believed that the essentials of religious truth proceeded and transcended rationalistic scientific truth. "The function of Christianity", says Ritschl, "is to make morality possible". Morality is understood here to mean "the assertion of man's spiritual freedom", a point of view coinciding significantly with the individualism of liberalism. Also like Ritschl, Baader believed that the true function of Christianity was being jeopardised by both church and state. Although by no means an occultist, Baader probably agreed with Morgenstern who "still fixed his hope in inquiries that might prove scientifically the reality of the spirit". Blavasky and the Theosophic movement and her follower, Rudolph Steiner, founder of the later Anthroposophic Society, are systematic and organised versions of this impulse. And these found their counterparts in the Christian-Social movement originating out of both religious and secular circumstances; for example, Stoecker's "*Christlich-soziale Arbeiterpartei*" and Hiller's "*Rat geistiger Arbeiter*", respectively, the latter of which was parodied by Raoul Hausmann and Baader in their own creation of *ARDUA* ("*Anationaler Rat unbezahlter Arbeiter*"). See Pascal 1973 (especially chapter seven: "Religion and the Churches").

[4] But beyond his service to Dada, he had, by 1918, his own rather developed programme to serve. Thus, on July 30, 1918, Baader, with the sanction of Club Dada, presented himself for the Nobel Prize. The text for the action, "*Ein Brief an den Dichter Paul Ernst*", clarifies many of Baader's convictions and strategies and provides an important conceptual access to his pictorial work as well; pictorial work that normally served as visual texts for live events. Furthermore, it details the combined grounds, theological, philosophical, and scientific, upon which he perceived the "avant-garde" was best and most significantly able to act. The programme, in its essentials, is not so very different from St. Simon's. Like the latter (at least the late career), Baader's concerns centre largely on the spiritual and religious aspects of society; aspects whose laws, however, were discoverable through science. Both rejected an atomistic, in favour of a synthetic, concept of the universe. Both advocated a new social system based on universal associations. Likewise, in his perception of Ernst Haeckel as such a "founder of the new Christian Church", Baader is certainly looking well past Haeckel to such ultimate sources of Monistic thinking as St. Simon, whose *Nouveau Christianisme* (1825) served as basic text for the massive discontent with the orthodox church in early twentieth century Germany.

[5] In February 1919, a broadside entitled "Dadaists against Weimar" ("*Dadaisten gegen Weimar*") was issued by Club Dada, the official house organisation of the Berlin Group. The document called for the immediate end of the Republic ("We shall blow Weimar sky-high") and illustrates that

even at this relatively early point in the movement's history, Baader served the others as the nominal "head" or symbolic focus of the movement. He is defined here both as "Oberdada" and as "*Präsident des Erdballs*" ("President of the Globe"). A veritable confabulation of avant-garde attributes — although admittedly something of a parody of the historical avant-gardist — the Oberdada was, in his irony, a highly sophisticated rendering of profoundly felt but equally frustrated avant-garde intentions. It was the latter which prompted Richard Huelsenbeck's remarks, made in a rage, that "Baader had nothing whatsoever to do with art". (Cf. Huelsenbeck 1974: 67).

[6] By late 1919 and early 1920, Baader's work had achieved its greatest clarity in his *Der Verfasser des Buches Vierzehn Briefe Christi in seinem Heim*. Fragments formerly composing the very elements of his work are now consigned to the background, yet classified and arranged in a way not unlike their development in his earlier photocollages and photomontages. Traces of his earlier, more textual works are confined to the "D" (far left, centre top), the residual, but ubiquitous "*Dadaisten gegen Weimar*" always lying just below the surface. The materials pinned to the back wall are the front page of *Die freie Strasse* 10 (December 1918) and a picture spread from the newspapers. Although no more important than other items, they do call explicit attention to the press, the then reigning media paradigm, which directly and indirectly suffuses Baader's work on all levels; as content, as form, and to a considerable degree, as process and medium. *Die freie Strasse*, noted above, and the slightly later collage, *Gutenberggedenkblatt* (1920), illustrate Baader's use of the media both as format and as subject. Social realties for Baader, become largely a question of media realities. The newspaper format, as a "collage of events", is crucial to a proper understanding of Baader's visual work and of the relationships taken between his printed texts and announcements and their incorporation into his actions and photomontage.

[7] *Club der blauen Milchstrasse*, dating from 1920, pictures Baader's 1906 *Welttempel* (upper left), the broadside, "*Dadaisten gegen Weimar*" (centre) and the announcement of the *HADO*. Two important and new features appear here, however. The first difference involves the appropriated photomontage by Grosz and Heartfield, *Korrigiertes Meisterbild* (1920), an altered reproduction of a painting, *Myself: Portrait Landscape* (1890) by Henri Rousseau, proverbial in modernist circles as the "primitive of a new age". The gesture, for Grosz and Heartfield and for Baader, clearly alludes to Dada's (and Baader's) new era of peace and the new beginnings of the Berlin Dada movement. It might be, in addition, a pun or clever allusion to J. J. Rousseau, to whom the concept of the avant-garde, as understood by St. Simon, was so much indebted. The second difference involves the tying

of Baader's and Dada's programmes to the live event, indicated here by the announcement (top) of a March 12, 1919 manifestation (perhaps commemorating the foundation of the *Anationaler Rat unbezahlter Arbeiter*) and the lecture times at Dada's offices (lower right). Both references serve as concrete spanners between Baader's visual works and his live actions, manifestations and performances. The work is executed on the Hausmann poster.

[8] Hausmann makes a point of this in reference to Baader's authorship of the Manuel du Super-Dada (HADO). "En 1919 Baader commença à faire des photomontages. Ses montages dépassaient toute mésure par leur quantité formidable et leurs formats. Dans ce domaine il était comparable à Schwitters. Partout, où il pouvait, il arrachait des pancartes entères des murs et des colonnes d'affiches et les rapportait chez lui, où il les classait soigneusement. Entre autre il a fait un Manuel du Super-Dada (HADO): sur un fond fait de centaines de quotidiens, il collait journellement des documents nouveaux, des taches colorées, des chiffres et même des représentations figuratives de sa moisson d'affiches. Avec cela il créa une sorte de collage-littérature ou collage-poésie. Il serait regrettable, quo son Manuel soit perdu. Le premier HADO fut terminé le 26 juin 1919, le second le 28 juin 1920, comme Baader, avec son exactitude coutumière l'avait noté dans le catalogue de la Foire-Dada." (Hausmann 1958: 79).

Bibliography

Foster, Stephen C.

1980 "Johannes Baader: Kunst und Kulturkritik". In: *Dada: Sinn und Unsinn*, ed. W. Paulsen. Bern/Munich: Franke Verlag, 153-176.

1984 "*Mediale Wahrnehmung und städtische Realität: Die Kunst des Johannes Baader.*" *Die Zukunft der Metropolen.* Berlin: Dietrich Reimer Verlag, 528-531.

1985 "Johannes Baader: The Complete Dada". *Dada / Dimensions*, ed. Stephen C. Foster. Ann Arbor: UMI Research Press, 249-271.

1986 "hausmann-baader: *Der eigentliche Dada*". In: *Kurt Schwitters Almanach*, ed. Michael Erlhoff. Hannover: Postkriptum Verlag, 163-189.

1988 "The Prerequisite Text." *The Avant-Garde and the Text, Visible Language*, vol. XXI, no. 3-4, 313-333.

Hausmann, Raoul
1958 *Courrier Dada.* Paris: Le Terrain Vague.

Huelsenbeck, Richard
1974 *Memoirs of a Dada Drummer*, ed. Hans J. Kleinschmidt. New York: Viking.

Pascal, Roy
1973 From Naturalism to Expressionism. New York: Basic Books.

Riha, Karl, Hanne Bergius and Norbert Miller (eds.)
1977 *Johannes Baader, Oberdada.* Lahn-Giessen: Anabas-Verlag.

CRUCIAL MOMENTS, CRUCIAL POINTS: WALTER BENJAMIN AND THE RECOGNITION OF MODERNITY IN THE LIGHT OF THE AVANT-GARDE

BERND KIEFER

I.

In his *Theory of the Avant-Garde* Peter Bürger presents Walter Benjamin as a prominent theorist of the avant-garde. He discusses Benjamin's notions of the vanishing of the „aura" of art through the advances of technological reproduction, the new foundation of art in politics, and his theory of allegory as a theory of the avant-garde work of art. For Bürger Benjamin is above all a theorist of a politically motivated reintegration of art into social life, a theorist of the surrealists' revolution. This coincides with the particular interest which Bürger pursues in his own theory. Bürger's contention is that all avant-garde movements adhere to the same principle set out by surrealism: the reintegration of social life and art which was to serve as a basis for social revolution. That particular avant-garde project failed. However, Bürger's theory of the failure of the avant-garde is a theory of nostalgia post-1968, it is a the revolution's necrology.

Walter Benjamin's works were rediscovered by the student movements at the end of the 1960s and became the works of a revolutionary critic of the "moment". Especially Benjamin's great essay on *Surrealism* was highly influential as critique of contemporary and everday life of modernity in the light of the avant-garde. Surrealism, as Benjamin wrote, was a kind of explosion of the contemporaneous moment which drove the forces of art into life in a moment of crisis. In 1968 that moment was *now*, and, as Karl Heinz Bohrer wrote, it was the mystic moment of a cultural revolution, that was more inspired by romanticism, surrealism and pop-culture than by Marx or Lenin (Bohrer 1968). Bürger regards his *Theory of the Avant-Garde* as an extension of a book on French surrealism which he published in 1971. In the introduction to this book Bürger explains that the events of May 1968 ran parallel to certain aspects of surrealism: the revolt against society, the will to transform all human relationships, and the tendency to unite art and life (Bürger 1971: 7). When that revolt failed in the moment of 1968, surrealism had failed again and also Benjamin. It was then that surrealism and Benjamin became topics of historical academic interest. This marks the first crucial moment, the first crucial point. Bürger's reconstruction of the avant-garde and its consequent failure are deeply rooted within a historical post-1968 moment, profoundly connected to the utopian hope that avant-garde art, as well as its theory, could act upon political life. But that moment, reflected by Bürger in 1974, can now be described as the end of high art and the rising of pop art, of popular culture and media culture. That post-1968 moment can now be understood, as Susan Sontag or Leslie Fiedler and Arthur Danto point out, as the moment when pop and camp became the first manifestations of postmodernism, the current form of everyday life *without* the prospect of social revolution.

II.

The writings of Walter Benjamin have been regarded and interpreted as a body of work diveded into three distinct periods of thinking (cf. Kiefer 1994: 19-33). The first period spans from 1911 to 1928 and can be seen as a theological and metaphysical phase reflecting on the end of religion. Young Benjamin's task was to re-establish the notion of *full experience of being* in a theory of language, inspired by Cabbalistic and Messianic thought, and to develop a form of criticism, inspired by early German romanticism and Friedrich Schlegel, that envisages every work of art as a fragment of a wholeness that is never fully attained. In 1928 that phase reached its peak with two books: *Ursprung des deutschen Trauerspiels* and *Einbahn-*

straße (One-Way Street). *Ursprung des deutschen Trauerspiels* develops a theory of allegory as a poetic concept of the seventeenth-century fragmentation of time, space and human body caused by historical and religious upheaval during a time of war: allegory is thus portrayed as an expression of decline. *One-Way Street is* an allegorical piece of writing on the fragmentation of social time, space and human body during the Weimar Republic. *One-Way Street* is an avant-garde text, it is *écriture avant-gardiste*. Benjamin combines Louis Aragon's *mythologie moderne*, taken from Aragon's *Le Paysan de Paris*, with his own intentions of a recognition of modernity in decline. *Decline* is the key-word in *One-Way Street*, and *redemption* the magic word. The modern world lies in fragments, everthing natural gets wasted. But between *Ursprung des deutschen Trauerspiels* and *One-Way Street* there is a gap. Benjamin now aimed to give the social phenomenon of *fragmentation* a political, a marxist interpretation. It was not only Georg Lukács' theory of *reification* that impressed Benjamin. He was aware of a much broader confrontation between man and technology, he was aware of the possibility that all social technologies — mechanisation of labour and media of communication such as photography, film and radio — would not only transform the way a human body perceives and enacts reality, but also how the human body perceives and enacts itself.

The second period of Benjamin's work was initiated by his essay "Das Kunstwerk im Zeitalter seiner technischen Reproduzierbarkeit" (The Work of Art in the Age of Mechanical Reproduction). This essay represents a crucial moment Benjamin's oeuvre. Conceived as an outline of his theory of modernity in the light of the avant-garde, the text not only represents an intervention within aesthetics, but also within the politics of modernity: Benjamin concentrated aesthetics and politics into a *theory of modernity as theory of shock*. The modern age of technology submits man to the reign of total mechanisation, and the human body and human consciousness are completely transformed under the permanent influence of moments of shock. To Benjamin, the experience of *shock* is synonymous to the experience of *modernity*.

In the third and ultimate period of his life, Benjamin wrote his book on modernity in the light of the avant-garde: *Das Passagen-Werk* (The Arcades Project). It was published in 1982, more than forty years after Benjamin's suicide in 1940. It was neither planned as a philosophical work, nor as a complete theory of modernity, but as a book constructed upon of fragments and quotations of modernity. Benjamin is the first historian of modernity to write about the intermixture of high art and everyday life, of the politics of revolt and everyday life (cf. Buck-Morss 1993: 308-346). The structure of the book comprises a *montage* of voices calling from the past, of human voices of utopia, now saved from oblivion. But this is not a book as we know it. It deliberately breaks away from the traditional mould. Benjamin's intention was to collect modernity's past in a moment of historical crisis in order to allow utopian voices *now* to become the forces of revolution. But the crisis of modernity came with fascism and with the advent of the war. In the last years of his life, when in exile in Paris, Benjamin saw technology as a means of ending humanism, mankind and history. This marks another crucial moment, another crucial point.

Benjamins recognition of modernity in the light of the avant-garde, in the light of surrealism, is now historic. Modernism is gone, so is the impulse of the avant-garde to give modernism a revolutionary form by transforming art into everyday life and everday life into art. Past utopian voices can no longer be heard calling for an utopian revolution of the perception of the senses, as the voices of Charles Fourier and Charles Baudelaire do in the *Arcades Project*, and as those of the surrealists did. A genuine transformation of the perception of the senses took place with the end of humanism and history. But Benjamin was right in one point: the question posed on the last page of "The Work of Art in the Age of Mechanical Reproduction" is still profoundly pertinent: what is to become of the human perception of the senses as it is completely transformed by technology?

III.

For Walter Benjamin the first task of the critic was always to pinpoint the *crucial moment* that motivates and sometimes determines his criticism and interpretation of a given phenomenon. The critic has to identify his "now of recognition". In our time, this "now of recognition" is a crucial point, a critical moment. In his contribution to *Kunst ohne Geschichte*, a reply to Hans Belting's book *Das Ende der Kunstgeschichte*, Bürger again quotes Benjamin's concept of the "now of recognition" as well as Adorno and Horkheimer's notion of the "rock of the now, of the present". This peak, this rock, Bürger continues, is shattered. A theoretical overlook is no longer possible. The present is a plain, the plain of *postmodernism*, of the pluralism of the "anything goes", or even of the *post-histoire*, where everything has been said and done. We can indeed thus say that everything is over. But that would be taking Benjamin's philosophical theories of art and of the present state of art for granted.

In my opinion we have to reconsider *our* "now of recognition". What is our *now*? What is the crucial moment that motivates our attempt towards a reassessement of the European avant-garde? Why *now*? What is *my now* of recognition that motivates *my* attempt of a reassessement of Benjamin's recognition of modernity in the light of the avant-garde.

IV.

Today, in the year 2000, Johannes Gutenberg appears as the "Man of the Millenium". In Mainz the the 600th birthday of Gutenberg was celebrated. There were many exhibitions, conferences and lectures bordering on such subjects as the culture of books, writing, printing, reading and the connection between humanism and book culture. But other questions were also raised: What will the fate of humanism be if the culture of books, writing and reading vanishes as we enter the realm of artificial images? In what way is humanism connected with media history?

Throughout his entire œuvre Walter Benjamin is concerned with these issues. In *One-Way Street* Benjamin wrote about the forthcoming end of books in the age of film and advertising and about the vanishing shape of the human body in such an age. He wrote about media, about books, about the historical content of books, about the sedimentation of historical experience in language and writing. He wrote about and for the radio, for education programmes for children, about literature and photography, about theatre and film, and he even wrote, in his notes to "Der Erzähler" (The Storyteller), about the new medium of television. Television will draw an end to story-telling as we know it, an end to "wisdom" through the telling of stories, and so, Benjamin concludes, “we are afraid of it”. But then he adds: “Tant mieux. Nicht weinen” — “It’s for good, don’t cry”.

Benjamin’s texts oscillate between a form of a *destruction* and a form of revolutionary nihilism. This is a reflection of the avant-garde position which calls for an end to (bourgeois) humanism through the use of new media, *and* is reminiscent of the position of one who collects the vanishing fragments of humanism — a Cabbalist, who reads the unwritten history of the arcades, a critic, who wants to “save” things, that are determined to sink into oblivion.

V.

In September and October 1999, the debate between Peter Sloterdijk and Jürgen Habermas took place. Sloterdijk gave a talk at a conference on Heidegger and Lévinas, in which he closely connected humanism with the culture of the letter, the book, the written word. The humanism of books, writing and reading, of teaching and learning appears to him as the only way of taming the human. But *now* — this is the *now* of Sloterdijk — not only do we have to confront the new setting of new media, we also have to face the *end of humanism* and a new kind of *social avant-garde*. Although Sloterdijk does not use this notion, what he means is very clear: *anthropo-technology* and *bio-genetics* are about to accomplish the unfulfilled prophecy of the avant-garde movements: the reintegration of art into the practice of life through the creation of artificial life. Let me remind you of Dziga Vertov’s *Kinoglaz* Manifesto from 1923: “I am kinoglaz, I will create man, more perfect than Adam, I will create thousands of different me […]. Through montage I will create the new, the perfect man.” That was a utopia of avantagarde film.

In his debate with Habermas — Habermas was strongly opposed to Sloterdijks proclamation that classical humanism had ended — Sloterdijk also declared the end of critical theory in the tradition of the Frankfurt School along with their “antiquated” concept of humanism. In my opinion, Walter Benjamin is the first philosopher of modernity to give modern humanism a new shape despite the rapid process of the fragmentation of life, despite the aesthetics of life and life-style caused by the advent of the new media and the perverse Pyrrhic victory of the avant-garde movements. They did not succeed in a revolutionary transformation of social life, although futurist, dadaist and surrealist, even punk elements of the avant-garde could be integrated into what one might call post-bourgeois life-style. It may well be that this is what we call *postmodernism*: the *everyday avant-garde life-style* without aiming at a social revolution, all the while encouraging technology. This could be what we now call *post-histoire*: *post-capitalism* without an intent for revolution which recycles every pre-modernist, modernist and avant-gardiste gesture as a quotation, an allusion, a pastiche, even a *reproduction* of man, "more human than the human" (see *Blade Runner*).

Was Benjamin aware of this? Did he and could he anticipate this? I believe, he did. In the last paragraphs of *The Work of Art in the Age of Mechanical Reproduction* he quotes from a manifesto of Marinetti in which the latter celebrates war, "because it initiates the dreamt of metalisation of the human body". Benjamin brands this an „aestheticisation of politics", more specifically of fascist politics. In the light of his other texts, this is the counterpoint of Benjamin's concept of modern humanism — in the light of the avant-garde.

VI.

The destruction of the form and shape of the human body in the age of modernity is embodied by *work*, work on the re-shaping of the contour of the human body. What constitutes modern man? According to Benjamin's studies on Baudelaire, modern man is "betrayed of his experiences", and he wants to be rid of experience to be free to feel pure *sensations*. The *in between* is the crucial point of Benjamin's humanism: he conceives man not as "metallic", but as an open body aware of his own mortality, knowing that he will have to deal with fragments of life without in the end being able to form a life-style, a whole life, out of the fragments. Benjamin's modern humanism consists in *practising life* as a work of art, in *telling* life as a work of art, thus sharing life in being told and telling it — the open I and the open you, the open eye and the open ear — just as storytellers did before the stories were written and printed and could be taken away from him.

VII.

Now, we experience "Global Benjamin". We can read three volumes (2000 pages) of international criticism of Benjamin in Klaus Garber and Ludger Rehm's edition of the contributions to the 1992 conference on Walter Benjamin (Garber and Rehm 1999). Benjamin can be linked to nearly everbody and to nearly everything. We have "Global Benjamin" as a subject, that can be divided into a thousand pieces, crucial moments, crucial points.

Throughout his entire body of work, Benjamin's intention was, as he wrote in a letter to Adorno, the philosophical recognition of modernity. He concentrated on this recognition through the notions of *experience* and *body-space*. There is, in all of Benjamin's theology, philosophy of language, politics of writing, philosophy of the media and philosophy of history a strong interest in *materialistic anthropology* as the basis of *modern humanism*. To conceive this theory — not as a "great theory", a "méta-récit", as Jean-François Lyotard would say — Benjamin let himself be inspired by the avant-garde movements. But he was never a follower of any avant-garde trend: not of expressionism, futurism, dadaism or constructivism, not even of surrealism. Benjamin's approach to the avant-garde is a pluralistic and eclectic one. For Benjamin, the avant-garde movements not only explored new ways of expanding the boundaries of art, of turning art into life, but also new ways of the *conditio humana*, of *la condition moderne*. They investigated the bursting of the old life structures as well as the superposition of the 'father' in the experience of social reality and identity (expressionism); the dominance of contingency and the experience of *shock* in the attempt to construct a life (dada); the confrontation of the human body with modern technology (futurism); and the opening of the realm of dreams and the subconsciousness in order to explore everyday life as a kind of reverie (surrealism).

VIII.

So what did Benjamin do with all these avant-garde inspirations? Firstly, I would say, in some sense Benjamin was overwhelmed by them, he was convinced that all those intentions and elements of the avant-garde movements, all those outsider positions, could be set against the new shape of capitalism in the 1920s and early 1930s. But at this crucial point we have to read one more time Benjamin's texts, for example the text on Georges Sorel: "Zur Kritik der Gewalt". Let us read it *closely*, read it against the grain as Jacques Derrida did. We will then find Benjamin's avant-garde fascination with destruction, his will for making *tabula rasa* with humanism and democracy, his "ambiguity", as Derrida calls it (Derrida 1991: 60). But I would also say that Benjamin in his later texts drew a line between the avant-garde's destructive intentions and his own intention of revolutionary redemption of the potentials of modernity. We can find this intention in *The Work of Art in the Age of Mechanical Reproduction* and in Benjamins intended *opus magnum*, the *Arcades Project*.

The Work of Art in the Age of Mechanical Reproduction is a landmark in the history of media theory, but Benjamin conceived this text as an outline of his *theory of modernity* as a *materialistic anthropology* and an *essay on humanism*. He therefore concentrated on all the subjects that were dear to him: on perception, the consciousness of the senses and the history of the senses, and on experience, the experience of the word as it is and as an image. Benjamin's text has been interpreted in different, contradictory ways: as a manifesto celebrating photography and film as the media of modernity in the future, but also as a critique of the destruction of the aura of the work of art through technical reproduction. I would propose a further reading: to read the text as a *poetic* text, as an avant-garde text of our *moment*, of the *moment* of human beings with a lost centre. *We* seem to be the actors who live in permanent reproduction, without knowing what we have lost. *The Work of Art in the Age of Mechanical Reproduction* is a text about the end of art, which man needed to shape himself; it's about the end of the history of art, which man needed as a concept of *Bildung*. *Now* — and that is Benjamin's *now*, not mine — *now* man no longer needs art, he no longer needs art history, for all art now is present in the form of medial reproduction. What man needs *now* is a form of sensual life that can resist to be reproduced.

IX.

I think that Walter Benjamin gave modern humanism, which is determined by existing in the age of reproduction, but wishes to resist being reproduced, a form. Benjamins *Arcades Project* represents this form. The *aesthetics* of the text is its *ethics*. There is history in the quotations from all books of the modern world; there is montage and collage of text fragments to testify the free will of the author, who no longer wishes to be an author; and there is also the reader who is invited to read this page or any page, the reader who is free to move, to read this book that no longer is a book, read it like no other reader has read it before him or will ever read after him. That represents modernity for Walter Benjamin. If there is anything left of that modernity that tries to stay in contact with the impulses of the avant-garde, it may not be art anymore. It may be a life in total awareness of what Benjamin wrote in 1928 in his book *One-Way Street*: We have to live now with what is left over. And we have to grasp it with our left hand.

Bibliography

Bohrer, Karl Heinz
1997 "1968: Die Phantasie an die Macht? Studentenbewegung - Walter Benjamin - Surrealismus". In: *Merkur*, 1997, no. 12, 1069-1080.

Bürger, Peter
1971 *Der französische Surrealismus. Studien zum Problem der avantgardistischen Literatur*. Frankfurt am Main: Athenäum.

1984 *Theory of the Avant-Garde*. Minneapolis: University of Minnesota Press.

Kiefer, Bernd
1994 *Rettende Kritik der Moderne. Studien zum Gesamtwerk Walter Benjamins*. Frankfurt am Main: Peter Lang.

Buck-Morss, Susan
1993 *Dialektik des Sehens. Walter Benjamin und das Passagen-Werk.* Frankfurt am Main: Suhrkamp.

Garber, Klaus, and Ludger Rehm (eds)
1999 *Global Benjamin. Internationaler Walter-Benjamin-Kongreß 1992.* München: Fink.

Jacques Derrida
1991 *Gesetzeskraft. Der "mystische Grund der Autorität".* Frankfurt am Main: Suhrkamp.

II.

INNOVATIONS AND MANIFESTATIONS OF THE AVANT-GARDE

APOLLINAIRE AND CUBIST INNOVATION: RESETTING THE FRONTIERS, CHANGING THE PARADIGM

IAN REVIE

So much of Bürger's theory of the avant-garde rests upon his location of his "historical avant-garde" that to demonstrate the existence of its characteristics at an earlier moment is not merely to quarrel with his definition in terms of literary and cultural history, it is to take issue with the nature of avant-gardism as Bürger has defined it and in so doing to raise questions that are of vital importance in allied areas. The nature of modernism — its very viability as a term — and therefore that also of postmodernism will be called into question just as much by a recontextualising of the notion of avant-gardism or by a revalorising of the term, so that the recent assertion by Anne Friedberg that avant-gardism is a troublesome (i.e. merely distracting) third term in the modernism-postmodernism debate (cf. Friedberg 1993: 162-168) is turned on its head and avant-gardism as defined here will emerge as the central concept.

The present essay will show the early and continuing existence of motifs in the poetry of Guillaume Apollinaire, which begins with the century itself, as fundamental to the attraction between the poet and the Cubist painters, particularly Picasso, and as crystallising concepts central to the work as to the notion of the avant-garde. The intention is not to claim that Apollinaire is father to it but to relocate the definition of avant-gardism. This is not to say that the historical context is negligible. It is, after all, of primary importance to see the emergence of the term in relation to social, political and cultural activity in just such a context, if we are to understand why we speak of the avant-garde (and not the vanguard etc.). The term, of course, is French and its emergence firstly into this area of discourse and its secondary acquisition of its presently accepted currency need to be related to contemporary events. It would be a superficial response which simply accepted the cultural hegemony of "belle époque" France as reason enough; the birth of the term has been studied in a richly complex perspective by the monumental work of Michel Décaudin, *La Crise des valeurs symbolistes*.

Among other things, Décaudin draws attention to the fact that the first years of the century, up to and including the birth of Dada, saw an explosion in the number of "isms", whether launched, as famously were both Impressionism and Cubism, by negative reaction in the press, or by conscious manifesto and rallying cry. Yet, as the title of his study shows, for Décaudin this phenomenon is best understood in the context of the slow death of a dominant cultural climate — at least as far as Paris was concerned — while more recent studies, in particular Antoine Compagnon's *La Troisième République des Lettres*, have stressed the creation of a generalised climate, within which a conscious cultural policy aimed at consolidating the values of the state emerges. It is precisely this aspect and the early resistance to it, which must be re-explored, in order to explain the slippage of the term from its culturally positive and therefore politically acceptable face — where the vanguard leads, soon others will follow — to the oppositional sense with which it is now most commonly used. Although it is not just the moment when the French Third Republic began to use cultural and educational policy in this way which would suffice as a defining starting point for the question we address any more than would the recognition of conscious artistic disobedience or misbehaviour in its presence.

Of course, Bürger does distinguish precisely this aspect in his attempt to differentiate avant-gardism from modernism. In making this distinction in terms of the assault on language and the assault on the institutions of art, Bürger fails completely to allow for the revolutionary impact of Cubism's assault on the central tenet of almost five hundred years of Western art — the primacy of single point perspective. And in failing to see that the figure of "le flâneur" — so important in Friedberg's otherwise highly convincing study of late-nineteenth and early twentieth century developments in the environment of cultural production — he singularly neglects an important body of evidence, which, when properly evaluated, removes the neat historical beginning attributed by him to the avant-garde and which therefore challenges its definition. The present essay is intended only as a modest beginning to an eventual redefinition of the term avant-gardism and in just such a direction.

Two studies — one recent and the other now some fifteen years old — Peter Read's *Picasso et Apollinaire* and Willard Bohn's *Apollinaire et l'homme sans visage* have made substantial progress in reclaiming for the poet a more central position in relation to developments in the visual arts than had generally been attributed to him in the years after his death in 1918. For while, during his lifetime, Apollinaire was widely associated with the birth of Cubism and allied movements such as Simultanism (as well as the parallel Futurism), both through his championing of the works of the artists and through the pivotal role he played in drawing together Braque and Picasso in 1905, Picasso, in particular, was inclined to be dismissive of his understanding of what "we" were doing, once Apollinaire was no longer there. Read's work has excellently drawn on archive materials to show that not only did Picasso find in Apollinaire's poetry, when he was alive, much that for him was closely allied to his own artistic researches, but that those aspects of the poetry continued to feed the painter's own work throughout his life.

Bohn's less recent study demonstrates the emergence in a famous work by the French poet of a motif — that of the faceless man — which was to be so fundamental to the paintings of Giorgio di Chirico as to constitute Apollinaire as the inspiration for the Italian's lifetime project. The faceless man who is found in the course of a stroll round one of Apollinaire's favourite quarters — the area surrounding the church of Saint-Merry now sacrificed largely to those representations of urban modernism or postmodernism, the Pompidou Centre and the Forum des Halles — is indeed central to much twentieth century iconography. And while *Le Musicien de Saint-Merry* dates from 1914, the mysterious figure, who, in Bohn's view, dominates the poem can be shown to have many avatars in Apollinaire's work stretching back to some of his earliest poems while also being accepted by Read and others as a powerful

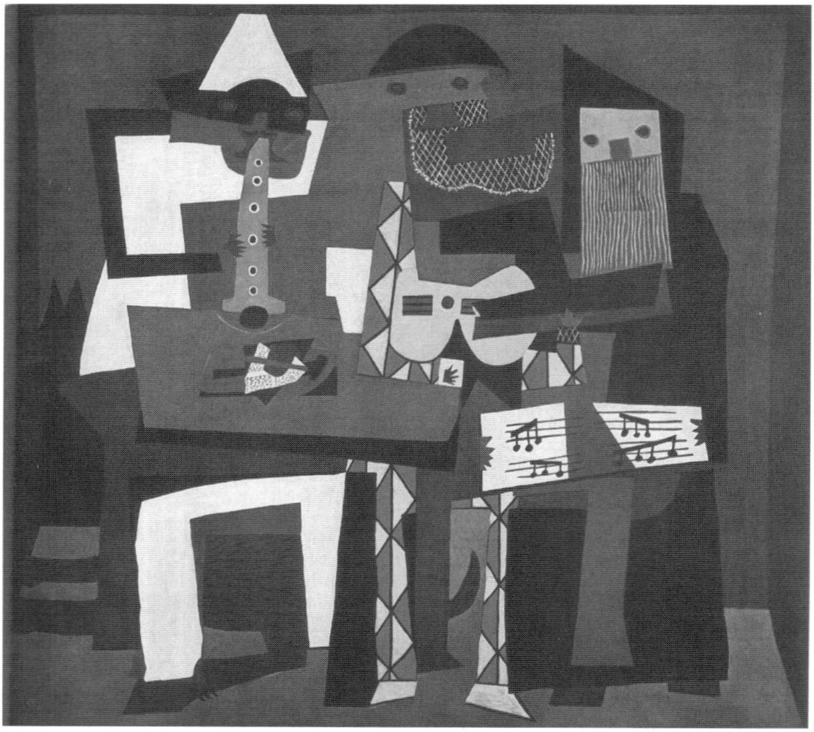

8 Pablo Picasso: *The Three Musicians*. 1921

source of Picasso's inspiration in creating his *Trois Musiciens* in 1921. Similarly the poetry written both prior to the encounter with Picasso in 1905 and that written during their subsequent friendship encompassing the birth of Cubism and its evolution, depends to such a degree aesthetically on similar figures, who in their wanderings, so clearly are the counterpart to the loss of single point perspective, as to make it possible to assert the fundamental role played by Apollinaire in the creation of the avant-garde in the dawn of the century. This is, as Read draws out, not to assert that Apollinaire was Picasso's inspiration but to show the convergence of their work. It is moreover in the refusal by both men — poet as much as painter — to let their art remain confined within the boundaries of a new style, however revolutionary, that we find one of the fundamental characteristics of the true avant-garde, which, whether expressed in a fleeting return to a modified classicism or in other forms of restless changeability, is the rejection of a fixed position, of the simple replacement of the old language by the new. Here indeed is the assault upon language and upon the institutions of art that can be seen to be embodied in Apollinaire's poetry not only in faceless, enigmatic and wandering figures but also in the constant themes of loss and forgetfulness as necessary and positive in modern life:

> Où est le Christophe Colomb à qui l'on devra l'oubli
> d'un continent.
>
> ("Toujours", Apollinaire 1965: 237)

While many lines chosen from many of the poems in the latter sections of *Calligrammes* (subtitled *Poèmes de la paix et de la guerre* and published in 1917) might serve, as does the above, to illustrate this aspect of Apollinaire's poetry, because Read's focus is much more on the impact of Apollinaire on Picasso, and because Bohn's study focuses almost exclusively on the one poem, it is equally important in advancing the present hypothesis, to present the case for the very early presence and central importance of similar themes in Apollinaire.

> Quand un homme sans yeux sans nez et sans oreilles
> Quittant le Sébasto entra dans la rue Aubry-le-Boucher
> Jeune l'homme était brun et ce couleur de fraise sur les joues
> Homme Ah! Ariane
> Il jouait de la flûte et la musique dirigeait ses pas
> Il s'arrêta au coin de la rue Saint-Martin
> Jouant l'air que je chante et que j'ai inventé
>
> ("Le Musicien de Saint-Merry", Apollinaire 1965: 188)

Thus Bohn's focus on while it certainly reveals the degree of identification between the poet, his poetry and the faceless musician, also needs to be brought into contact with such early and intensely personal pieces as "L'Emigrant de Landor Road", written from the experience of the failure of Apollinaire's love for the English woman Annie Playden, and first published in 1905 (although containing elements going back to 1902):

> Le chapeau à la main **il** entra du pied droit
> Chez un tailleur très chic et fournisseur du roi

Ce commerçant venait de couper quelques têtes
De mannequins vêtus comme il faut qu'on se vête
[...]
Mon bateau partira demain pour l'Amérique
Et **je** ne reviendrai jamais
("L'Emigrant de Landor Road", Apollinaire 1965: 105)

Its opening lines (my emphasis) reveal the same insistent multiplication of the self and the confrontation with mutilation and violence, which, while they can be read as externalisations of the poet's inner turmoil because of the loss of the object of desire, need also to be read as centrally connected to a position which systematically denies a centred self and a single perspective on the world. Read, that is, as fundamentals of the poetry and the poet, rather than mere adjuncts of a contingent experience.

Exactly the same is true of the opening to "La Chanson du Mal Aimé", which many consider to be Apollinaire's greatest poem, and which certainly arose from the same unsuccessful pursuit of the timid English governess, but which goes on to reconfigure time and space, past, present, London, Paris, Germany, the city and the Steppes, Earth and the Heavens, in as radical and challenging a manner as any early Cubist work or, indeed, the later Simultanist art of both Delaunays. And this work too, while its first publication dates from 1909, has been shown to belong to the years 1903/4.

Un soir de demi-brume à Londres
Un voyou qui ressemblait à
Mon amour vint à ma rencontre
Et le regard qu'il me jeta
Me fit baisser les yeux de honte

Je suivis ce mauvais garçon
Qui sifflotait mains dans les poches
Nous semblions entre les maisons
Onde ouverte de la mer Rouge
Lui les Hébreux moi Pharaon

Que tombent ces vagues de briques
Si tu ne fus pas bien aimée
Je suis le souverain d'Egypte
Sa soeur-épouse son armée

Si tu ne fus pas l'amour unique
("La Chanson du Mal Aimé", Apollinaire 1965: 46)

The refusal to accept any position fixed in space, time or self, is carried over into the instabilities of language itself via the play on the possible interpretations of "Je suis" (I am or I follow). And the finale is shot through with an ironic modern, yet jester-clad vision of the city:

J'erre à travers mon beau Paris
Sans avoir le coeur d'y mourir

Les dimanches s'y éternisent
Et les orgues de Barbarie
Y sanglotent dans les cours grises
Les fleurs aux balcons de Paris
Penchent comme la tour de Pise

Soirs de Paris ivres du gin
Flambant de l'électricité
Les tramways feux verts sur l'échine
Musiquent aux long des portées
De rails leur folie de machines

Les cafés gonflés de fumée
Crient tout l'amour de leurs tziganes
De tous leurs siphons enrhumés
De leurs garçons vêtus d'un pagne
Vers toi toi que j'ai tant aimée

Moi qui sais des lais pour les reines
Les complaintes de mes années
Des Hymnes d'esclaves aux murènes
La romance du mal aimé
Et des chansons pour les sirènes
("La Chanson du Mal Aimé", Apollinaire 1965: 59)

Here clearly we can see much that may well have appealed to Picasso, because resembling his own art, in this poetry, but it far outstrips the pink and blue period paintings in their attempt to deal with similar themes.

While several studies — including one of my own: "The Banality of Modernism" in *Poetry in France* — have pointed up the relationship of Apollinaire's *saltimbanques* with the figures from these pre-Cubist phases of Picasso's work, this has tended to place the emphasis on what in the painter drew the sympathy and abiding interest of the poet. If now we begin to look on pre 1910 Paris as a significant challenge to the frontiers laid down by Bürger, then that emphasis needs to be reversed. This would be equally true, even were we to look for evidence in the area of graphic presentation as a highly significant characteristic of all the arts of the period, for even here, the emergence of lettering in early Cubist painting, and even more so in the use of newspapers in collage, is prefigured in another aspect of Apollinaire's work (whose fascination with the random and the daily is alluded to in the title of my earlier essay) which can be shown to have been of primary importance in the definitions offered by a range of critics (from Bürger to Friedberg) as characteristic of both modernism and avant-gardism. This is, of course, the influence of the layout of the newspaper page — without wishing to discount the importance of the earlier typographical experimentalism of Stéphane Mallarmé — which, when viewed from outside the conventions of the typesetters (who figure in some of the most challengingly modern poems of both Apollinaire and Cendrars) presented such feats of aesthetic daring as to belittle the poets' efforts to break with the conventions of versification and challenge a centred readership perspective. Perhaps because Apollinaire himself long nurtured his project to publish a volume of verse arranged according to essentially graphic criteria under the title *Anch'io son pittore*, many have seen this aspect of his work to be essentially due to the influence of painters (whether Italian or Spanish). Typical of this perspective is that presented by one of the most commonly available studies in English of Apollinaire — Francis Steegmuller's *Apollinaire, Poet among the Painters*.

The urgent task now, and here Friedberg is right in the links she draws between technological and urban innovation and the contemporary arts from the end of the nineteenth century onwards, is to re-evaluate the impact of the daily, the banal in their irruption into an aesthetic domain, which, as Décaudin knew, Symbolism had tried to maintain in its unbreachable isolation. For reasons such as this, Décaudin locates the emergence of the Parisian avant-garde as c.

1910. Following on the Futurist manifesto and the crystallisation of an anti-bourgeois spirit (Décaudin 1960, ch. iv). In this sphere too, the relations between the poetry of Apollinaire and numerous embodiments of early avant-garde activity — not least the appearance of various manifestos — require us to relocate and redefine the accepted views of the origins of avant-garde and of the celebrated Bürger definition of the "sublation of the practice of art within the praxis of life". The frequently repeated injunction in Apollinaire's work to take all aspects of the modern as the vanguard of radicalism, because not held within conventions of the aesthetic, and to accept the discontinuity and fractured nature of contemporary experience as the true basis on which to re-align the arts, must however also be seen in the context of his sometimes painful, sometimes joyful opening up to those aspects of the modern which pulled the rug from under the feet of the single-point perspective artist:

> O mon amie hâte-toi
> Crains qu'un jour un train ne t'émeuve
> Plus
> Regarde-le plus vite pour toi
> Ces chemins de fer qui circulent
> Sortiront bientôt de la vie
> Ils seront beaux et ridicules
>
> ("La Victoire", Apollinaire 1965: 310)

Poems such as "La Victoire" almost always also contain the references to the inadequacy of language, the demand that it should be subject to violent assault, which has lead partisans of Apollinaire to stress his role as precursor of both Dada and Surrealism, despite the adherents of these movements having dismissed him as too timid, or worse. But to enter into that argument now and from that perspective would be to neglect the more radical possibility of leaving aside claims of historical precedence in favour of a reshaping of the notion of avant-gardism. For what, to those who point to the enduring presence of the octosyllable, with its complex music, in Apollinaire's verse, and who not infrequently buttress their arguments with reference to the apparent backtracking from his radical past that took place particularly in the period between his trepanning and his death, is evidence of timidity, can be shown to be more persuasive evidence of a distrust of the idea that the "new style" (or *Esprit nouveau* to accept Apollinaire's own and perhaps over-inclusive label) once discovered would be stable, self-perpetuating. In this respect also, Picasso's periodic willingness to return to more classical forms and perhaps especially his late-period dialogue with masters of earlier epochs can be seen to have been foreshadowed by Apollinaire and to constitute one of the essential characteristics of the avant-garde.

However, since the main focus here is on the need to move beyond Bürger, it becomes particularly illuminating to take first of all an apparent side-step in to another debate and to look, in the light of Anne Friedberg's recent study *Window Shopping* at the way in which a parallel failure to recognise what the primary characteristics of the period really were has lead to the conclusion of the rejection of avant-gardism as an appropriate category. Friedberg's fascinating — but nonetheless teleologically overdetermined — study leading into a discussion of postmodernism and, essentially, the cinema, locates the emergence of "le flâneur" and the creation of the department store together with the "Passage" — an early precursor of the shopping mall — as the key elements in the development of what she terms "the mobile virtual gaze", which is in turn the principal defining characteristic of modern spectatorship and therefore of postmodernism. However, her failure to distinguish between the manifestations of "le flâneur" in the poetry of Baudelaire and that of Apollinaire leads her to overlook, as Bürger has done, key developments in the early years of the twentieth century. Where Baudelaire's itinerant observer of Paris retains an essential unity (or perhaps painful duality) of the self, his observations being caught in the contradictions of *Spleen* and *Idéal*, Apollinaire's flâneur undergoes a de-centred experience of multiple identification and loss that can be found even in the texts, of the most whimsical journalistic kind, as exemplified by many of those in *Le Flâneur des deux rives*, but this same sense also permeates the volume *Alcools* which he published in the same year as his often disparaged as too poetic *Les Peintres cubistes*.

It is curious that, while Friedberg may be forgiven on the grounds that she merely perpetuates an already long history of Anglo-American assimilation of the roots of the inspiration for Anglo-American modernism to that same phenomenon in the face of the persistent failure of the term modernism to take hold in France,

Bürger should attempt to separate the avant-garde from the modernist through the same failure to recognise the importance, more even the nature, of what happened in Paris in the years preceding the outbreak of the First World War. There are critics who, like Malcolm Bradbury, rather than try to understand the essentially continental phenomenon which was to inspire the English language writers to create a movement for which the label "modernist" does have some genuine value, go so far as to proclaim that modernism is quite simply an Anglo-American phenomenon. How odd then that Pound, Eliot, Joyce and Stein should have this need of Europe, of Paris, of Cubism and of French poets from Laforgue to Apollinaire! Yet here is Bürger with his "historical avant-garde" overlooking all that the early years of the century, and not solely in Paris and Cubism, but also in Russia and in Germany, needs to be assimilated to the phenomenon so that we may be free from the cloud of falsely based historical distinctions in which we presently exist.

As was stated at the outset, the purpose of this essay was never to erect Apollinaire as the father of the avant-garde nor yet to claim that 1900 is a real boundary, since neither proposition would be true. But in taking away Bürger's starting point, in refusing a radical epiphany to Dada, in favour of emphasising a more gradual emergence of numerous factors, social, urban and artistic, which precede the leap to Cubism's abandonment of single point perspective (in which I have not even tried to establish the well acknowledged role of Cézanne and other predecessors) I have wanted to suggest that what has been called avant-garde, while not denying it that label, has been wrongly presented and to suggest also that the first characteristic of the avant-garde is its permanent instability and its refusal of a merely stochastic response. When, in 1917, Apollinaire writes:

> A l'institut des jeunes aveugles on a demandé
> *N'avez-vous point de jeune aveugle ailé*
>
> O bouches l'homme est à la recherche d'un nouveau langage
> Auquel le grammairien d'aucune langue n'aura rien à dire
> ("La Victoire", Apollinaire 1965: 309-310)

— he was saying essentially the same thing as Picasso when the latter emphasised the primacy for him (but also for others) of the artist's activity as a constant search for something that is not yet and which, if found, cannot be repeated. A fairly striking, but nonetheless little noted, example of this can be found in the mark made by that other "Modernism" (Art nouveau, Jugendstil) in the work of the Paris-based avant-garde. Virtually its sole reflection, and that an indirect one, consists in the use of the title Nord-Sud which celebrated the opening of the metro line linking the two seminal foyers of Monmartre and Montparnasse — the architecture and decoration of the metro being characterised by its art nouveau approach. That which had become or was becoming a style is not to be found in their work. Yet to conclude too quickly that what is under discussion here is merely a quest for innovation or novelty would be to ignore the evidence that abounds in the work of Apollinaire and Picasso of the willingness to return to the classical, in whatever shape or form. Each line written, each canvas approached is both dialogue with its predecessors and an attempt to find that which will stand alone.

It would appear, therefore, that the label "modernism" has been a serious barrier in the past and continues to be so in the present to a fruitful understanding of the avant-garde. It may well be that crossing oceans, or merely the English Channel, makes for a more intelligible re-alignment of the term with the idea of the avant-garde than is the case in Europe. As Freidberg shows, this fault-line is still active to the present day. To attempt, therefore, this enterprise of redefinition, is clearly not merely a matter of literary and cultural history; it is to address our understanding of the art of the present, of the category of a neo-avant-garde and to wrest from the grasp of the modernism — postmodernism debate the crucial question of the status of all culture and its objects. High modernism, if we surrender to the term, is seen as attempting to preserve high culture from the pressures of the masses; avant-gardism abandons this opposition. The enthusiasm with which Picasso, Apollinaire and many others embraced the comic-strip, the newspaper page, the infant cinema and the scandalous public event, fore-runner to the Happening, clearly shows us the need to change with our historical perspective our present understanding, the need to re-define our terms.

BIBLIOGRAPHY

Apollinaire, Guillaume
1965 *Œuvres poétiques*. Paris: Gallimard.

Aspley, Keith, and Peter France (eds)
1992 *Poetry in France*. Edinburgh: Edinburgh University Press.

Bohn, Willard
1984 *Apollinaire et l'homme sans visage*. Rom: Bulzoni.

Compagnon, Antoine
1983 La Troisième Républiques des lettres. Rom: Editions du Seuil.

Décaudin, Michel
1960 *La Crise des valeurs Symbolistes*. Toulouse: Editions Privat.

Friedberg, Anne
1993 *Window Shopping*. Berkeley: University of California Press.

Read, Peter
1995 *Picasso et Apollinaire* Paris: Editions Jean-Michel Place.

Steegmuller, Francis
1963 *Apollinaire: Poet among the Painters*. London: Rupert Hart-Davis.

CUBIST PAINTING, AUTOMATIC WRITING AND THE POETRY OF GERTRUDE STEIN

DIETRICH SCHEUNEMANN

Pablo Picasso's *Les Demoiselles d'Avignon* has been described as the "turning point" in a five hundred year old tradition of painting, and as the "most important pictorial document" of the 20th century (cf. Fry 1978: 16; Golding 1981, 53; Daix 1982: 31). As an unfinished *work in progress* it displays a number of the artistic innovations which signalled a decisive breakaway of the cubist painters from the conventions of their métier. With the representation of the human body reduced to geometrical forms of lozenges and triangles, and with a face depicted as a mask, the figure to the left of the picture immediately introduces two new astonishing elements in the composition. The figures in the centre add what will arguably become the most important change in the history of painting for almost 400 years: the one-point perspective creating the traditional spacial illusion on a flat canvas is replaced here by a combination of multiple viewpoints. The central figures in *Les Demoiselles* introduce this fundamental shift in pictorial representation in a rather moderate way by combining a profile view of the nose with a frontal view of the rest of the face. The figure in the lower right-hand corner displays all these elements in a radicalised form. The body is composed out of geometrical shapes. The face is depicted in the form of a mask. The whole image combines a rear view of the body with a profile and frontal perspec-tive of the mask-like face. Although clearly indicating the "turning point" in the

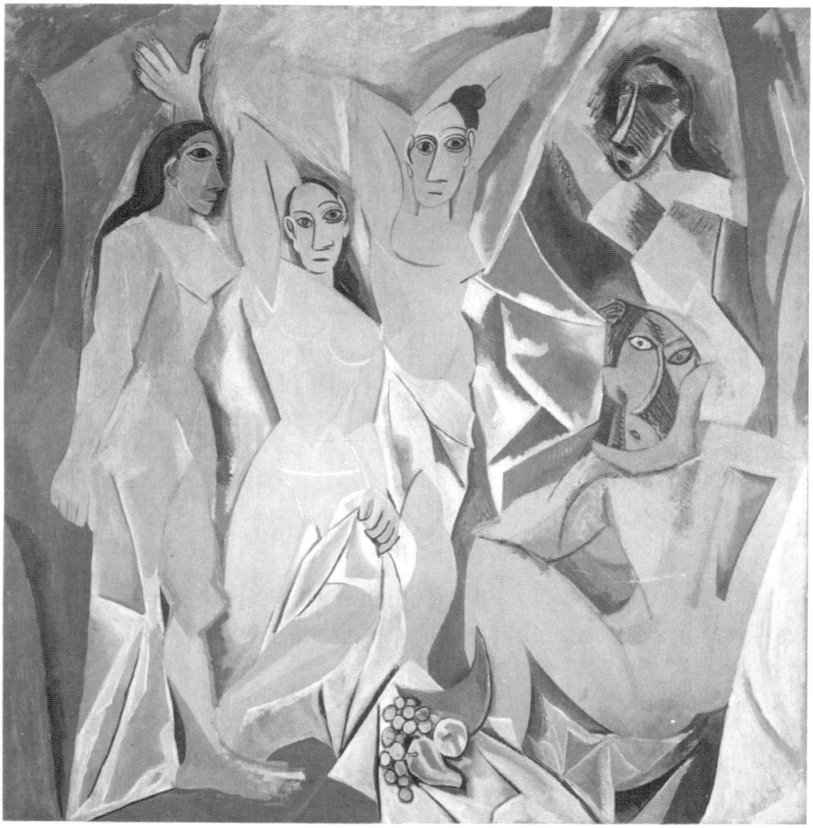

9 Pablo Picasso: *Les Demoiselles d'Avignon*. 1907

history of painting, *Les Demoiselles d'Avignon* represents just the starting point of a series of innovations which Picasso and Braque put forward in the short period between 1907 and 1913. The abandonment of the classical norms of representing the human body and the departure from the one-point perspective of pictorial representation were soon followed by a dissolution of the contours of objects and the fragmentation of images. In spring 1910 letters appeared for the first time since the Middle Ages in a painting, indicating the name of the newspaper GIL B(LAS). And in 1912 Picasso and Braque added the invention of collage and of *papiers collés* to the range of cubist innovations which changed the course of painting so dramatically.

The innovations of the cubist painters marked the beginning of the historical avant-garde and remained a continuous point of reference providing orientation and direction to subsequent movements from futurism and the Russian cubofuturist movement to dadaism and surrealism. While it is characteristic for all these movements to embrace painters and poets alike, cubism is characterised by its achievements in painting alone. However, the notorious *bande à Picasso*, well known in Montmartre since 1904/5, comprised writers and literary critics as well. "Any separation between avant-garde art and literature in Paris early in the twentieth century", Linda Wagner-Martin therefore rightly points out,

> is artificial. Friendships among the artists [...] are evidence of the great reciprocity that existed between innovative painting and writing. (Wagner-Martin 1995: 74)

And legend tells that the writers played a considerable part in the genesis of the *Desmoiselles*. In an early, anecdotal sketch of the picture Max Jacob is supposed to have entered the "philosophical brothel" with a book in his hand. André Salmon apparently suggested the final title of the picture, with which Picasso was always extremely happy. In 1905 Apollinaire wrote his first enthusiastic article on the "young painters", with particular emphasis on Picasso. In the same year, the latter was invited to Gertrude Stein's salon, and was to paint her portrait in 1906. Gertrude Stein expressed her thanks in 1909 with a literary portrait of Picasso: "One whom some were certainly following was one who was completely charming..." (Stein 1971: 203). An exchange of thoughts, ideas and attitudes between the painters and writers could scarcely not have taken place. Particularly in the case of Gertrude Stein and Guillaume Apollinaire these exchanges had a discernible impact on their literary production.

Not surprisingly, the question has therefore been raised from time to time, whether the poems of Stein, Apollinaire and Jacob can be described as "cubist poetry". In his "Introduction" to *The Yale Gertrude Stein*, Richard Kostelanetz made a case for it:

> Stein [...] recapitulated in literature the evolution of modernist painting. Her earliest works could be considered "cubist" in their syntactical radicalism, the redistribution of traditional emphases and the distortion of space-time representation. (Stein 1980: xxiii)

In his book *Apollinaire – Poet among Painters*, Francis Steegmuller makes a similar suggestion relating to Apollinaire's work. In an interview Steegmuller had asked Georges Braque with disarming candour: "Would you say that Apollinaire sometimes wrote *cubist poetry*?" When Braque replied that some of the poems which were printed in the shape of guitars or other objects used in cubist still lifes could be described as such, or perhaps better as "cubist typography", Steegmuller agreed with the "more strictly pictorial" suggestion by Braque (Steegmuller 1963: 150-151).

The fact that Fernand Léger contributed a "cubist Charlie Chaplin" to one of Man Ray's experimental films, has lead critics to extend the qualification cubism even to cinema. Standish Lawder discusses avant-garde films of the 1920s under this label (cf. Lawder 1975). The creation of ever new branches of cubist activity represents, in my view, an all too forceful attempt to structure the development of the avant-garde in little unified and convenient compartments.33 While the films discussed by Lawder emerged as part of the activities of cubist as well as dadaist and surrealist artists and therefore represent truly *avant-garde cinema*, the writings of Stein, Jacob and Apollinaire have obtained such an aura of originality in their own right and in their specific métier, that attributing them to a movement which indicates its pictorial nature so unmistakably in its name would seem inappropriate. However, this reservation does not undermine, rather, it supports the legitimacy of the question to what extent the rapid succession of innovations in cubist painting, and the changes to the whole notion of art which they entailed, contributed to the development of the writers' experimental style, the question also whether the literary experiments of the authors concerned achieved a degree of innovation and progressive change in their métier which might be considered as comparable to the advances in cubist painting.

In one of the first and most remarkable comments on Gertrude Stein's writing Mabel Dodge maintained that "Gertrude Stein is doing with words what Picasso is doing with paint" (Dodge 1986:

27-28). Gertrude Stein herself repeatedly claimed that she expressed "the same thing in literature" which her friends, the cubist painters, conveyed on their canvasses (cf. Hoffman 1986: 180). At the same time she was adamant that an artist "can only have one métier" (Stein 1966: 85), and always emphasised in her comments the particular properties of her own medium, writing. Consequently, she never referred to any similarities in technique or style between her own and the cubist painters' endeavours. It is on the level of general artistic principles and a "new vision" of twentieth-century reality that she feels akin to Picasso. The ability "to see the things in a new way" rather than merely presenting them differently was in her view characteristic of Picasso's art as well as her own. It is this ability that, from Stein's view, created what she considered their shared "understanding of things" (Hoffman 1986: 180).

The "new way" of seeing things implied the dispensation of the traditional mode of representation in art. The departure from the age-old mimetic function, which literature and painting had shared since the times of Aristoteles, characterises Stein's work as it does Picasso's. It is this feature that links Stein's work with one of the major properties of avant-gardist aesthetics.

Stein may actually have perceived the first signs of Picasso's adventurous geometricalisation of human forms in her own portrait. While the body and the surroundings are painted in a rather conventional style, some of the facial features, which Picasso added several months later to the portrait without the model being present, are simplified and reduced to geometrical forms. There is hardly a poem that adopts this attitude of simplification and reduction to basic forms of the medium used in a similar convincing fashion than Stein's

> A rose is a rose is a rose is a rose.

Together with Apollinaire's "Lundi rue Christine", Chlebnikov's "Incantation Through Laughter" and Hugo Ball's "Karawane", this poem has come to epitomise avant-garde poetry. It is a poem which, in keeping with the conventions of its genre, eulogises a flower. As in the portraits and still lifes of the cubist painters, artistic innovations emerge in Stein's poetry on the occasion of depicting familiar objects. Nothing could also be more conventional for a poem about a flower than to be concerned with a rose.

A number of things happened to the poem in the meantime. Gertrude Stein herself transformed it into the shape of a ring, so that the sequences perpetually repeat themselves (Stein 1971: 136). As Reinhard Baumgart observes, the poem was adopted in an advertisement for a popular motorcar, which "...runs and runs and runs..." (Baumgart 1968: 52). The advert borrowed the evenly flowing, wave-like intonation of the poem and obviously employed the sequential repetition as a method of persuasion. However, while the advertisement tells something about the genuine properties of the advertised automobile, Stein's poem is remarkable in that it refrains from relating anything about its object. The rose even appears cheated of its poetic legacy to stand as a symbol of love — with thorns or without. It evidently stands for itself and nothing else.

A student of the University of Chicago, keen to learn more about the rose, questioned Gertrude Stein about the poem. She in turn was not at a loss for an answer: "I'm no fool", she declared,

> I know that in daily life we don't go around saying "...is a ...is a ...is a ...". Yes, I'm no fool; but I think that in that line the rose is red for the first time in English poetry for a hundred years. (Stein 1971: 7)

Words had become worn out in centuries of their literary use, Stein explained, and were, in conventional use, no longer suitable for describing objects. One of the foremost tasks of the modern writer therefore is to develop a creative method that brings back intensity and vitality to the language. To this end Stein employs neither an extensive description of objects depicted nor a "complicated" method of presentation, but she goes back to one of the basic material properties of language, to the rhythm and the melody of words. The rhythm and the melody of the sequential repetition serve as persistent assurance of the identity of the rose, caressing it and shielding it at the same time from its traditional loaded symbolism.

Another poem about a rose, one from *Tender Buttons*, written in 1911/12, extends the investigation of the same object and also turns rather unexpectedly into an investigation of the material aspects of language:

Red roses
A cool red rose and a pink cut pink,
a collapse and a sold hole, a little less hot.
(Stein 1971: 172)

The principle of text construction is different here. Assuring repetition gives way to contrasting variation and ultimately to an accumulation of text elements which have no immediately obvious coherence and connection. It is easy for the reader to imagine the cool red of the rose. The dark vowels clearly evoke the colour. The change from long, dark vowels to the light, staccato "pink cut pink", however, signals the contrast, the speckled pink of a carnation. The poem achieves what Stein said of Shakespeare's sonnets: "You hear the beauty you see the sound" (Stein 1971: 304). In the ensuing sequences the initial contrast is blended with further textual fragments, whose origins and coherence can scarcely be determined by the reader. The *poème en prose* thus presents itself as put together from fragmented, discontinuous textual elements.

Fragmentation has been noted as one of the aesthetic principles which came to the fore in cubist painting. In the context of the abandonment of one-point perspective it presented itself as the distinguishing feature of a new form of compositional organisation, allowing for the combination of multiple views of an object into one image. Given Stein's high regard for Picasso and his work, one is tempted to attribute the use of fragmented, discontinuous text in Stein's poetry to the influence of cubist painting, and I do indeed believe that Stein has been encouraged to experiment with the device of fragmentation in her own field of artistic activity by the pictures of Picasso. However, this exercise in fragmentation does not only take place in a different medium and obviously for different artistic purposes, but it also seems to have another, a second source of inspiration.

When Stein sent the pieces of prose and poetry that became *Tender Buttons* to Donald Evans, who had just founded his new press, Claire Marie, she added a biographical note to her letter in which she referred to two important events in her life. As a student at Radcliffe College, a Harvard Annex, Stein pointed out, she had participated in psycho-technical experiments in *automatic reading* and *automatic writing*. Coming to Paris, she continued, she had come to know Matisse and Picasso and there existed a "particularly strong sympathy between Picasso and myself as to modern direction". Wagner-Martin assumes with good reason that the profile given by Stein suggests that she herself saw both lines of experience converge in her writing and that "readers would relate her writing to both" (Wagner-Martin 1995: 116-117). In the *Autobiography of Alice B. Toklas* Stein establishes an explicit link between the experiments in *automatic writing* and the particular style which she developed in her work:

> She was one of a group of Harvard men and Radcliffe women and they all lived very closely and very interestingly together. One of them, a young philosopher and mathematician who was doing research work in psychology left a definite mark on her life. She and he together worked out a series of experiments in automatic writing under the direction of Münsterberg. The result of her own experiments, which Gertrude Stein wrote down and which was printed in the Harvard Psychological Review was the first writing of hers ever to be printed. It is very interesting to read because the method of writing to be afterwards developed in *Three Lives* and *Making of Americans* already shows itself. (Stein 1966: 86)

Reading the article which Leon Solomon and Gertrude Stein published in the *Psychological Review* clearly substantiates this claim.

The set-up of one of the experiments included writing at dictation, while "the subject's attention" was simultaneously occupied by reading. The experiment was designed to investigate the possibility of mentally absorbing two texts at once. The evaluation emphasised a marked concentration of the subject on the sound of words without becoming aware of their meaning. Particularly "Miss Stein", the article points out, "has a strong auditory consciousness, and sounds usually determine the direction of her attention" (Solomon 1896: 500). The evaluation of one of the other experiments designed to test *spontaneous writing* while being distracted by reading includes the notion, that the result shows "a marked tendency to repetition", also the observation that "the stuff written was grammatical, and the words and phrases fitted together all right, but there was not much connected thought" (Solomon 1896: 506). Not only in the "marked tendency to repetition" and the emphasis on the sound of words as opposed to their meaning, but also in the continuous blending of textual fragments of different origin the experiments in the Harvard Laboratory clearly anticipate the creative method which Stein developed in her novels as well as her prose poems. A comparison of a few specimens from the laboratory with one of the *Tender Buttons* reveals this:

> When he could not be the longest and thus to be, and thus to be, the strongest. (Solomon 1896: 506)

> This long time when he did this best time, and he could thus have been bound, and in this long time, when he could be this to first use of this long time. (Solomon 1896: 506)

> If lilies are lily white if they exhaust noise and distance and even dust, if they dusty will dirt a surface that has no extreme grace, if they do this and it is not necessay it is not at all necessary if they do this they need a catalogue. (Stein 1971: 164)

Although there is "not much connected thought" to be found — neither in the texts from the psycho-technical experiments nor in the prose poem — both texts show that Stein was aware of the aesthetic attraction which the blending of textual fragments of different origin holds. She had also experienced that dealing with words does not necessarily involve their semantics, that aspect of language which normally dominates its use. For the purposes of the psycho-technical experiments as well as for Stein's poetry the recognition of the sound qualities of words takes the lead over their meanings.

The contrast in vowels at the beginning of the poem "Red Roses" establishes this principle very clearly. Words are to be heard and word sequences are organised primarily by tonal relations. Of course, sound and rhythm have always been constitutive elements of poetry. But it is the "simultaneous construction of meaning and tone", which is normally considered the epitome of poetic craftsmanship (cf. Allemann 1971: 207). The isolation and exposure of the sound qualities of words and word associations was the risk Gertrude Stein took in the face of poetic tradition. Cummings rightly observes that Stein arranges words according to their beauty, "the beauty of their sound" (Stein 1980: xx). The juxtaposition of long and dark with short and light vowels at the beginning of the poem are followed by textual fragments which pick up the tones of the opening once more, repeating them, varying them and ultimately dispersing their tension. They are similar sounds which leave the carnation speckled pink, and the hole sold. "A sold hole" is at the same time also linked to the cool rose as a variation in "ou". Likewise the counterpoint of the beginning finds its resolution in the wonderfully layered vowel sequence and rhythmically insistent combination of "a little less hot", further supported in its tonal splendour by an alliteration.

Sound relations thus prove to be the "driving wheels and belts", the "lifts and drops" which E.A. Poe, the forefather of modern verse, attributed to poetic production (cf. Enzensberger 1970: 58-62). Sound relations organise the textual fragments into a poem. After two centuries of culture dominated by writing, printing and reading — cultural activities in which poetic language had become mute — the exposition of the sound qualities of language was an unexpected as well as invigorating undertaking. Bringing sound to language again and playfully unfolding its musical energy: these were the distinguishing artistic features of *Tender Buttons*. At the source of this new creative method, however, we find both Stein's experience in *automatic writing* as well as her obvious encouragement through *cubist painting*.

Any comparison between poetry and painting needs to take into account the difference of the media and the different context and status of corresponding changes in the art forms. The emergence of the principle of *fragmentation* and its application to painting and poetry is certainly a case in point. While in cubist pictures fragmentation is above all a necessary accompaniment of the combination of multiple viewpoints, in Stein's poetry it emerges as a means of creating a melody of words unimpeded by syntax and semantics. What both applications have in common, however, is that they are integral parts of an intensive exploration of the aesthetic properties of the artistic material of the painter and the writer, respectively. It is this investigation of the material's properties, the two-dimensional nature of the canvas, the implications of the rules of the one-point perspective, the whole geometry of lines, planes and volumes, with which the cubist painters had opened the gate to their innovations and to the development of the great wealth of new artistic forms and techniques in subsequent avant-garde movements. The fact that the artist's material becomes the object of an intensive inquiry is a consequence of the competition in which he finds himself with a new medium, photography. With the search for the energies of the sound of language which Stein displays so strongly and impressively in *Tender Buttons* she adopts the same attitude towards her artistic material.

Admittedly, the painters had no interest in sound qualities, in spite of the fact that they frequently arranged violins, clarinets, sheet music and strings in their still lifes. However, that in one instance roses are made to ring out, and in the other the geometric contours of violins are examined, makes the comparison all the more attractive. By displaying the sound energy of words and word sequences, Gertrude Stein steered poetic production onto the field of material experiments which the cubist painters had tilled with their investigations. It would be apposite to describe the explorations in both art forms as "analytic", were it not for the fact that since Kahnweiler's comments on cubist painting this term has been associated with the objects of pictorial depiction rather than the devices and materials of the artist. It is here, though, that Stein's achievements lie. The impuls which she gave to the exploration of the aesthetic properties of the artistic material of poetry are the most important contribution which she made to the development of the avant-garde in its formative years.

Both the fragmentation of text and its organisation under the primacy of sound and rhythm turned out to become distinctive features of avant-garde poetry in the years which followed. In 1913, the Russian cubo-futurists made it their task to focus attention on the "phonetic characteristics" of words and syllables and to discover the poetic dimension of language in the "living, spoken word" (Chlebnikov 1972: 108). Chlebnikov, whose poem "Incantation Through Laughter" was widely circulated and translated, undertook in particular to derive new meaning from the sound of words and syllables. He did not remain alone in this approach. Huelsenbeck records Hugo Ball's conviction that the sounds he strung together to form "Karawane" were better suited to being generally understood than familiar words and phrases which had lost any true meaning (Huelsenbeck 1984: 15). The *poème simultan* which Richard Huelsenbeck, Tristan Tzara and Marcel Janco presented on the first evening of the *Cabaret Voltaire* made the simultaneous recital of texts in English, French and German language their particular strategy of stripping the words of their conventional meaning, of preventing a conventional, semantic use of language and exposing sounds and rhythm instead as language's more reliable properties.[17] Kurt Schwitters' lovingly articulated *Urlaute* and Majakovski's powerful sailors' cries soon joined the simultaneous sounds of the Zurich dadaists.

It took less than a decade until the avant-garde experiments with sound entered the store of aesthetic devices of major literary projects of the time. James Joyce's *Ulysses*, this "modern epic", revealed its point of reference not only in the musically composed chapter of the song of the sirens. Sound associations played a considerable part in producing the complex fabric of allusions and cross-references in the novel from "met something with hoses" to "yes I said yes I will Yes". *Finnegans Wake* lives virtually exclusively from the caprioles of spoken language and contains arguably the most beautiful chapter based on the qualities of sound of any novel in modern literature: the chapter on "Anna Livia Plurabelle", in which the chatter of the washerwomen magically passes over to the murmur of the river Liffey. Not the murmur of the Spree, but the clumsy rhymes of a ballad singer encounter the reader of Döblin's *Berlin Alexanderplatz* on the original cover of the novel and in all chapter titles. Döblin expressed his opinion on the "creative powers" of spoken language also in a speech given to the *Prussian Academy of the Arts*:

> The book is the death of real language. The most important, inventive powers of language escape the epic writer who merely writes; for a long time, my motto has been: away from the book, however, I see no obvious course for the contemporary epic writer, unless it is the way to a – new form of theatre. (Döblin 1963: 132)

Fortunately, Döblin ultimately did find another solution to incorporating "living, real language" in the book – which in turn gave Walter Benjamin cause to contemplate the "oral tradition" of epic works and the wealth of everyday experience which was stored within it (Benjamin 1999: 299). What began with the exposure of sound qualities of everyday language, an everyday American English, in the poetry of Gertrude Stein eventually crystallises into a widely promising literary agenda and a major project of avant-garde writing.

In his book on *Gertrude Stein and the Literature of the Modern Consciousness* Norman Weinstein has fiercely rejected any relationship between Stein's experiments in *automatic writing* and her literary style. Weinstein was also adamant that "so-called 'automatic writing' as practiced by the surrealists bears no similarity to the definitions of *Tender Buttons*" (Weinstein 1970: 59-60). However, Breton who celebrated the "invention" of the new technique of automatic writing in the first surrealist manifest, was as aware as Stein that automatic writing was an inheritance of psycho-technical experiments that had appeared "at the end of the 19th century" (Breton 1948: 177). While Stein learned the blending of textual fragments in the laboratory of William James, Breton came across a similar technique in Pierre Janet's writings on "psychologic automatism", which served as his source of inspiration. Although both writers have certainly adopted different aspects of the technique, Breton hoping that it might accomplish the surfacing of the unsciousness in the act of writing, while Stein had turned the same technique into a conscious aesthetic practice of great novelty and charm, one should perhaps not overlook the fact that both avant-gardist styles have been encouraged by the same source, by the latest scientific experiments into automatism.

Breton and also Louis Aragon were also aware of the fact that the experiments in *automatic writing* were closely linked to contemporary developments of the media. Breton even called *automatic writing* an "inheritance of the media" (cf. Waldberg 1981: 80). This draws attention to the fact that the rediscovery of the sounds of poetry occured in the wider context of the invention of technical media which made it possible to transmit, record and reproduce sound. By the end of the 19th century the telephone, the phonograph and the gramophone had emerged. Together, Marshall McLuhan maintains in his study on *Understanding Media*, these "talking machines" gave a new "stress and importance to actual speech rhythms in music, poetry and dance alike". The new machines, he underlines, "did so much to recover the vocal, auditory and mimetic world that had been repressed by the printed word" (McLuhan 1987: 276-279). With its new emphasis on the sound of language, avant-garde poetry responds to the emergence of these new media of sound communication, exploring the significance and

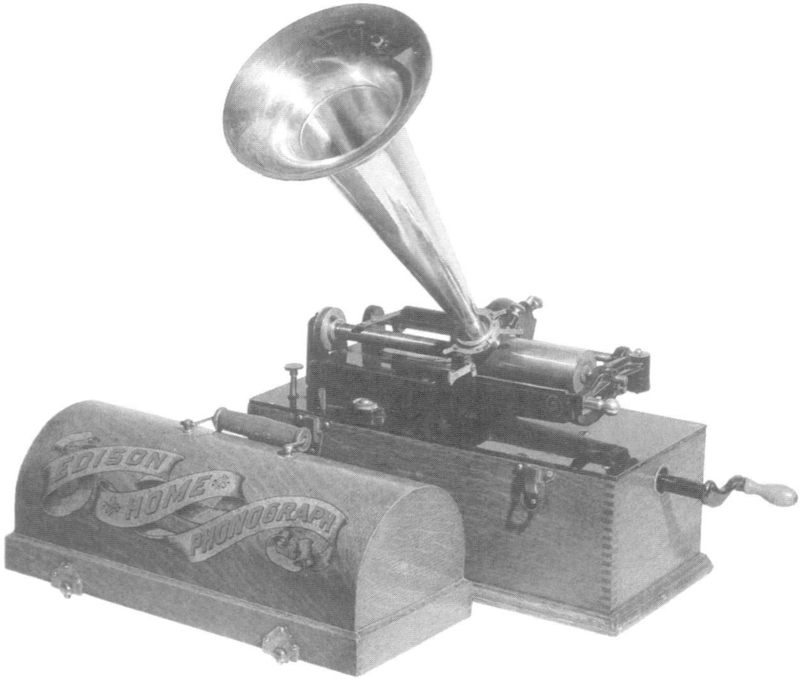

10 *Edison Home Phonograph*. Model A. 1897

poetic energies of the "spoken word" on their own terrain. Just as the cubist painters took up the challenge of photography in their traditional medium of painting, so did the poets by exploring the beauty of the sounds in their traditional medium of the "printed word". In both cases, however, the old forms of artistic expression did not remain unaffected by their respective explorations. As a consequence of these, not only the style, the techniques and attitudes towards artistic production, but also the essential material constitution of the works produced experienced a profound change. "In certain phases of their development", Benjamin maintaines in his essay on *The Work of Art*, the traditional art forms "work toward effects which later are effortlessly attained by the new ones"(Benjamin 1973:251). Stein's as well as Breton's experiments in *automatic writing* have certainly a share in this.

Bibliography

Allemann, Beda (ed.)
1971 *Ars poetica*. Darmstadt: Wissenschaftliche Buchgesellschaft.

Baumgart, Reinhard
1968 *Aussichten des Romans oder Hat Literatur Zukunft*. Neuwied: Luchterhand.

Benjamin, Walter
1999 *Selected Writings, vol. 2: 1927-1934*. Cambridge, Mass.: Harvard University Press.

1973 *Illuminations*. Bungay: Fontana.

Breton, André
1948 "Max Ernst". In: Max Ernst, *Beyond Painting*. New York: Wittenborn, 177.

Chlebnikov, Velimir
1972 *Werke 2*. Reinbek: Rowohlt.

Daix, Pierre
1982 *Der Kubismus in Wort und Bild*. Stuttgart: Klett-Cotta.

Döblin, Alfred
1963 *Aufsätze zur Literatur*. Olten: Walter.

Dodge, Mabel
1986 "Speculations, Or Post-Impressionism in Prose". In: Hoffman 1986, 27-31.

Enzensberger, Hans Magnus
1970 *Gedichte / Die Entstehung eines Gedichts*. Frankfurt am Main: Suhrkamp.

Fry, Edward F.
1978 *Cubism*. London: Thames and Hudson.

Golding, John
1981 "Cubism". In: Nikos Stangos (ed.), *Concepts of Modern Art*. London: Thames and Hudson, 50-78.

Hoffman, Michael J. (ed.)
1986 *Critical Essays on Gertrude Stein*. Boston, Mass.: Hall & Co.

Huelsenbeck, Richard (ed.)
1984 *Dada. Eine literarische Dokumentation.* Reinbek: Rowohlt.

Lawder, Standish D.
1975 *The Cubist Cinema.* New York: New York University Press.

McLuhan, Marshall
1987 *Understanding Media. The Extensions of Man.* London: Routledge and Kegan Paul.

Solomon, Leon, and Gertrude Stein
1896 "Normal Motor Automatism". In: *Psychological Review*, vol. 3, 492-512.

Steegmuller, Francis
1963 *Apollinaire. Poet among the Painters.* London: Ruper Hart-Davis.

Stein, Gertrude
1966 *The Autobiography of Alice B. Toklas.* Harmondsworth: Penguin Books.

1971 *Look at Me Now and Here I Am. Writings and Lectures 1909-45.* Harmondsworth: Penguin Books.

1980 *The Yale Gertrude Stein.* Selections, with an Introduction by Richard Kostelanetz. New Haven: Yale University Press.

Waldberg, Patrick
1981 *Der Sürrealismus.* Cologne: DuMont.

Wagner-Martin, Linda
1995 *"Favored Strangers". Gertrude Stein and Her Family.* New Brunswick, N.J.: Rutgers University Press.

Weinstein, Norman
1970 *Gertrude Stein and the Literature of the Modern Consciousness.* New York: Frederick Ungar.

SCREECHING VOICES: AVANT-GARDE: MANIFESTOS IN THE CABARET

MARTIN PUCHNER

There is a consensus among modern writers and theorists that the artwork should pretend not to be aware of its audience. What they have found so distressing about forms of literature and art that address themselves directly to the audience is the exhibitionistic quality inherent in such a taste for public display. All too soon the artwork finds itself personified as actor and ends up assuming the pose of a vain diva ready to count artistic success by the number of bouquets flung on the stage. It is thus that the theatre and its lust for audiences finds itself cast in opposition to the values demanded of art.[1] I do not want to follow the numerous apologists for the theatre who critique anti-theatrical positions as misguided value judgements. Even if one wonders at times what kind of theatre these anti-theatricalists imagine when they launch into their diatribes against theatricality, their perceptions and sentiment provide useful insights for understanding the nature and value of the theatre and of the arts.

The controversy about the use of the theatre for art recurs with particular urgency when it comes to the avant-garde. While other critics reject theatricality because it threatens to estrange art from itself, the avant-garde sees in this estrangement the theatre's redeeming quality, for it enables the avant-garde to critique the institution of art. We can, therefore, detect an uneasy alliance between anti-theatricalists and the avant-garde, both of whom agree that art and theatricality are at odds with one another and that embracing the one means keeping the other at a distance. The genre that openly subsists on such a kind of theatricality and that most successfully accomplishes this critique of the institution of art is the avant-garde manifesto.

The history of the manifesto is twofold: originally, it indicates a declaration of state, issued from the position of power. This meaning is still at work when Kaiser Franz Joseph declares what will become World War I through a text called *Manifest.*[2] The "we" of this type of manifesto is the royal "we", speaking with full and unchallenged authority on behalf of the collective which it represents. This royal "we" is then, in a second step, turned into its opposite, namely a revolutionary voice of dissent. In England, the first manifestos using this revolutionary "we" were issued by the Levellers around the 1648 upheaval. This second type of manifesto gains momentum through the French and American, and later the Russian, revolutions, which were instrumental in shaping the manifesto into a collective, revolutionary, and polarising appeal directed against the status quo and those who preserve it.[3] In the nineteenth century, the most famous and certainly most effective of such manifestos was the Communist Manifesto, which remains one of the standard models of the genre. What these manifestos have in common is that they mimic the royal "we" of the first type, trying to emulate its representative authority. However, what the revolutionary "we" stands for remains uncertain, as does the authority by which it represents.[4] This uncertainty has far-reaching consequences for the rhetoric and tone of the revolutionary manifesto, which compensates for this lack of authority and this absence of an existing, coherent "we" through the demonstrative over-confidence and aggressiveness that will remain the marks of the genre.[5]

It is under the influence of the French Revolution and its manifestos that Romanticism becomes the first movement in the history of art and literature to adopt the revolutionary rhetoric of the manifesto in order to stage a radicalised conflict between the "old" and the "new", using a language of rupture. When Coleridge complained, for example, that the *The Preface of Lyrical Ballads* did not adequately represent Wordsworth's poetry, he did not recognise that the divergence of theory and practice was not an oversight but strategic choice. During the nineteenth-century, with the rise of what is called the political and artistic avant-garde, the aggressive tone of the manifesto gains particular momentum in the revolutionary manifestos of the Paris Commune; from then on it oscillate between politics and art, between Zola's "J'accuse" and his manifesto-like call for naturalism. By the time Jean Moréas writes his *Le Manifeste symboliste* (1886), the term manifesto has become the standard form for art and politics alike in which to voice dissent, demand a rupture with the status quo, and to gain control over the writing of an alternative history.

When Marinetti published what would become the first manifesto of futurism in *Le Figaro* in 1909, he not only continued the history of the political and artistic manifesto, but he initiated one of the most astonishing and also most consequential phenomena for the avant-garde: the proliferating use of and therefore dependence on the second, revolutionary type of manifesto (the first type of manifesto re-emerges in the second and third surrealist manifestos through which the autocratic leader of the movement, Breton, controlled the movement single handedly). The dozens of Italian futurist manifestos were followed by the manifestos of dadaism, vorticism, and surrealism only to name the most widely known. By means of the foundational power inscribed into their history, manifestos proclaimed and called into existence the collective "we" of movements, groups, schools, and associations labelled Lef, Stijl, Purism, Zenitism, 41°, Wir, Synthès, Constructivism, Kuri, and Poetism. These manifestos differ from earlier manifestos in that they push their attributes — the anxiety of constituting these collectives, the rhetoric of rupture, the re-writing of history, and the overcompensating confidence and exaggerated tone — to an extreme. The proliferation of manifestos is the most distinct mark of the historical avant-garde, but it is by no means confined to this particular period. After World War II, a large number of new movements from the situationists to fluxus were instituted, named, and proclaimed by manifestos. The twentieth century concluded with a new and astonishing manifesto called Dogma, which was written and signed by four Dutch film makers who confined themselves to a particularly ascetic use of technology. Its overwhelming success, culminating in a *Palm d'or* at Cannes 2000, has ensured that today a growing number of films are shot along the lines of the Dogma manifesto, which is shown before each film with the signatures of the authors attached.[6] Why did the avant-garde invent the manifesto, what desire did this manifesto fulfil, and what were its continuing effects on the development of twentieth-century art?

The first two questions can be answered by reformulating part of Peter Bürger's still influential *Theory of the Avant-Garde*. Bürger makes extensive use of the manifesto — he quotes from the manifestos of futurism, dadaism, and surrealism — but he does not reflect on the manifesto's generic form and structure. In virtually ignoring the generic constitution of the manifesto, Bürger's theory is no exception; the study of avant-garde art, indeed of twentieth-century art, has by and large failed to understand the ramifications of the manifesto, which becomes a central and consequential form of expression.[7] In Bürger's theory, the omission is particularly striking since the sudden emergence of this genre confirms some of his claims, in particular his thesis that in contrast to modernism, the avant-garde attacks the institution of art in an attempt to overcome the distinction between art and life. I will argue that the manifesto is the genre that is most instrumental not only for formulating this project, but for partially achieving it.[8]

When Marinetti writes his first manifesto in 1909 he uses, adopts, and co-opts a genre that fulfils a function in the public, political sphere. The avant-garde begins to rely on the manifesto just at the moment when the split between a political avant-garde and an artistic one has become irrevocable. The historical avant-garde is eager to regain its connection to politics and there is no better way of establishing this link than by adopting the overtly political genre of the manifesto. Many avant-garde manifestos thus borrow phrases and modes of address from political discourse. The founders of futurism participate in the political process by voicing their anarcho-syndicalist inclinations through a manifesto called "Political Program of futurism", which begins with an appeal to "Futurist Voters" and proceeds to promote such political positions as "Absolutely sovereign Italy" and "Patriotic Education of the Proletariat" (Asholt 1995: 65). Berlin dada includes similarly direct political forms of address and positions, listed, in the fashion of the Communist Manifesto, in numbers, a form which becomes one of the defining features of the genre: "1. International, revolutionary unification of all creative and intellectual humans of the world on the basis of a radical communism" (175). Later manifestos still use this rhetoric, albeit in a more distanced manner, such as h. hoerle's manifesto entitled "Dilettantes, rise up" (200). The desire of the manifesto to inherit the Communist Manifesto is, perhaps, most visible in the Russian Lef (Left Front of the Arts), which published manifestos dedicated to such symbolic days as May 1, and regularly addressed the audience as "Comrades, Reformers of Life!", celebrating, for example, the fifth anniversary of the October Revolution (301).[9]

This use of revolutionary politics, whether anarcho-syndicalist, proto-fascist, or communist does not mean that the avant-garde manifesto becomes fully co-extensive with political agitation. The relation of Lef to official, revolutionary Russia, of Berlin dada to the German communist party, or of Marinetti to Mussolini remain a complex affair. What is clear, however, is the desire on the part of the avant-garde to participate directly in the political sphere. And it is this desire that motivates the use of the avant-garde manifesto and its particular strategies, turning it into a privileged form of expression. The manifesto not only articulates but also enacts what Bürger considers its grand project, namely overcoming the difference between art and life; it allows for a degree of engagement that far surpasses even the most generous and hopeful notion of engaged art, such as the one proposed by Sartre.[10] As a genre, the manifesto trumps any engaged novel because political engagement is inscribed into its very history and structure. What is most compelling about the manifesto, however, is that it escapes being pigeon-holed as art and instead is situated across the divide between art and public life.[11] When we consider Bürger's theory through the lens of the manifesto, it becomes necessary to criticise the Hegelian terms in which he articulates the avant-garde's critique of the institution of art:

> The avant-gardists thus intend a sublation (*Aufhebung*) of art — sublation in Hegel's sense of the word: art is not simply to be destroyed, but enclosed in the practice of life, where it will be contained, albeit in a transfigured form. (67)

It is not surprising that Bürger himself judged this project, which implies not only the transformation of art but also of life as having failed (134). It is possible, however, to reformulate this project in terms of genre. Due to its generic history and its modes of circulation and performance, the manifesto actually manages what remains impossible for the other arts, namely to evade, if not to erase altogether, the divide between the institution of art and the public sphere of politics.[12] This evasion allows us to consider not so much the failure of the avant-garde, but the effects and specific strategies it implemented in pursuit of its impossible goal.

II.

The weight I put on the genre of the manifesto rather than on its content raises the question of whether the manifesto is altered once it is adopted by the avant-garde. For one could object that the avant-garde does not believe in the genre of the manifesto, that it does not stand behind it the way the Communist Party stood behind the Communist Manifesto, and the question then becomes whether the avant-garde just played around with the manifesto. This objection is particularly pertinent to dadaism. Almost all dada manifestos are also meta-manifestos, they show an awareness of the manifesto's defining features, such as the critique of the status quo, the galvanising appeal to the audience, and the brevity and explicitness, which Marinetti singles out in his "arte di far manifesti." While Marinetti thinks about the manifesto in letters, Tristan Tzara transposes this type of reflection to the manifesto itself, beginning, for example, with the opening of his *Manifest Dada 1918*:

> To put out a manifesto you must want ABC
> to fulminate against 1, 2, 3 [...]
> to sign, shout, swear, to organise prose into a form of absolute and irrefutable evidence. (Motherwell 1989: 76).

What disrupts the manifesto even more than such forms of self-referentiality are those moments when the manifesto's central name and terms are strategically replaced by pure negations, themselves parodies of Hegelianism, such as in the 1921 manifesto *DADA hebt alles auf* (DADA sublates everything): "DADA does not speak, DADA does not have a fixed idea" (cf. Asholt/Fähnders 1995: 223-224). The signatories, amongst them Man Ray and Marcel Duchamp, not only leave the central name DADA unexplained, but use the term "nothing" where other manifestos use all of their rhetorical power to drive home a particular agenda. dada manifestos even go so far as to claim that they are not manifestos at all.

These manifestos certainly seem generically impure, disrupted, and displaced. The mechanisms of these generic displacements and subversions could be best articulated by means of Jacques Derrida's polemics against John R. Searle, a reading devoted to showing the instability of contexts and therefore the ineradicable possibility of irony or parody in any given speech act, including, I would add, the speech act of the manifesto. As convincing as this argument may be in its principled rigor and its universal claims, it should not keep us from registering that the manifesto is particularly invested in its own speech act and that this investment is at work even in the most distanced and self-referential dada manifestos. The manifesto quoted above, for example, is addressed to "Citizens" (Asholt 1995: 225) and tries hard, this time in a more communicative mode, to differentiate dada from expressionism, simultaneism, futurism, unanimism, neo-classicism, and many others competing movements. This manifesto also reminds us that the strategy of negation—"DADA does not speak DADA does not have a fixed idea"—is in fact widely used by the manifesto, which usually knows better what it is against than what it is for. This manifesto continues to communicate to the audience what dada is not and therefore remains within the manifesto's generic limits.

In order to give contours to this claim that the avant-garde does not simply play with the manifesto, I will argue that the avant-garde manifesto remains distinct from the sphere of avant-garde art on the one hand and from the domain of theory on the other. In her important essay "'Violence and Precision': The Manifesto as Art Form", Perloff shows to what extent futurist and dadaist manifestos borrow from other avant-garde genres such as visual poetry, becoming futurism's privileged art form, "the movement's literary genre par excellence (90)". I agree with Perloff's claim that the manifesto and the art forms of the avant-garde are closely intertwined — but I would place even more emphasis on the manifesto's distance from the aesthetic than she does. As much as the manifesto uses bold letters and arranges them all over the page, there remains a fundamental difference between the typography of the manifesto and of avant-garde lyric, between futurist manifestos and its *parole in libertà*. This difference lies in the fact that the manifesto not only remains within the sphere of political discourse but that it also continues to be almost desperately committed to communication.

This communicative desire of the manifesto, which Tzara recognises in its "absolute and irrefutable evidence" forces the manifesto to steer clear of most techniques of avant-garde lyric.

While we thus must distinguish the manifesto from art, it is even more crucial that we not consider it as a kind of theoretical appendix devoted to explaining the basic aesthetics of a given movement in a more or less discursive manner. It is this common misperception against which Perloff directs her argument, by insisting on the fact that the manifesto does not supplies the theory for an already existing art movement. The difference between the manifesto and the theoretical treatise — or the preface, apology, or essay — is its programmatic function, a function directed towards a future development. When Marinetti published the first futurist manifesto, no futurist artwork had yet been created. Not only, then, do most futurist manifestos not have available to them an existing object, they also do not possess a proper vocabulary in which to talk about the object they imagine. For this reason, the language of the manifesto is always insufficient, a condition which it compensates by its characteristically excessive rhetoric.

This theoretical insufficiency can best be demonstrated by means of J. L. Austin's *How to Do Things with Words*. If any genre attempts to do things with words, it is the genre of the manifesto. This fit between Austin's notion of speech acts and the manifesto's direct speech is almost too perfect because the manifesto's desperate eagerness to change the world drives it to overdo what Austin would consider a proper speech act. And indeed, Austin did not recognise the manifesto as speech act, because — one could speculate — its exaggerated rhetoric, screeching voice, and over-the-top layout would not have convinced him to take it seriously. Austin's neglect of the manifesto thus parallels in many ways his neglect of the theatre. And just as the theatre has come to haunt his theory, because his scenarios for speech acts — baptising, wedding — are social rituals and thus participate in the theatricality of social life, it may not come as a surprise that the manifesto has come to haunt his theory as well.[13]

What would the manifesto look like if we consider it through the lens of speech act theory? Austin distinguishes the act of enunciation (locutionary act), the immediate performative direction (illocutionary act), and the further consequences and effects of that illocutionary act (perlocutionary act). When seen through this schema, one can see that the manifesto is particularly concerned with the revolutionary effects it might have.[14] Both the locutionary utterance and the illocutionary command are thus in the service of this hyper-perlocutionary goal, which never must be threatened by indirect communication or misunderstanding. Its investment in the effects of its speech acts leads the manifesto not only to subscribe to Tzara's "absolute evidence", but also to an obsessive use of aggressive and performative verbs: we declare, we announce, we demand we proclaim, we denounce, we are against, we destroy, down with. These proclamations are usually integrated in the speech act of command: one must, one must not, go, do this or that. The most ingenious example of a fusion of all of the above is BLAST, which is built entirely around a verb that is, at the same time, performative, declarative, and also a command. In this sense, manifestos are textbooks for performative speech acts, but speech acts in the state of hyperactivity.[15]

What drives the manifesto to its performative and illocutionary excesses also effects the locutionary act, causing the "screaming" which Tzara mentions as the other defining feature of the manifesto. It is here, in the locutionary dimension of the manifesto, that the distinct tone of the manifesto comes into focus, a tone that is replicated in the bold layout and advertisement-like use of typography.[16] Again it is BLAST that best captured the speaking voice of the manifesto most systematically by capitalising and enlarging this central performative verb on every page. The other effect of this structure is the never ending use of exclamation marks — the defining punctuation mark of the genre. In addition, many of the more self-referential manifestos refer to their own screeching voice. In *Death to Moonshine*, Marinetti includes a narrative description of scenes, scenes in which he describes himself "screaming" to the inhabitants of Paralysia: "Cowards! Cowards!" (Asholt 1995: 7). This original scream of futurism sets the tone for the ensuing genre of avant-garde manifestos. The "Manifesto of futurist Painters" opens with "The Scream of Rebellion, which we utter", which is followed by manifestos that refer to their own performance as making noise, cursing, yelling, shrieking, crying, and howling. The most extensive such list appears in Russolo's manifesto "The Art of

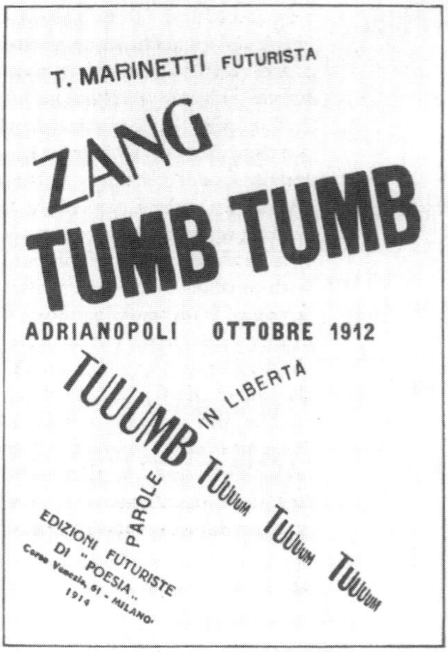

11 Filippo T. Marinetti: *Zang Tumb Tumb* (title-page). 1914

Noise", which demands "2. Hisses Puffs 3. Whispers Murmurs [...] 4. Screeching [...] 6. Voices of animals and humans: Shouts, Shrieks, Moans, Yells, Howls, Laughs, Groans, Sobs" (Kirby: 171-172). Any further attempt to define the modes of theorisation at work in the manifesto must take into account the screeching tone and theatricality of the manifesto; it must address the question of what kind of theory, or philosophy, can be produced by the manifesto's screeching tone.[17] While I will not be able to address this question here, I will devote the remaining space of this essay to the theatricality of the manifesto that resides in this screeching tone.

III.

Famously, the first futurist manifesto was published in *Le Figaro* in 1909, and newspapers, preferably with large circulation, remained a favourite mode of publication.[18] In addition, manifestos were simply handed out on the street as flyers, for example Mayakovsky's famous "Slap in the face of public taste" before it became part of the first collection of Russian futurist writing. Manifestos also appeared on bill-boards, as ads, and as press-releases. More particularly, futurist manifestos were distributed during a exhibition in Petrograd 1915 (the supremacist Manifesto of the last futurist exhibition), and a manifesto by Khlebnikov "against Marinetti" was handed out before Marinetti's lecture in Petersburg 1914. Marinetti, as always, was the most creative of distributors: he climbed up the clock-tower of Venice in order to let his manifesto, "Against a passéist Venice", rain down on its inhabitants.[19] His favourite mode of distribution, however, was, not surprisingly, to throw manifestos out of the window of a racing car.

While it may seem that the manifesto's proper medium was the flyer, with its flashy layout and advertisement-like ways of grasping attention, there was a second mode of distribution, and that is the oral reading or performance of manifestos on the stage. As early as 1910 the authors of the "Manifesto of futurist painters" (Carra, Russolo, Boccioni) read their manifesto aloud, and they did so in the Theatro Chiarella in Torino. They were perhaps the first, but by no means the last, to use the theatre for manifesto-speeches. The theatricality of the dada manifesto is perhaps most clearly visible in the "Manifesto of Mr. Antipyrine", which was an integral part of a dada play-performance at Zürich (Waag-Saal) entitled *La Première Aventure céleste de M. Antipyrine*. The collective "we" identifies itself as "circus directors", and addresses its audience as "Dear Listeners" (122), not as readers. Most dada manifestos were part of dada soirées, screamed at the audience which was always ready to scream back.[20] Hans Richter observes:

> Tzara had skillfully arranged things so that this simultaneous poem closed the first half of the programme. Otherwise there would have been a riot at this early stage in the proceedings and the balloon would have gone up too soon. (Richter 1965: 78)

Richter then proceeds to describe the performance of his own manifesto-like speech: "I started the second half with an address, 'Against Without, For Dada.' In this address I cursed the audience but with moderation." Even though "cursing" was part of many dada performances, the manifesto usually took over sooner or later because it remained the most effective and direct way of provoking the audience.

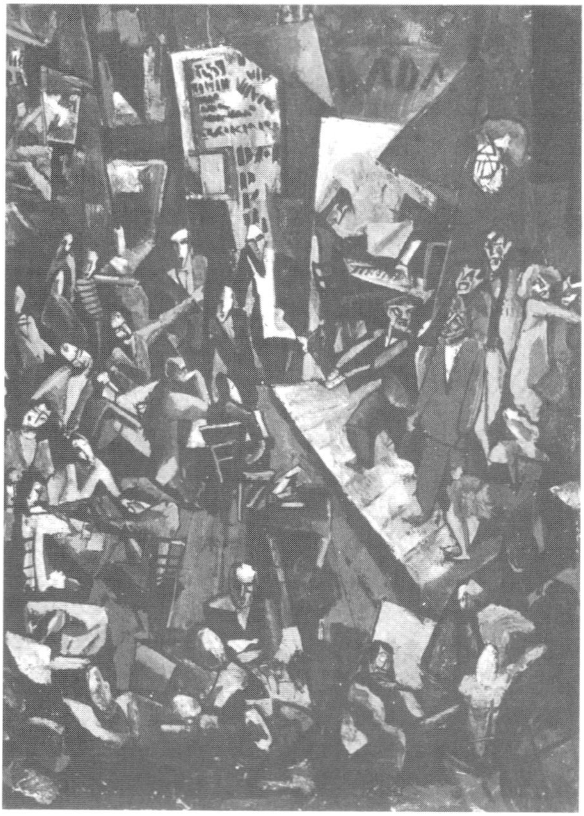

12 Marcel Janco: *Cabaret Voltaire*. 1916

Not only the manifesto but the entire avant-garde began to move into the theatre. The signal for this move, as always, came from Marinetti, who declared that "everything of any value is theatrical." Due to Günter Berghaus's careful and comprehensive reconstruction of futurism's theatrical activities, it is now possible to appreciate the extent to which various forms of theatricality, from the cabaret to street agitation, defined the various phases of futurism. This dedication to the theatre and forms of theatricality had many ramifications, which have not yet been explored in detail. It heavily influenced futurist poetics, especially the *parole in libertà*, which, along with the "acted out poem" (202), were conceived explicitly as a poetics for the stage. Similarly, the simultaneous poem of dadaism, inheritor of the *parole in libertà*, is only possible as performed poetry on the stage. In fact all the arts, from poetry to painting, are put on the stage. This operation of theatricality was applied most rigorously to the first avant-garde movement, namely cubism, so that the dadaists could claim triumphantly that "dadaism turned cubism into a dance on a stage" (146). In order to assess what this theatricality means for the avant-garde it may be useful to remember the anti-theatrical polemic I mentioned at the beginning. The theorists and critics suspecting that the theatre was not simply one form of art among others, but rather a condition that threatened all the arts, and must, therefore, be exorcised from them, had something in common with the avant-garde. The avant-garde shares their understanding insofar as they considered theatre not as an art form apart, but an operation, or condition, that can be applied to the other arts, an operation which ruthlessly exposes their structure and their limits to an audience.

Even as the avant-garde embraces the theatre and seeks to drag all the arts, from poetry to cubism, onto the stage, it is important to specify that the avant-garde stage is preferably the stage of a cabaret. The cabaret is an alternative to the bourgeois theatre, for it is political, rough, it provokes and reacts to the audience, and it is a place for satire, spontaneity, and brevity, qualities celebrated by futurism and dadaism alike. Finally, the cabaret is less concerned with preserving the integrity of the aesthetic and does not shy away from forms of loud, screeching direct speech. Even architecturally, as Manfredo Tafuri has shown, the cabaret is located at the centre of various projects of redesigning the bourgeois stage, proposed by such reformer as Georg Fuchs and Kurt Hiller (Tafuri: 98), whose manifesto on the "Neophathetisches" Cabaret celebrates the cabaret as a space resounding with Nietzschean laughter. One should speak, therefore, not only of a "cabaretic modernism", as Peter Jelavich has done, but also of a "cabaretic avant-garde", so that more traditional turn-of-the-century cabarets such as *The Chat Noire* and *Die 11 Scharfrichter* can be seen as the predecessors of the Cabaret Voltaire.[21] It was only later that futurism and, by extension, the avant-garde began to envision other places of performance, also modelled on political agitation, such as street theatre and street demonstrations. The avant-garde's most extravagant proposal to regain the public sphere was the futurist Aerial Theatre, promoted by the Fedele Azari, the self-proclaimed "futurist pilot aviator" (Kirby: 218). In this sense, futurism critiqued the institution of theatre while at the same time promoting the theatricalisation of life, of which the theatricalisation of the arts would be one form.

If the manifesto and the theatre mark two strategies that intersect in the performed manifesto, we may take those manifestos that speak directly about the theatre and theatricality as a privileged type of manifesto. Futurism expresses its dedication to theatricality in two manifestos, one for the futurist variety theatre and one for the synthetic theatre. Not surprisingly, both do their utmost to distance themselves from the bourgeois institution of theatre and instead envision a theatre based on what Marinetti calls *fisicofollia*, or body-madness, as well as a number of futurist values such as speech, constant transformation, electricity, condensation, and the "absolute value of novelty" (Kirby: 201). Neither of the two major futurist manifestos and none of the dada manifestos, however, refer to the *serate* or soriées as examples of the kind of theatre they envision.[22] The reason for this neglect lies in the fact that the theatricality these manifestos envision is different from the theatricality on which they subsist. While the futurist variety theatre is invested in "body-madness" and a circus-like atmosphere, the manifesto has no body or any other representational content that could be staged.[23] In contrast to such a theatre of bodies, the manifesto's theatricality is derived from performed speech. As Berghaus (134) has shown, Marinetti drew on his pre-futurist engagement with the art of declaiming poetry for the performance of manifestos and indeed it is this art to which he devotes one of his earliest theatre manifestos. The theatrically-declaimed manifesto occupies, therefore, a special place in the avant-garde theatre: while the stage is occupied by Marinetti's 'body-madness' and its inheritors, desperately trying to break with the history of the theatre, the manifesto with its theatrical declamation and screeching tone has already turned the cabaret into a arena for agitation. The avant-garde relied so much on the manifesto and its insufficient capacity to theorise that it forgot to theorise its own use of the manifesto. This failure to theorise is precisely what shows the extent to which the avant-garde relied on and was invested in the manifesto.

Viewing the difference between the avant-garde and modernism through the lens of the manifesto and its specific kind of theatricality raises one central issue: doesn't this understanding of the avant-garde privilege the verbal art of the manifesto and its theatrical performance at the expense of those arts that by their nature tend to shy away from discourse and language, such as the visual arts, sculpture, or music? I would like to respond to this objection in an indirect way by considering the ways in which the reliance on the manifesto affected the arts. While I insisted that we consider the manifesto as more than a genre of art amongst others and that while I pointed out the difference between futurist theatre and the performed manifesto, as well as between futurist and dadaist lyric and the language of the manifesto, I would like to suggest now that the manifesto infected the artworks of the avant-garde even as it kept its distance from them. Like the manifesto, much of avant-garde art is not directed at subtle audiences or close readers. In a simultaneous performance, all the arts must compete for the attention of the audience, always distracted and usually overwhelmed by the excessive rhetoric and theatricality used on the stage. No form of expression manages to scream louder and speak more directly to the audience than the manifesto.[24] In this sense, the avant-garde acquired its screeching voice from the performed manifesto, a tone that infused avant-garde art with a number of manifesto-like qualities, such as explicitness and directness.[25] Bürger seems to register such a quality in Duchamp's *Urinoir*, which was not, he claimed, a "work of art, but a manifestation" (71). Similarly, Roman Jakobson once remarked in an essay on futurism that "futurism offers picture-slogans, pictorial demonstrations" (147). I find hidden in these remarks the seed of a theory of the avant-garde that would take its point of departure from the manifesto and that claims that all artworks of the avant-garde aspire to the condition of the manifesto.[26]

Claiming that the avant-garde artwork aspires to the condition of the manifesto may seem counter-productive to those who have attempted, against all odds, to practice close readings of avant-garde art, imposing onto it modes of reception that are taken from the modernist canon and its cult of difficulty. I am not suggesting that it is not worth while to pay close attention to the individual artifacts, even if they are separated from their original theatrical context, left to us by the historical avant-garde. However, I would suggest that a substantial part of avant-garde art, guided by the genre of the manifesto, was not meant to be contemplated in private, that its screeching voice upsets our close-reading sensibilities. The most important difference between this type of "manifesto-art" and the canon of modernism is the fact that the manifesto and manifesto-art is not geared towards the act of interpretation. While Joyce calculated the interpretative challenge of his oeuvre, the manifesto and manifesto-art act as if interpretation can be circumvented altogether. This does not mean, of course, that manifest-art cannot or should not be interpreted, but that its interpretation should take into account that the implied audience of manifesto-art may still be the audience of street agitation, or of the avant-garde cabaret.

NOTES

[1] Nietzsche separates the theatre from art in his polemic against Wagner. Michael Fried does the same in his essays in *Artforum* from the sixties and as recently as his introduction to a collection of his essays on modern art (1998). Adorno likens actors to apes in his *Ästhetische Theorie* (181), while Stein explains her suspicion of the theatre in her essay „Plays."

[2] Walter Fähnders (1997) details this history of the manifesto, including the „Manifest Kaiser Franz Josephs" from July 28, 1914 declaring war to Serbia (19).

[3] Hubert van den Berg (Asholt 1997) discusses in more detail the history of the term avant-garde and argues that the political origin of the manifesto in the French Revolution remains a point of reference even for avant-garde manifestos (61). The print culture and political manifestos and pamphlets around the French revolution is discussed by Roger Chartier and Antoine de Baecque. Both consider the rise of political manifestos during the French revolution.

[4] This switch from the *pluralis majestatis* to the revolutionary "we" may give some insight into what Derrida (1984: 20) called the un-decidable structure of the *Declaration of Independence*, namely the fact that it both states and produces the independence of the "good People", who are its presumed signatories and speakers. This difficult of the *Declaration of Independence* in constituting its own "we" can be explained by situating it

within the history of the manifesto, for the *Declaration of Independence* is located precisely between the royal, authoritative declaration and the revolutionary appeal: while it gives voice to dissent, the speakers and signatories are already in a position of power at the time of their foundational speech act. Its "we" is, therefore, not only an act of military authority, as Derrida (27) argues, but also the attempt to constitute a coherent voice of dissent.

[5] Janet Lyon (23) devotes some attention to the precarious "we" of the manifesto and emphasises that the manifesto creates a generic speaking position for the *vox populi*.

[6] A few month ago, Rem Koolhaas received the Pritzker prize, which has been termed the Nobel prize of architecture. The primary achievement cited by the awarding committee was not his architecture but the publication of his text *Delirious New York*, with its paradoxical subtitle *A Retroactive Manifesto for Manhattan.*

[7] It is only through the work of Wolfgang Asholt and Walter Fähnders that the discussion of the manifesto as genre has begun to attract systematic critical and theoretical attention. Insightful studies have been devoted to this genre by Claude Abastado, who edited a 1980 special issue of *Littérature* on the manifesto, Marjorie Perloff, and Mary Ann Caws, who is preparing the first substantial collection of the manifestos of the historical avant-garde in English.

[8] Asholt and Fähnders view the manifestos as a similarly instrumental genre, as does Alfons Backes-Haase (Asholt 1997: 257) in his essay on dada.

[9] The most valuable work on Russian futurist manifestos has been done by Anna Lawton and Herbert Eagle in their collection of futurist manifestos.

[10] It is interesting to note the uneasy relationship between various forms of engaged art and the more explicitly engaged genre of the manifesto. As Idt (Abastado 1980: 61ff) points out, Sartre criticised the typical school manifesto, but did not denounce the manifesto as engaged art, since he thought manifestation to be part of what is human. Bürger (137) observes that Satre's and Zola's manifestos remain embedded in their respective interest in the novel and do not take over the way they do in the avant-garde.

[11] In situating itself across the divide between art and the public sphere and thus across the divide of art and politics, the manifesto can be said to politicise art. This effect of the avant-garde's move of the manifesto calls for a reassessment of Benjamin's formula that fascism aestheticises politics and communism politicises art (241-242). Benjamin comes to this assess-

ment by reading Marinetti's manifesto that propagates the aestheticisation of war; however, Benjamin too fails to reflect the generic history and form of the manifesto and the fact that it imports politics into the art of the avant-garde and even to some extent replaces the artwork with the hybrid form of the manifesto.

[12] Murphy (33ff), in his excellent recent study, points to an inherent ambiguity in Bürger's Hegelianism. Murphy proposes two models of sublation, one in which transformed art functions as the ideal of life, the other in which life swallows art. He also criticises Bürger's insistence that a vaguely sublation functions as "goal" rather than simply as an "orienting principle" (259). My reflection on the manifesto arrives at a similar critique of Bürger's Hegelianism, which causes, I would add, Bürger to disregard the genre of the manifesto and the concrete way in which it seeks and also manages to evade the difference between public life and art.

[13] Amongst the many "theatrical" readings of his theory feature most prominently the work of Judith Butler, but also a collection of essays on performance and performativity edited by Sedwick and Parker.

[14] This concern with the perlocutionary effect and the resulting clarity and commitment to communication can be seen as a reformulation of the type of intentionality at work in the manifesto, an intentionality that has received recent attention in an excellent collection of essays edited by van den Berg and Grüttemeier (1998).

[15] Wagner (Asholt 1997: 51) discusses the performative function of manifestos, including their frequent use of performative verbs. Ultimately Wagner judges the genre of the manifesto to become mere quotation for postmodernism (55). While I agree that many so-called postmodern manifestos maintain an ironic attitude towards the manifesto, as did many dadaist and other avant-garde manifesto, I find that the persistent use of manifestos from fluxus to Dogma points towards a continuous use of the form across the divide between the historical avant-garde and post-modernism.

[16] Here I agree with Wagner (49), who sees in the printed form of the manifesto elements of its original theatrical context.

[17] One may be reminded, here, of Kant's pamphlet against the "noble tone" of mystical philosophers, a tone that will be, he predicts, the death of philosophy. A reflection on the different tones of philosophy and theory must be undertaken in order to define the types of theorisation that the manifesto produces. Such a reading should take into consideration Derrida's (1983: 29) reading of Kant's essay, which shows that what bothers Kant about the mystics he criticises is no so much their lack of

argumentative rigor of the falseness of their tone, the fact that they imitate a tone, taken from theology, that is not theirs.

[18] Berghaus (45) points out that Marinetti managed to publish his first manifesto in *Le Figaro* because of family connections.

[19] Modes of publication and distribution are derived from the invaluable collection of manifestos by Asholt and Fähnders (1995).

[20] Meltzer's study of dadaist and surrealist performance provides the best account of the different activities that were part of the diverse dada soireés, from declaimed poetry to manifestos.

[21] Segel gives a detailed account of the Cabaret's history as it culminates in the Cabaret Voltaire.

[22] Berghaus (156ff) argues that the 1913 and 1914 manifestos on futurist theatre mark turning points in the development of futurist theatricality: away from the *serate* and a theatricality built around political agitation and the provocation of the audience towards a renewed interest in such traditional theatrical topics as drama, acting, and mise-en-scène.

[23] In her fascinating study on the Latin American avant-garde, Unruh identifies what she calls "performance manifestos", a hybrid genre between drama and manifesto that works by personifying different contentious positions, while, at the same time, privileging one of them. These types of performance manifestos are close to didactic drama, for example Brecht's *Lehrstücke*, differing from them, perhaps, by their greater commitment to the forms of direct speech that characterise the manifesto.

[24] While the founding moments of the avant-garde are thus the *serate* of the futurists and the evenings at the Cabaret Voltaire, theatricality remained a central feature of other avant-garde venues, for example the avant-garde exhibition. The First International Dada Fair, the origin of Berlin dada, for example, had much of the theatrical atmosphere of the Cabaret Voltaire; and even the surrealists continued to practice street happenings such as the mock trial of Maurice Barrés. Also compare, for example, Altshuler's discussion of the exhibition space of the avant-garde.

[25] Claude Abastado (1980) speculates about a "manifesto effect" of works of art (5).

[26] Asholt and Fähnders use a concept of the manifesto large enough to include what they call a "Bildmanifest" by Styrksý (XIX).

Bibliography

Abastado, Claude ed.,
1980 *Les Manifestes*, special issue of *Littérature*, no. 39, Paris: Librarie Larousse.

Adorno, Theodor
1986 *Die musikalischen Monographien.* Frankfurt am Main: Surkamp Verlag.

Altshuler, Bruce
1994 *The Avant-garde in Exhibition: New Art in the 20th Century.* Berkeley: University of California Press.

Asholt, Wolfgang, and Walter Fähnders (eds)
1995 *Manifeste und Proklamationen der europäischen Avant-Garde* (1919-1938). Stuttgart: Metzler Verlag.

1997 "*Die Ganze Welt ist eine Manifestation*": *Die europäische Avantgarde und ihre Manifeste.* Darmstadt: Wissenschaftliche Buchgesellschaft.

Austin, J. L.
1962 *How to do things with words.* Cambridge, Mass.: Harvard University Press.

Backes-Haase, Alfons
1995 „wir wollen triezen, stänkern, bluffen…". In: Asholt and Fähnders 1997: 256-274.

Benjamin, Walter,
1961 *Illuminationen: Ausgewählte Schriften.* Frankfurt a. M., Suhrkamp Verlag.

Berghaus, Günter
1998 *Italian Futurist Theatre 1909-1944.* Oxford: Clarendon Press.

Bürger, Peter
1974 *Theorie der Avantgarde.* Frankfurt am Main: Surkamp Verlag.

Butler, Judith
1990 Gender Trouble: Feminism and the Subversion of Identity. New York: Routledge.

Calinescu, Matei
1977 *Faces of Modernity: Avant-Garde, Decadence, Kitsch.* Bloomington: Indiana University Press.

Caws, Mary Ann (ed.)
1974 *Le Manifeste et le chaché: langages surréalistes et autres*. Paris: Minard.

Chariter, Robert
1991 *The Cultural Origins of the French Revolution*, translated by Lydia G. Cochrane. Durham: Duke University Press.

Chartier, Roger, ed.
1989 *The Culture of Print: Power and the Uses of Print in Early Modern Europe.* Princeton: Princeton University Press.

De Baecque, Antoine
1989 "Pamphlets: Libel and Political Mythology". In: Robert Darnton and Daniel Roche (eds), *Revolution in Print: The Press in France 1775-1800.* Berkeley: University of California Press, 165-176.

Derrida, Jacques
1983 *D'un ton apocalyptique adopté naguère en philosophie.* Paris: Édition Galilée.

1984 *Otobiogrpahies: L'enseignement de Nietzsche et la politique du nom propre.* Paris: Édition Galilée.

1988 *Limited Inc..* Evanston, Il.: Northwestern University Press.

Fried, Michael
1998 *Art and Objecthood.* Chicago: University of Chicago Press.

Idt, Geneviève
1980 "La ‚littérature engagée', manifeste permanent". In: *Littérature 39*: 61-71.

Jakobson, Roman
1997 *My Futurist Years*, edited by Bengt Jangfeldt and Stephen Rudy. New York: Marsilio Publishers.

Jelavich, Peter
1985 *Munich and Theatrical Modernism: politics, playwriting, and performance, 1890-1914*. Cambridge, Mass.: Harvard University Press.

Koolhaas, Rem
1988 *Delerious New York: A Retroactive Manifesto for Manhattan*. New York: Monacelli Press.

Lawton, Anna, Herbert Eagle (eds)
1988 *Russian Futurism through its Manifestoes, 1912-1928*. Ithaka: Cornell University Press.

Lyon, Janet
1999 *Manifestoes: Provocations of the Modern*. Ithaca: Cornell University Press.

Meltzer, Anabelle Henkin
1976 *Dada and Surrealist Performance*. Baltimore: Johns Hopkins University Press

Motherwell, Robert (ed.)
1989 *The Dada Painters and Poets*. Cambridge, Mass.: Harvard University Press.

Murphy, Richard
1998 *Theorizing the Avant-Garde: Modernism, Expressionism, and the Problem of Postmodernity*. Cambridge, UK: Cambridge University Press.

Nietzche, Friedrich
1973 *Der Fall Wagner*. Stuttgart: Reclam Verlag.

Parker, Andrew and Eve Kosofsky Sedwick (eds)
1995 *Performativity and Performance*. New York: Routledge.

Perloff, Marjorie
1986 *The Futurist Movement: Avant-Garde, Avant-Guerre, and the Language of Rupture*. Chicago: The University of Chicago Press.

Richter, Hans
1965 *Dada Art and Anti-Art*. New York: McGrath-Hill.

Segel, Harold
1987 *Turn-of-the-century Cabaret: Paris, Barcelona, Berlin, Munich, Vienna, Cracow,Moscow, St. Petersburg, Zürich*. New York : Columbia University Press.

Senelick, Laurence ed.
1989 *Cabaret Performance: Volume I. Europe 1890-1920.* New York: PAJ Publications.

Tafuri, Manfredo
1990 *The Sphere and the Labyrinth: Avant-Gardes and Architecture from Piranesi to the 1970s*, translated by Pellegrino d'Acierno and Robert Connolly. Cambridge, Mass: The MIT Press.

Unruh, Vicky
1994 *Latin American Vanguards: The Art of Contentious Encounters*. Berekley: University of California Press.

Van den Berg, Hubert
1997 "Zwischen Totalitarismus und Subversion. Anmerkungen zur politischen Dimension des avantgardistischen Manifests". In: Asholt and Fähnders 1997: 58-80.

Van den Berg, Hubert, and Ralf Grüttemeier (eds)
1998 *Manifeste: Intentionalität*. Amsterdam/Atlanta.

Wagner, Birgit
1997 "Auslöschen, vernichten, gründen, schaffen: zu den performativen Funktionen der Manifeste". In: Asholt and Fähnders 1997: 39-57.

Wolfe, Don M. (ed.)
1967 *Leveller Manifestoes of the Puritan Revolution.* New York: Humanities Press.

PAINTERLY CONCEPTS AND FILMIC OBJECTS: THE INTERACTION OF EXPRESSION AND RE-PRODUCTION IN EARLY AVANT-GARDE FILM.

DAVID MACRAE

Film is afflicted with objectivity. That is to say that filmic images, however stylised or manipulated, inevitably capture and reproduce the objects of their directly denotative attention. The pioneering European film works of the early 1920s were utterly conceptual, based as they were upon the progressive painterly aspirations their creators had previously been developing upon canvas. The *conceptual* and the *objective*, then, are two elements of crucial significance in this context, which require specific analysis in order to more clearly consider their key implications for avant-garde theory.

The graphic and geometric excursions on canvas, made by certain avant-gardiste innovators, were characterised by a fascina-tion with the nature of the peripheral boundaries of representation and expression. This largely involved a process of experiencing the *sensation* of imagery rather than purely the *imitation* of imagery. These images, then, intrinsically involved the role of the sensory in both their creation and reception. However, in the transition to the new medium of film, the original avant-garde visions would undergo a dramatic alteration, not necessarily of appearance, but certainly of perceptual status and significance. To view an example of early avant-garde film may still be to witness the forms and structures consonant with a cohesively progressive visionary ethos now mobilised in a spatio-temporal sphere, yet it is also to witness these structures through a glaze of technical mediation.

Questions of perceptual status and significance have, of course, been central to the development of theories of the avant-garde. Peter Bürger's *Theory of the Avant-Garde* has become well established as an incisive key text in regard to such questions, yet devotes conspicuously little attention to the critical role of avant-garde film. The aim of this paper is to consider Bürger's theories in relation to the phenomenon of avant-garde film, and to examine the issues and contentions they raise in the particular areas of "negation of the autonomy of art" and the problematics of the categorisation of avant-gardiste "works". The focus of this methodology will be upon the concept of constructive collision of expression and reproduction as revealing crucial evidence about the perceptual status of the filmic medium in the context of avant-garde artistic creation and reception.

The notion of painterly conceptualism, and the ways in which this is distinguished from objective representation, initiates a range of challenging questions. It is a matter of extremely obvious fact that an abstract painting, and a filmed recording of an abstract painting hanging on a gallery wall, are two forms of visual experience which exist at significantly different perceptual levels, yet this apparently obvious fact conceals a series of complex evasions of precise definition. Frequently, critical efforts to explain the perceptual distinction achieve little more than affirm the fact that such a distinction indeed exists. The common ground between these levels, which seems most abundantly obvious, is their status, as processes of *visual* experience. In *Theory of the Avant-garde*, Bürger places an early emphasis on the concept of a dichotomous separation, in the visual arts, between realist representation and artistic creation — between "art" and "real life". He states:

> Whereas during the period of realism, for example, the development of art was felt to lie in a growing closeness of representation to reality, the one-sidedness of this construction could now be recognised. Realism no longer appears as *the* principle of artistic creation but becomes understandable as the sum of certain period procedures. The totality of the de-velopmental process of art becomes clear only in the stage of self-criticism. Only after art has in fact wholly detached itself from everything that is the praxis of life can two things be seen to make up the principle of development of art in bourgeois society : the progressive detachment of art from

> real life context, and the correlative crystallisation of a distinctive sphere of experience, i.e. the aesthetic. (Bürger 1984: 22-23)

This classic dichotomy, which Bürger reinforces, has established itself as a critical paradigm for the interpretation of modernism itself and specific avant-garde developments. But exactly how thorough is this granite paradigm which has long cast its influential shadow across twentieth century theorisation? From the privileged position of contemporary reflection we might detect the presence of a range of more diverse forces influencing the relationships between representation and creation, between real life and art. (Or as Stephen Foster has proposed, transcend the notion of any relationship at all in favour of a cultural continuum of functioning "fictional realities": cf. Foster's contribution in this volume, 49-67).

Of course, the advent of new reproductive representational media radically altered the forms and functions of the so-called fine arts, perhaps most significantly that of painting. Yet, as the forms of painterly visual communication and expression gradually evolved through the respective phases of impressionism, post-impressionism, fauvism, expressionism, cubism, and futurism, so the specific processes of visual reception and interpretation were reciprocally altered. These alterations of reception begin to show particularly interesting implications during that phase of painterly activity immediately prior to the full flourishing of German expressionism. Frequently cited as one of the most influential precursors of the cohesive expressionist movement, the Norwegian painter Edvard Munch is of particular note here as he was simultaneously intrigued by figurative representation (including symbolic narrativisation), and formal expression (including exaggerated linearity, angularity and disruptive perspectival regimes). To look at perhaps his most famous work, *The Scream* the viewer apprehends a representative object (allegedly Munch himself is a moment of autobiographic angst), and painterly expression (in the lurid and dramatic formal structure of the work itself). The variant layers of perceptual process active in the interpretation of a work such as this are enlightening in terms of how viewers would be equipped to comprehend the nature of later avant-gardiste endeavours. *The Scream* provides a forum for a nuanced range of visual responses. Consider some of the contrasting characteristics of these responses which reveal themselves in textual interpretation. The viewer witnesses a scream, when confronted by the painting. There are particular visual structures of the composition which focus the gaze upon the figure's shrieking face, and this face might be described as the *scream* itself — it *is* the scream. Yet there are further elements of the work which take the perceptual impact of the *scream* itself beyond its objects. To merely describe the face, or its expression and depiction as the meaning of the work is reductive and superficial. Despite its deploy-ment of *objective* forms, the work's most potent element is the presentation of *conceptual* effects.

Munch's *The Scream* serves here as a basic example of the ways in which a viewer of the painted image is simultaneously confronted by a multiplicitous range of perceptual layers, and the impaction of these layers is a factor which would emerge with particular force in avant-gardiste artworks in the early part of the twentieth century. Expressivity, then, is a perceptual layer which spreads itself across the surface of represented objects in the expressionistic painting, indeed it permeates the work and its objects — ultimately perhaps even *becoming* its central object. The act of witnessing an expressionist painting is a process which activates a variety of contrasting responsive factors: it involves seeing re-presented objects, acknowledging the actual objective origins of these objects, seeing the manipulated reconfigurations of the artist's own responses to the actual original objects, and also seeing the surface textures of the materials of representation — specifically the facture of the painted canvas. Therefore the viewer is concurrently witnessing the originally perceived object, the artist's creatively inflected interpretation, and the *actual* material medium. These various factors involve the viewer in a process of active acceptance and denial. Perception, recollection, inflection and medium, all reciprocally oscillate in the viewer's responses as representation is acknowledged yet denied in the acceptance that the image relies purely on the configuration of blobs of undulating pigment upon a stretched canvas surface. The representation is indeed there, but crucially depends, for its expressive impact, upon the abundant acceptance that it is not. These processes, of course, operate at a latent level. The viewer of an expressionist painting embraces the conscious procedure of apprehending the actuality of the manipulated picture surface and the illusory representation sus-pended within — it is both a suspension of disbelief and an affirma-tion of pictorial belief. Hans Richter's 1914 painting entitled *Revolution* (Berlinische Galerie, Berlin) presents the viewer with the depictive representation of figurative arrangements, architectural configura-tions, spatial depth, and a composition of visionary en-vironmental formation. Yet it also confronts the viewer with the factual fore-grounding of the painted surface itself. Richter's painted surface of oil on board still, however, invokes the viewer's projec-tion of the mind to the actuality of revolutionary fervour, both as fact and concept beyond factural techniques and textures. This might be described as a perceptual *projection,* which is an implicit com-ponent of viewing the painting. It is important to note that this is not a separately manufactured perceptual effort on behalf of the viewer, but an immediate response enmeshed within the apprehen-sion of the image.

In Hans Richter's avant-garde films, by contrast, the medium of representation itself invokes the viewer to engage with the imagery in an intriguingly distinct manner: the filmic images involve the per-ceptual acknowledgement of the nature of the medium as well as a perceived actuality of represented events. Thus the viewer accepts a process of apprehending events from the camera's location and angle, a situating device intrinsic to the authority of the medium whereby the filmic surface is denied in relation to perceived events.

Of course, this is merely a fragment of the entire perceptual pro-cedure. The painted surface, such as that in Richter's *Revolution,* expresses itself through its textural sensations as well as its extended appeal to the viewer's personal assimilations and imaginings. The painted surface, therefore, may be *experienced* in a dynamic manner which will have unique resonances for each individual viewer. There are important distinctions between the process of experi-encing the painting as surface effect and factual document: the imaginary effects of the painting may be said to exist largely in-dependently of the requirements of the depicted event. Consider, then, the validity or otherwise of gazing upon a Richter painting and asserting "That is the expressive *work* of Hans Richter", and also gazing upon the screen of a Richter film and asserting "That is the expressive *work* of Hans Richter".

Our perceptions of the *works* in question are, respectively, little more than the causal outcome of a dynamic experience of imagery involving the mediating agency of Hans Richter's thought processes. In terms of the perception of the painted image, not only is the viewer consciously acknowledging the nuances of surface texture and physical manipulation of medium, but there is also the active extension of personal assimilative sensation and meaning which reaches toward perceived actuality from recollection. Simultaneously, then, there is acceptance and denial of surface and illusion — the perception of paint becomes as one with dynamic experience of imagined event.

For Peter Bürger, the parameters of perceptual dynamics necessitates consideration of "the autonomy of art" and the nature of the category *work*. He states:

> With reference to the problem of autonomy, one should ask whether there is a connection between its two elements (the detachment of art from the praxis of life, and the obscuring of the historical conditions of this process as in the cult of genius, for example), and what sort of connection that may be. The emancipation of the aesthetic from the praxis of life could probably be most easily traced if one examined the development of aesthetic ideas. The nexus between art and the sciences that the Renaissance created would then have to be interpreted as the first phase of art's emancipation from ritual. In the emancipation of art from the direct tie to the sacral, one should probably see the center of that process that is so difficult to analyze because it required centuries for its completion, the achievement of autonomy by art. [...] It is true that Baroque art makes an extraordinary impression, but its connection with the religious subject has become relatively loose. This art does not derive its principal effect from the *sujet* but from the abundance of colours and forms. [...] There is yet another sense in which the process of emancipation of the aesthetic is a contradictory one. For as we have seen, what occurs here is not merely that a new way of perceiving that is immune to coercion of means-end rationality comes into existence. It is also that the sphere this opens up is ideologized (notion of genius, etc.). (Bürger 1984: 40-41)

Bürger's approach emphasises the aesthetic separation, then, from original subject, in his recurring fixation with the idea of "praxis of life". This detached insularity of *praxis of life* from the aesthetic sphere is problematic in that it suggests a bizarre socio-cultural scenario involving unconvincing processes of creative transition and constricted routes of access into the fictional or imaginary. For Bürger, the obstruction of access to the aesthetic sphere from the praxis of life denies the perceptual extension of imagining the depictive. In confronting the avant-gardiste artefact, the viewer apprehends various perceptual perspectives, or levels, and these *become* the catalyst of the *work's* meaning. In Bürger's framework, these variant perceptual levels have, in themselves, created a detachment from the "praxis of life" and therefore the viewer is obstructed in relating each level to the other or, indeed, of interpreting the nature of their very relatedness. Bürger continues:

> An art no longer distinct from the praxis of life but wholly absorbed in it will lose the capacity to criticise it, along with its distance. During the time of the historical avant-garde movements, the attempt to do away with the distance between art and life still had all the pathos of historical progressiveness on its side. But in the meantime, the culture industry has brought about the false elimination of the distance between art and life, and this also allows one to recognise the contradictoriness of the avant-gardiste undertaking. (Bürger 1984: 50)

Yet there is a further contradictoriness involved here, and that is within the structure of Bürger's terminology of distinction and absorption between "art" and "praxis of life". The uses of the notion of distinction and subsequent absorption as somehow oscillating areas of definition in this regard suggests the necessity of a spectatorial process of recurrent transitions from one interpretative location to another. The idea of a distance between art and life which may be erased and/or re-established in order to define the terms of an aesthetic phenomena creates a reductive circularity in the scope of the debate. The aesthetic experience, from aestheticism through the historical avant-garde and into neo-avant-garde projects, involves interpretations from a variety of informed locations. These interpretative locations do not necessitate arduous transitions from "life" to "art" or vice-versa, but operate in unison. In observing a painting, whether by Picasso, Magritte, or Warhol, to cite some of Bürger's diverse choices of example, the viewer is certainly capable of acknowledging the processes of creative selection and material manipulation, as well as the processes of illusion and representation.

Each of these processes operate as intrinsic aspects of art and life, or life/art. There is no *enforcement* of excluding/including either one or the other. So, in contrast to the Bürger perspective, distance or separation are not *prerequisites* of critical apprehension; the principle is straightforward: the convergence of these elements does not require the idea of a mutually exclusive origin for the generation of meaning. Viewers of an avant-garde film work by Hans Richter, for example, are capable of perceiving the idea of the abstract pure shapes and forms he manoeuvres upon the screen as expressive extensions of the artist's creative *praxis*, and then additionally perceiving the technical medium of the visual presentation as a modifying influence each emerging from aspects of the aesthetic sphere, each intrinsic to the *praxis of life.*

In the event that we do allow for a perceptual obstruction from an awareness of praxis of life, and become enveloped in a pure sphere of aestheticism, there is no requirement for the viewer to struggle to locate some clandestine route back to a conventionalised sense of life praxis; to endeavour to pierce through an imaginary veil of perceptual isolation. It is not inevitably necessary, in terms of the avant-garde aesthetic experience, to trace the faded footprints of the artist's elusive presence back to the life practices of the technical phases of construction or selection. Consider, in this regard, the following claims by Bürger:

> The historical avant-garde movements negate those determinations that are essential in autonomous art: the disjunction of art and the praxis of life, individual production, and individual reception as distinct from the former. The avant-garde intends the oblation of autonomous art by which it means that art is to be integrated into the praxis of life. This has not occurred, and presumably cannot occur, in bourgeois society unless it be as a false sublation of autonomous art. (Bürger 1984: 53-54)

Surely it is perfectly clear, however, that when the specific artefact is confronted, whether avant-garde or otherwise, many of its constructed (or unconstructed) origins and communicative implications are not perceptually foregrounded, and the artefact, therefore attests to a pheonomenological immediacy of presence. In this sense, the questions of "autonomy" or "anti-aestheticism" are somewhat muted. Bürger concedes, though, that the avant-gardiste artefact may observe structural qualities other than obsessive exclusion or disjunction:

> Generally speaking, the work of art is to be defined as a unity of the universal and the particular. [...] The avant-gardiste work does not negate unity as such but a specific kind of unity, the relationship between part and whole that characterizes the organic work of art. (Bürger 1984: 56)

Thus, Bürger contends that in interpreting the avant-gardiste work of art the viewer must be involved in a process of separating the unity between part and whole which, he claims, is a characteristic of *organic* works of art. There is a questionable assumption here, however, about the relationship of the viewer to the work. The assumption is that the viewer must accede to a process of calculating an imaginary level of *organic* wholeness in terms of the work's naturalistic validity. Yet a work of art, whether avant-gardiste or *organic*, need not necessarily demand that the viewer must occupy a perceptual space located by the artist. Additionally, it is not a corollary of an art work that its stylistic methods of execution will always translate into a reciprocal style of interpretation. This ushers in the question of autonomy.

> The category 'autonomy' does not permit the understanding of its referent as one that developed historically. The relative disso-ciation of the work of art from the praxis of life in bourgeois society thus becomes transformed into the (erroneous) idea that the work of art is totally independent of society. In the strict meaning of the term, 'autonomy' is thus an ideological category that joins an element of truth (the apartness of art from the praxis of life) and an element of untruth (the hypostatization of this fact, which is a result of historical development as the 'essence' of art). (Bürger 1984: 46)

In the case of "praxis of life", Bürger's phraseology engages a notion of representative identification. This praxis of life appears to be a scope of imagery which initiates a series of *viewpoints,* whether of artist or recipient. In this regard of these indentificatory viewpoints of the *praxis of life* the viewer must therefore identify with the ideological framework of the artist, or indeed, that the artist accede to an imagined requirement of a potential viewer's ideological status. This appears to be an area in which Bürger's notion of 'praxis of life' becomes deficient. The viewer might identify with, or more precisely *project* their perceptions of certain events or objects, emphasising a selection of specific features which resonate in personalised terms. Furthermore, the modern viewer is abundantly *empowered* with the awareness of the relational status of the cultural artefact and its fictional reality: This awareness embraces both the idea of the viewer's personal responses and a consciousness of the role of the artist's selective decisions implicit to the work. Rather than negating any 'praxis of life', then, the avant-gardiste work *instructs* entirely by virtue of its open portrayal of a visual *experience.* It is an experience which, critically, transcends the idea of identifying with a representational or ideological stability consistent with the artist's own perceptually rooted status.

Layering, or superimpositions, of perceptual strata in relation to the avant-gardiste artwork is a matter which Bürger approaches most tantalisingly, if not entirely satisfyingly, in his consideration of the concept of montage. It is at this stage that Bürger notices, but fails to fully recognise, the significance of the filmic medium in the avant-gardist arsenal of visual ammunition:

> Film is the stringing together of photographic images that because of the speed with which they flow past the eye of the spectator, create the impression of movement. In the film, the montage of images is the basic *technical procedure.* It is not a specifically artistic technique, but one that lies in the medium. Nonetheless, there are differences in its use. It is not the same thing when natural movements are photographed as when simulated ones are created by cutting (for example, the leaping stone lion in *Potemkin*, which is edited from shots of a sleeping, an awaking, and a rising marble lion). In the former case, there is also a montage of individual shots but the impression created in the film only reproduces illusionistically the natural sequence of move-ments, whereas in the second case, it is montage that creates the impression of movement. (Bürger 1984: 73)

The critically absent concept in this account, however, is the fact that in the avant-garde film, montage is at the core of an active evolutionary expressive *event.* Certainly, it is much more than merely the "basic technical procedure", or "not a specifically artistic technique". The early avant-gardiste film deployed as perhaps its most striking effect the very fact of its extraordinary collision of the technical set of objective representational elements at a scientific level and the visionary spectacles of the imagination to produce the essence of an avant-garde statement. Furthermore, for Bürger to seemingly separate "technical procedure" into a detached compartment of definition is surely to deny an integral component of most modernist cultural phenomena itself. The early twentieth century's most radical creative and progressive impact depends heavily upon the reciprocality of the mechanical and the organic, the visionary expression and the technical reproduction.

There is considerable significance in the fact that much of early twentieth-century avant-garde development has an intrinsically filmic aesthetic. Fernand Léger, in an article first published in the journal *Soirées de Paris* in 1914, entitled "Contemporary Achievements in Painting", asserts the nature of the perceptual alterations initiated by modern life:

> If pictorial expression has changed, it is because modern life has made this necessary. [...] The thing that is imagined does not stay as still, the object does not exhibit itself as it formerly did. When one crosses a landscape in an automobile or an express train, the landscape loses in descriptive value, but gains in synthetic value. [...] The condensation of the modern picture, its variety, its breaking up of forms, are the result of all this. It is certain that the evolution of means of locomotion, and their speed, have something to do with the new way of seeing. (Léger 1966: 135)

For Léger, film was an extension to his cubist activity as a painter. Although his work in film was not particularly prolific, it was certainly influential. *Ballet Mécanique* (1924) is regarded as a key film-work of the early avant-garde and demonstrates Leger's em-bracing of the expanded potential of new media. The film subverts conventional temporal progression, accelerates and decelerates the movements of machine parts, and presents figures in repetitively looped sequences which subsume human physical action within the mechanised medium of their reproduction.

In *The Cubist Cinema*, Standish D. Lawder emphasises the way in which film was able to accommodate these avant-garde urges toward a visual aesthetic of motion, specifically assessing an earlier

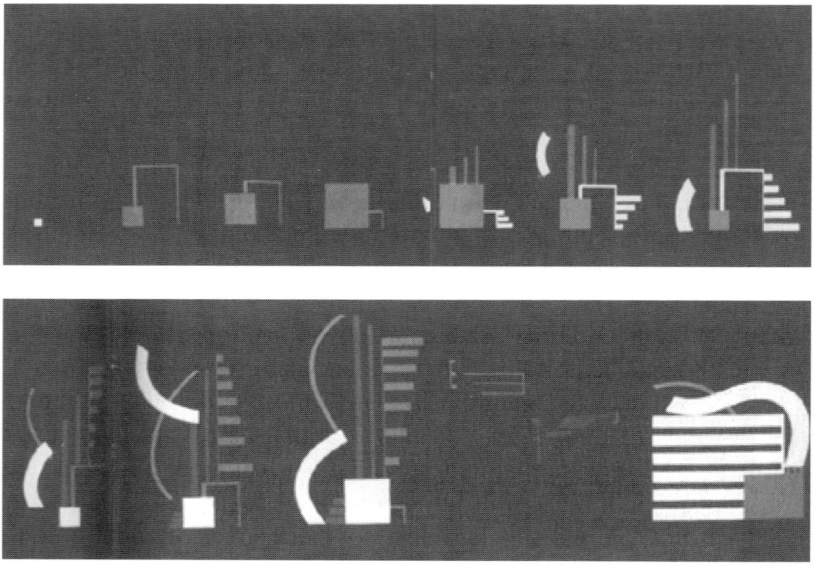

13 Hans Richter: *Rhythm 23*. 1923

filmwork by Hans Richter which serves as an exemplary demonstration of the implications of a collision of painterly subject and filmic object:

> Richter's first film, *Rhythm 21,* was a kinetic composition of rectangular forms of black, grey, and white. Perhaps more than in any other avant-garde film, it uses the movie screen as a direct substitute for the painter's canvas, as a framed rectangular surface on which a kinetic organisation of purely plastic forms was composed. For, normally, the movie screen is perceived as a kind of window, more or less arbitrarily circumscribed, and behind which an illusion of space appears; in *Rhythm 21*, by contrast, it is a planar surface activated by the forms upon it. Thus, its forms, like those of an abstract painting, seem to have no physical extension except on the screen, nor do we sense their lateral extension beyond the limits of the screen as is usually the case in images created by camera vision. The film is a totally self-contained kineticcomposition of pure plastic forms. (Lawder 1975: 49-50)

Richter was intrigued by the optical dynamism which film could contribute to his explorations of shape, tone, line, and form. He followed *Rhythm 21* with *Rhythm 23* (1923), which developed further his technical grasp of the filmic medium and shows the progress of his fluent language of mobilised visual structures, gradually integrating his painterly sense of composition with the spatio-temporal scope of the screen context.

Perhaps of most critical importance for the avant-garde visual aesthetic of the time, though, is the effect that such early experimental film work has in reconstructing the nature of inter-action between concept and object, both in terms of creation and reception of the avant-gardiste work. Bürger claims that

> montage does not introduce a new category meant to replace the concept of allegory. Rather, it is a category that permits a more precise definition of a particular aspect of the concept of allegory. Montage presupposes the fragmentation of reality and describes the phase of the constitution of the work. (Bürger 1984: 73)

Yet surely the achievements of early avant-garde film-works emphasise clearly that *montage* itself transcends the simplistic procedure through which the represented content remains the dominant factor in any phase of a work. This perspective challenges the established theorisation of the historical avant-garde, in which there is a tendency to emphasise aspects of creative technique and ideological functionality in relation to pre-existing aesthetic prac-tice. Furthermore, early examples of avant-garde film-works present themselves as literal paradigms of a demonstrative interface of concept and object, expression and reproduction. In its avant-gardist context, film became capable of operating in a mode of simul-taneous illusion and revelation, it both exposed and enclosed the perceptual processes of aesthetic interpretation. For film allowed for the veiled expression of reproductive objectivity, and for the actuality of a tangible environment irrevocably entrapped within the flickering glaze of mechanical construction and reconstruction. This is perhaps the most profoundly influential factor of the avant-gardist film — and indeed of the early avant-garde ethos itself — which is initiated by the very precision of reproductive imagery and which thus subordinates, and apparently ostracised, expressive form as a prime factor in creative process. It is precisely here, however, in this fact of transition of focus, that the renewed creative formalism resides.

Of such form/content perceptual transitions, Peter Bürger identifies the vital role of Marcel Duchamp:

> Duchamp's ready-mades are not works of art but manifestations. Not from the form-content totality of the individual object Duchamp signs can one infer the meaning, but only from the contrast between mass-produced object on the one hand, and signature and art exhibit on the other. It is obvious that this kind of provocation cannot be repeated indefinitely. The provocation depends on what it turns against: here, it is the idea that the individual is the subject of artistic creation. Once the signed bottle drier has been accepted as an object that deserves a place in a museum, the provocation no longer provokes; it turns into its opposite. (Bürger 1984: 52)

Had Bürger prolonged his exploration of Duchamp's diverse attentions, he would have revealed a considerably more rewarding vein of endeavour. Bürger consigns Duchamp's form/content transitions to a simplistic category of provocational self-obstruction, yet in the filmic medium Duchamp deploys the processes of perceptual transition with strikingly expansive implications. Marcel Duchamp collaborated in the development of various avant-garde films and made an appearance in the René Clair film entitled *Entr'acte* (1924), however his own most significant contribution to the medium is the 1926 film *Anémic Cinéma.* This remarkable piece of film was developed from Duchamp's bizarrely convoluted exploration of the illusory impacts of geometric shapes painted upon rotating glass discs. When set in motion at alternating directions and speeds, these mechanised discs generate sensations of dynamic dilation and contraction, projection and recession, surface and spatiality. P. Adams Sitney elaborates on the film's visual structure and its implications:

> For Duchamp the word "cinema" yields the anagram "anemic". [...] Eight disks of different graphic spirals alternate with eight on which elaborate puns have been printed spirally, so that each sentence begins at the perimeter and ends at the center of the revolving circle. The motion of the camera records their illusionary movement. Although there is no ontological difference between

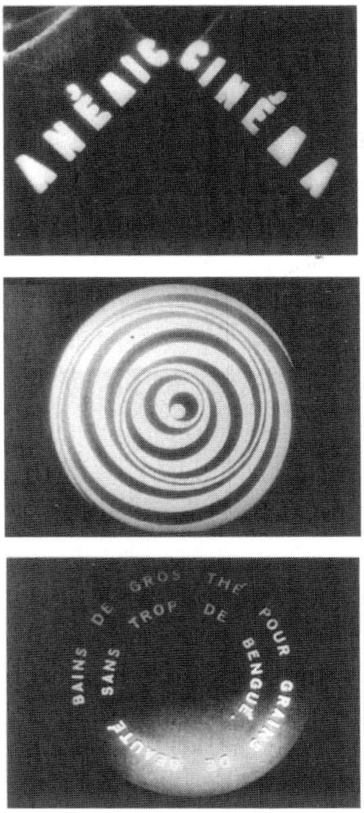

14 Marcel Duchamp: *Anémic Cinéma.* 1926

> the image of a moving disk with concentric (and eccentric) circles and the image of a similar disk with letters rather than straight lines, the automatic optical response of the viewer shifts at each change from spirals to words, and this is the main point of the film. [...] The optical illusion of depth generated by the graphic spirals corresponds to the "translation" of the letters into sounds, words, and meaning in the act of reading. (Sitney 1974: 399)

In contrast to Bürger's restricted assessment of Duchamp's ready-mades as shallow, static statements of provocational opposites, *Anémic Cinéma* reveals an ingenious dynamic interaction operative between space and surface, sign and sense, interpretation and allusion, fact and form, process and presentation. Indeed it is an incessantly informative presentation of the acts of assimilation — the reflexive oscillation of perceptual levels. The stifled closure which Bürger proposes, as provocation merely turns into its opposite, becomes swept into an entirely different mode of resonance in the sphere of avant-garde film. Superfluous self-referentiality is transcended by the cinematic surge of persistence of vision — urgently empowering the viewer with the oxygenating active awareness of imagery, meaning, and the mechanised terms of their respective generation.

These mechanised terms of image generation and meaning, intrinsic to the avant-gardist film-work, are essential components of the historical avant-garde endeavour itself: reconstituting the dynamic interface between form and content, between concept and object. Indeed, it is within the technical factuality of the filmic process, i.e. the persistence of vision, and its constant collisions of related successive images that this dynamic perceptual process becomes foregrounded for the viewer. Yet, in contrast to preceding practices of aesthetic structure and interpretation, where a harmonic convention of representation — whether depictive or authorial — prevailed, the mechanisms of the avant-garde film experience deployed radical tensions and subversions to enforce the pressure upon and between the viewer's various levels of perception. Man Ray's 1923 film, *Return to Reason,* for example, simultaneously exploits the conscious pressure between film as an exposed malle-able material, representational tool of illusionary spatiality, and semiotic structure of encoded imagistic symbolisms. *Return to Reason* shows Man Ray's famous 'photogramming' technique: a variety of objects and implements are printed directly onto the filmstrip, foregrounding the concept of film as materialist medium and surface of textural illusion. These sequences contrast drama-tically with those of representational dimensions of depth in the spinning lights of a fairground, the chiaroscuro shadows of sculpture and figure.

Early avant-garde film is of such critical importance in any thorough theorisation of avant-garde aesthetics as a precise result of its recurrent invocation of both the physical and the cerebral: it urges an empowered, active engagement of the viewer's faculties, which transcends the conventionalised closed-circuit aesthetic treadmill interlocking the artefact with the authorial presence of the artist and onlooking passive participation of the viewer. Perhaps more than any other examples of early avant-garde artefact, such as photomontage, assemblage, installation, or ready-made, it is the avant-garde film which most lucidly — if unsettlingly — presented itself as a work of art purely by inviting, strangely and seductively, the urge to participate in the process of understanding vision through embracing construction of image. This is a point perhaps best elucidated with a contrast. Of his own ready-made urinal, Marcel Duchamp wrote: "an ordinary article of life, placed [...] so that its useful significance disappeared under the new title and point of view", thus creating a "new thought for that object" (cf. Harrison and Wood 1992: 248).

Although enlightening in itself, Duchamp's assertion seems considerably more profound when contrasted with an intriguingly similar statement by theorist Peter Gidal regarding avant-garde film:

> The assertion of "film as material" is predicated upon representation, inasmuch as "pure" empty acetate running through the projector-gate without image, for example, merely sets off another level of associations. These can be abstract, or not. But they are, when instigated by such a device, no more materialist or anti-illusionist than any other associations. (Gidal 1989: 118-119)

Ultimately, therefore, the nuanced dynamic interactions of expression and reproduction unique to avant-garde film might expose the quintessential qualities of the early European avant-garde ethos, as its most profound achievement is possibly not within the presentations of creative concepts but the transitions of perceptual objects.

Bibliography

Bürger, Peter
1984 *Theory of the Avant-Garde*. Minneapolis: University of Minnesota Press.

Gidal, Peter
1989 *Materialist Film*. London: Routledge.

Harrison, Charles, and Paul Wood (eds)
1992 *Art in Theory 1900-1990: An Anthology of Changing Ideas*. Oxford: Blackwell.

Lawder, Standish D.
1975 *The Cubist Cinema*. New York: New York University Press.

Léger, Fernand
1966 "Contemporary Achievements in Painting". In: Edward F. Fry, *Cubism*. London: Thames and Hudson, 135-139.

Sitney, P. Adams
1974 *Visionary Film*. Oxford: Oxford University Press, 2nd edition.

THE WORLD "OUTSIDE OF FICTION": GEORGES BATAILLE AND SURREALIST PHOTOGRAPHY SCULPTURE

MARA DE GENNARO

> The facts and theories of ethnology have always exerted on Georges Bataille a sort of fascination.
>
> Alfred Metraux[1]

> In so far as they manifest themselves in a social milieu, the impulses that are identified *in practice* by heterology as the *raison d'être* of man can be regarded in a certain sense as antisocial (to the same degree that sexual perversions or even delights are regarded by certain individuals as a waste of vigor, for example the great ritual destructions of goods in British Columbia or, among civilised peoples, the pleasure of crowds convening in the night at great fires). Yet the impulses that go against the interests of a society in a state of stagnation (during a phase of appropriation) have, on the contrary, social revolution (the phase of excretion) as their end.
>
> Georges Bataille[2]

Around the time Georges Bataille was finishing work on the last issue of his short-lived journal *Documents: Archéologie-Beaux Arts-Ethnographie-Variétés,*[3] he wrote an essay in which he challenged André Breton's "Second Surrealist Manifesto" with a concept that, though previously unnamed, had pervaded *Documents* throughout its two-year run. In this essay, "The Use Value of D.A.F. de Sade", Bataille gives the name "heterology" to "the science of what is completely other", a theory of knowledge "opposed to any homogeneous representation of the world, in other words, to any philosophical system" (1970b: 61, 62).[4] Though he refrains from attacking Breton directly, he makes clear that any "total poetic conception of the world" is pseudo-revolutionary in that it wrongly sets poetry at odds with what it implies to be an "inferior vulgar reality", thereby perpetuating the idealist framework traditional to the very bourgeois systems of thought ostensibly being opposed (1970b: 62). Bataille had made a similar but more explicitly anti-Bretonian argument not long before in "The 'Old Mole' and the Prefix *Sur*", writing that although surrealism is exceptional philosophically thanks to its "contribution of base values (the unconscious, sexuality, filthy language, etc.)", it unfortunately "gives these values an elevated character by associating them with the most immaterial values", as its very adoption of the prefix *sur* attests (1970b: 103).

The consignment of surrealism to a sphere of merely "poetic agitation" Bataille attributes to Breton's wrong-headed conception of existence as "*purely* literary", as seen in his appeals for the mental resolution of contraries, which Bataille insists is tantamount to a childish appeal to "*annihilate* the healthy contingencies as well as the unhealthy contradictions of nature" (1970b: 105-106). Here as in his "Critical Dictionary", Bataille criticizes those who uphold repressive conventional conceptual categories even as they seek to oppose an abstract "bourgeoisie" or "civilisation". In his "Materialism" entry he writes:

> Most materialists, although they had wanted to eliminate the entire spiritual entity, came to describe an order of things whose hierarchical relations give it a specifically idealist character. [...] It is time, when the word materialism is used, to designate a direct interpretation, *excluding all idealism*, of raw phenomena and not a system founded on the fragmentary elements of an ideological analysis elaborated under the sign of religious relations. (1970a: 179-80)

It is this "direct interpretation" of "raw phenomena" or "base matter" that Bataille, in promoting his oppositional "base materialism" during these years between the wars, consistently distinguishes from idealist systems of conceptualising and representing that matter: "Base matter is external and foreign to ideal human aspirations and refuses to let itself be reduced to the great ontological machines resulting from these aspirations"("Base Materialism and Gnosticism" in 1970a: 225). Hence his disdain for the "most open apologists of Sade" who praise his poetic power even as they deny "the practical application" of the acts he describes. In relegating Sadean practice "outside of and above all reality", Bataille argues, these intellectuals hypocritically "affirm that the flashing and suffocating value that [Sade] wanted to give to human existence is inconceivable outside of fiction" ("The Use Value of D.A.F. de Sade" in 1970b: 55, 57).

Bataille's delineation of "heterology" and of the closely related "base materialism" coined prior to it has been much discussed in recent years, but as with his writing in general, broadly suggestive and ambiguous as it often is, some pertinent phrases and passages have tended to be privileged to the relative neglect of others. Of the remarkable passage that concludes "The Use Value of D.A.F. de Sade", for instance, Yve-Alain Bois (1997: 263n14) writes only that "as many critics have remarked, a certain ethnological naïveté dominates Bataille's texts at the time". Here is Bataille's passage:

> Now communities of color, once liberated from all superstition as from all oppression, represent in relation to heterology not only the possibility but the necessity of an adequate organisation. All formations that have ecstasy and frenzy as their goal (the spectacular slaughter of animals, partial tortures, orgiastic dances, etc.) will have no reason to disappear when the day comes that a heterological conception of human life is substituted for the primitive conception; they can only transform themselves as they are becoming generalised under the violent impetus of a moral doctrine of white origin, taught to men of color by all those Whites who have become aware of the abominable inhibition that is paralyzing their [*leur*, i.e., the black] race's communities. It is only starting from the collusion of a European scientific theory and black practice that there may develop institutions which will serve definitively as outlets, with no other limitation than that of human force, for the impulses that today require Revolution by fire and by the blood of social formations the whole world over. (1970b: 69)

The centrality of heterology to Bataille's thought and its usefulness as a concept through which to interpret numerous vanguard art texts and trends are persuasively demonstrated in *L'Informe: Mode d'emploi*, the critical collaboration of Bois and Rosalind Krauss which began as a 1996 exhibition at the Centre Georges Pompidou and was later published as a book, first in French and subsequently in English as *Formless: A User's Guide*. So it is curious that so provocative a passage, a passage clearly anticipated from the start of Bataille's essay,[5] would be quoted only in a footnote, and that the commentary on it would prove so cursory.

In response, Brent Hayes Edwards has considered the quotation at greater length in his perceptive essay "The Ethnics of Surrealism", but he, too, downplays what he calls the "bizarre quality" of Bataille's "somewhat rootless 'tribal' reference", arguing that really Bataille is interested not so much in evoking the primitive as in identifying the revolutionary potential of "civilised" blacks (115). Though arguing for the potential of blacks once they have been initiated into a scientific mode of thinking is indeed Bataille's emphasis, and glorifying or denigrating a seemingly "primitive" world remote from "civilisation" is not, Bataille's argument nevertheless depends on an assumption that there is such a thing as a "primitive conception" or set of beliefs and values by which "men of color", presumably Africans, make sense of their ritual practices and the psychological effects of these practices; he makes clear, too, that this conception is distinct from his own. It is not ritual practices themselves that he considers primitive, at least in a negative sense, but the conventional religious and philosophical justifications that ritual practitioners fail to question, justifications that for him amount to "superstition" and the "abominable inhibition" to which superstition gives rise.

Thus his skepticism, in this essay and elsewhere, of traditional or common-sense ideologies applies not only to those idealist and spiritualist ones of his own culture but also to those of others, even as their collective ceremonial itself interests him as an expression of more fundamental psychological impulses and desires than the idealist conceptual framework of the ceremonial acknowledges. For him, the explanatory force of a readily familiar and accessible knowledge system, philosophical, religious, or aesthetic, obfuscates the system's own "irreducible waste products",or all that violates the ideological confines of the system and shows it to be fictitious. The result of this process is a "consistent homogeneity, which man established throughout the outside world by everywhere substituting outside objects, *a priori* inconceivable objects, with classified series of conceptions or ideas" (1970b: 60). The potential *pratique nègre* elaborated vaguely but insistently in the passage quoted above appears to represent for Bataille one waste product of bourgeois culture, in that it would owe its revolutionary social force to a vaguely defined *théorie scientifique européenne* despite the legitimising functions that science tends to have for that bourgeois culture. Hence black practice, once transformed by white Europeans educated in "scientific theory" and able to appreciate its subversive possibilities, would exemplify the heterological, or that which is wholly other *within* a repressive and rigidified norm that without it would be unquestioned.

Clearly, those who are to impart this education to blacks have in common an awareness of the repressive prohibitions of their own culture and hence some degree of liberation from them. They share also the intention of retrieving from an inauthentic "primitive" conception of ritual violence and eroticism — presumably a religious explanation that imposes prohibitions of its own — what is useful and valuable, namely the libidinal catharsis produced by an enlightened enactment of such rituals. Thus Bataille, in hoping to mobilise blacks as a subversive force by replacing what he sees as their primitive belief-systems with one that, in his view, "generalises" or democratises rather than polarizes and hierarchizes, is indeed reacting against the colonialist mission of attempting to influence non-Europeans to adopt the beliefs and goals dominant in Christian Europe. But even as he seeks to discredit those beliefs and goals rather than perpetuate them, he retains the colonialist assumption that the belief-systems of cultural others are false or inadequate, and ought therefore to be made to correspond with what their self-appointed educators conceive to be a more advanced agenda.

Though *Formless: A User's Guide* does not for the most part address the relationship of Bataille's theory between the wars to his contemporaneous interest in ethnography, it was Krauss whose seminal reinterpretations of surrealist sculpture and photography made known the significance of Bataille's formulations of "the base and the primitive" to *Documents* and to surrealist and dissident surrealist art more generally. In relating Bataille's thought to formal preoccupations of certain avant-garde artists familiar with his thought, she enabled readers to conceive of the widely heterogeneous "movement" of surrealism in a new way. Specifically, she identified as a vanguard reformulation of "the base" the horizontal sculptures that Alberto Giacometti produced between 1930 and 1933, and much of the surrealist photography of Man Ray, Jacques Boiffard, Brassaï, and Raoul Ubac. Through her recent collaboration with Bois she has continued to explore the relationship of Bataille's writings of the 1920s and 1930s to twentieth-century avant-garde art production.

But Krauss's focus is primarily on the transmission of formal and conceptual innovations in the art-historical tradition. Questions of the place of these structures in larger contexts of social and intellectual history have drawn little specific scholarly interest. An exception is a proliferation of feminist critiques since the 1980s of surrealist figurations of dismembered and mutilated women, critiques that have encouraged some shift of focus from form to gender thematics, but have often not extended their analyses beyond the interests of their immediate social agenda. A fuller exploration of the cultural functions of Bataille's work and his influence on avant-garde art may profitably begin with the recognition that the structures and figurations centrally featured in much of *Documents* and to some extent in later surrealist periodicals derive largely from categories that Bataille formulated in active dialogue with modern ethnographic theory and practice, and that the assumptions he drew from mainstream ethnography at the time put him, in this respect at least, at a remove theoretically from important areas of current criticism.

Krauss's "No More Play" considers in detail Giacometti's responses between the late 1920s and the mid-'30s to primitivist discourses,[6] and the relationship of the forms his sculptural innovation took during these years to Bataille's critiques of the hierarchical idealism he associated with Western philosophy since Descartes, and with Breton's conception of surrealism in particular. Krauss writes of Giacometti's *Spoon Woman*, "With this celebration of the primal function of woman seen through a primitivized formal logic, Giacometti had assumed the most vanguard of positions" (1985b: 49). Her preceding paragraph offers a clue why she considers this the most vanguard of positions:

> By taking the metaphor and inverting it, so that 'a spoon is like a woman' becomes 'a woman is like a spoon,' Giacometti was able to intensify the idea, and to universalise it by generalising the

forms of the sometimes naturalistic African carvings toward a more prismatic abstraction (48-49).

What accompanies this metaphoric reversal is what Krauss describes as a generalisation of aesthetic structures such that a universally common "primal function" may be discerned. Woman figured as primal *par excellence* was indeed a familiar sight in avant-garde art between the wars, but instead of responding to this phenomenon only by asking, as numerous critics of the last two decades have done, "Why woman?", we might also ask, "Why primal?"

Comparing *Spoon Woman* to Georges Henri Rivière's enthusiastic promotion of archaeology as the "parricidal daughter of humanism", Krauss traces the widespread primitivism of the visual avant-garde back to an "aggressive anti-Western stance" that entailed, she suggests, an opposition to humanism as it was currently formulated (49). But if *Spoon Woman* opposes humanism by exposing the cultural production of a unidirectional metaphoric logic as arbitrary, as her reading implies, the question still arises of why dissident surrealist transgression relies so often specifically on ethnological and primitivist themes. If an avant-garde artwork's transgression of a familiar logical sequence destabilises other, more broad-based systems of thought in which that sequence operates, then the "collapse of distinction" or "obliteration of difference"[7] effected by such transgression could be conflated with a poststructuralist mode of transgression were it not for other characteristics of avant-garde transgression that distinguish its anti-humanism from that of poststructuralism. *Spoon Woman* indeed reverses, hence denaturalises, the production of a monologic common sense familiar to Western consumers of primitive art. But its function may be more plausibly understood, in the context of European modernism, less as absolute denaturalisation than as a stripping away of the distinctions and peculiarities of a particular culture to reveal a common ground of structures recognisable across cultures. That Giacometti would shortly go on to explore themes of ritualised eroticism and violence, themes central to *Documents*, enabled him to continue this project begun in the late 1920s of exposing a base of commonalities. Increasingly, though, he attended not just to the identification of formal affinities and the degrounding of Western standards that this implies, but to the confrontation of consumers of Western art with stark figurations of decontextualised sado-erotic conjunctions of objects, conjunctions designed to underscore fundamental instincts shared by those consumers.

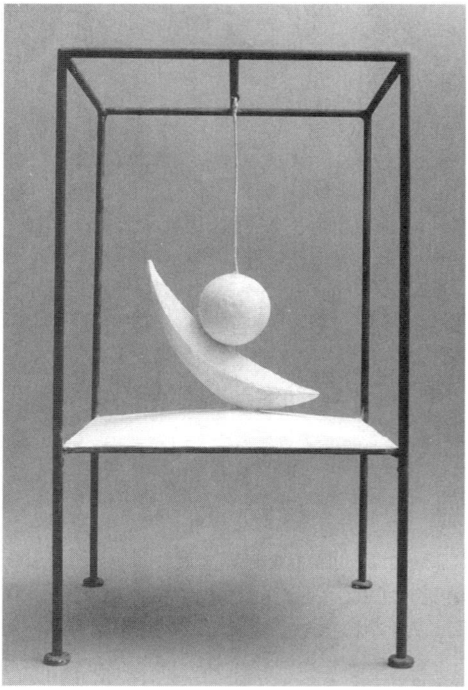

15 Alberto Giacometti: *Suspended Ball*. 1930-31

Giacometti's *Suspended Ball*, at once closely connected with Bataille's theorisations of the sacred and the base and vastly influential among orthodox surrealists, is a case in point. With this sculpture Giacometti, recently initiated into *Documents* and befriended by editor and soon-to-be ethnologist Michel Leiris, generated a response directly pertinent to avant-garde primitivism. Of its first showing in 1930 Maurice Nadeau recalls, "Everyone who saw this object functioning experienced a strong but indefinable sexual emotion relating to unconscious desires. This emotion was in no sense one of satisfaction, but one of disturbance" (cited by Krauss 1985b: 57). *Everyone who saw it.* The resonance for orthodox surrealists of irrational libidinal drives has been obvious since the movement's inception, but we would do well to consider some implications of avant-garde spectators' responses to Giacometti's multiply suggestive "disconnection of the sexes".[8] The commotion Nadeau describes could occur only because of the general perception at the time that a feeling of disorienting sexual anxiety was being uniformly shared. Admirers of Bataille's work on sadism, beginning with Giacometti himself, recognised the sculpture's association of erotic pleasure and violence; in Krauss's words, "the sliding action that visibly relates the sculpture's grooved sphere to its wedge-shaped partner suggests not only the act of caressing but that of cutting" (1985b: 58). At stake in Nadeau's account, then, is a belief that an artwork can tap into unwilled, collectively shared, fundamentally human drives. These are the "excremental collective impulses (orgiastic impulses)" that Bataille argues are "in opposition with political, juridical, and economic institutions" ("The Use Value of D.A.F. de Sade" in 1970b: 58).

The reception of *Suspended Ball* indicates that such works served for the surrealists not as monuments to an abiding aesthetic but as experiments in transgressing accepted conceptions of ideal humanity — i.e., a divisive Eurocentric humanism — through the assertion of a base humanity shared irrespective of social and cultural affiliations. Indeed, as influential as Bataille's thought has been for poststructuralist thinkers from Foucault to Kristeva to Derrida, the base materialism of Bataille and company retains a faith in a core of human impulses that at once links it theoretically to "orthodox surrealism" and distinguishes it in important ways from later multiculturalist developments skeptical of attempts to classify manifestations of personal and communal instinct, erotic desire, and ritual violence as fundamentally human rather than historically contingent. In the case of *Suspended Ball* as well as Giacometti's earlier *Man and Woman*, an abstracted primitivism, ambiguously sexed components, and the implication of violence in the erotic disrupt a Eurocentric individualist contemplative mode of art reception by levelling human distinctions and marking collectively shared base impulses. Certainly *Suspended Ball* achieved the success it did among surrealists because, as James Clifford has noted about "ethnographic surrealism" more broadly, it "attacks the familiar, provoking the irruption of otherness — the unexpected" (1988: 145). But when Clifford describes Bataille and his circle as waging a "ludic warfare" that radically questions "any stable or essential grounds of human similarity" (148, 145), he obscures the fact that Bataille, Giacometti, and others affiliated with *Documents* attack the familiar Western modes of experiencing and interpreting reality by reference to impulses valued precisely because they are seen as extending across a collectivity broader than the culture in question.[9]

In this context, the widespread fascination among the 1930s avant-garde with the praying mantis is suggestive in several related ways. When Giacometti, Roger Caillois, Max Ernst, André Masson, Salvador Dali, and Hans Bellmer represented the mantis in media ranging from essay to collage, painting to sculpture, they evoked a violent eroticism highly compatible with that of *Suspended Ball* and *Man and Woman*. Here, too, avant-garde figurations of violent eroticism serve not primarily to exemplify cultural otherness, as Clifford implies, but to investigate the mysterious nature of a universalised eroticism in general; they mark not so much alternative realities as representative ones. It is true that in such works as Giacometti's *Cages* the female mantis's sometime practice of eating her mate during or after copulation is figured in terms of a single, isolated pair of mantises. But what resonates most powerfully in these *Cages* is not the singularity of the vengeance being exacted, but rather that this libidinal violence is both instinctive and routine. Disjoining and abstracting the bodies of his encaged subjects in a mode reminiscent of Oceanic art, Giacometti transforms the teeming cages kept by Breton, Dali, and Paul Éluard into a subtly anthropocentric prison in which a masculine mantis, represented by a sphere which Krauss has associated with a cranium, unsuccessfully wards off the irrational and destructive impulses of his mate. Just as the male mantis is doomed by his desire to pair himself with his antagonist and be defeated by her, the cranium is by nature conjoined in a necessarily weaker and more dispensible condition with these destructive impulses; the cage that literally bars his escape merely evokes an inevitable condition which outside in the wilds of nature would be unchanged. In other words, there is no outside of the base material, instinctual condition. By representing the female as no less encaged than her partner, Giacometti makes palpable the subordination of her rational will to the deep-seated libidinal forces that motivate her and, in the end, define her.

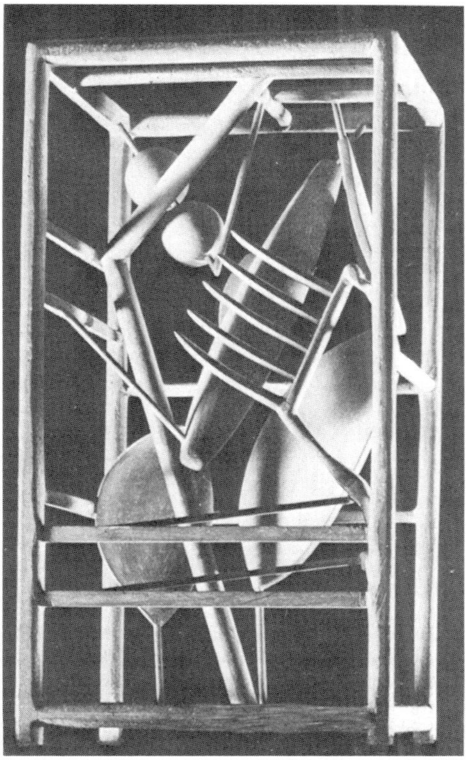

16 Alberto Giacometti: *Cage*. 1930-31

Like so many artists and writers publishing in *Documents*, *Variétés*, and *Minotaure* from 1929 through the 1930s, Giacometti seeks to engage that aspect of identity which is instinctive and common to one's kind. In so doing, he challenges an idealist and individualist humanism by offering a redefinition of the human as necessarily driven by base impulses. Bataille's own interest in the findings of psychoanalysis as potentially subversive both of reductive positivist categories and of the idealist humanism he associates with those categories is clearly echoed here. Giacometti's act of analogizing the cranium of an insect with that of a man, whose rationality had, since at least as far back as the Enlightenment, been regarded as his defining characteristic, dramatically contests Western idealist philosophical hierarchies. However, this act of contestation asserts not an intellectual or cultural relativism, but rather a new humanism deeply informed by both Freudian psychoanalysis and modern ethnographic reactions against colonialist interpretations of evolutionary anthropology.

Raoul Ubac's photograph of Masson's mantis-like mannequin more explicitly takes up the question of how these primal impulses operate within Western metropolitan culture. Again we see a figure of the fractured male mantis, this time in the form of a plucked flower, captive in the female mouth; and again the predator's voracity coincides with her own captivity. Ubac thus maintains Giacometti's focus on the inseparability of eroticism and violence, but dispenses with the *Cage*'s explicit treatment of the attack and instead develops the idea of the predator as herself captive. The shadows cast across her body as she stares out from behind bars convey, as Krauss notes in "Corpus Delicti", how "this mantis, which possesses, is simultaneously possessed by the mesh of space" (1985a: 74). Further, Ubac takes as his subject a mannequin already well-known among his surrealist contemporaries and thereby renders obvious the inanimateness of his already entrapped figure. He thus immobilises and sterilises the female mantis even as his photograph conveys the menace of her otherness. Transformed into a doll, frozen in space by the photographic medium that has reproduced her, and less easily read as consuming her prey than as gagged by it, the predatory mantis encaged by Giacometti has here been multiply, indeed superfluously, contained.

Such overcontainment can be persuasively linked to a "contempt for the feminine", and more precisely to "the self-contempt of a castratable subject violently resentful of a female other who, far from castrated, is uncastratable" (Foster 1993: 95). But if, as I would argue, the primacy of the female mantis over the male functions for surrealists in general as a figure for the primacy of deep-seated and collectively shared libidinal instincts over culturally specific modes of rational analysis, then the overcontainment of *Mannequin* may be something else again. For Ubac's choice of photographing a mannequin, infinitely replicable as photographs and mannequins always are, pointedly addresses what for dissident surrealists following Bataille is an anxiety at the heart of Western modes of representation. It is an anxiety not finally about the supremacy of female over male, but of what surrealists were able to signify and critique by

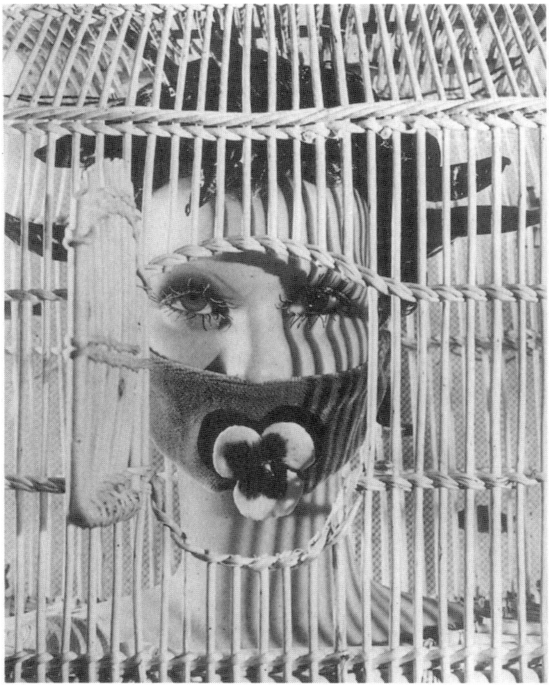

17 Raoul Ubac: *Mannequin*. 1937

reference to readily familiar conceptual categories of femininity andmasculinity, namely, an anxiety about the supremacy of common instinct over idiosyncratic will, of libidinal repetition over productive variation. The same may be said of the headless insectoid or crustacean subject of Giacometti's *Woman with Her Throat Cut*, whose elongated, spirally grooved neck recalls a mechanical screw far more than it does the organic connector between head and body, the physical origin of both words and screams. Both works, by positing a subject that is partly reminiscent of the female mantis, partly reminiscent of mass industrial products, challenge the modern Westerner's pretensions to an advanced individualist subjectivity. At the same time, their evocation of conventional gender binaries to recode the human puts them outside of a late twentieth-century multiculturalist framework.

When the surrealists consistently select the feminine as the quintessential representative of that which has been repressed or denied in Western idealist definitions of the human, they indeed exploit what seems to us today a highly conventional binary opposition between a masculine civilisation on the one hand and a feminine nature or wilderness on the other.[10] Feminist critiques by such critics as Susan Rubin Suleiman, Whitney Chadwick, Mary Ann Caws and others have pointed to the latent sexism of such figurations.[11] Suleiman, for instance, a generally enthusiastic interpreter of surrealism and of its enduring influence on postmodernist literature, has repeatedly indicted its "unmistakably male voyeuristic fantasies (as Surrealist paintings often are), representing female orifices and body parts, and scenes of extreme sexual violence perpetrated on the bodies of women" (1994: 137). She makes clear that

> if the world is really to change, it will have to start by imagining differently 'what it is to be a woman'—and a man. Differently [...] from the Surrealists, whose imaginative faculties faltered on the threshold of sexual roles. (139)

But, again, even as we recognise ways in which avant-garde professions of subversiveness are not subversive enough by our standards, it is important to try to situate historical movements not only in relation to our debates but also in relation to their own. Primitivist surrealist representations of female sexual predators, like Giacometti's praying mantis and Ubac's *Mannequin*, or of female victims of what appears to be sexual violence, like *Woman with Her Throat Cut*, operate within specific historical contexts, many of which differ from ours. Current discussions of avant-garde representations of women repeatedly bypass the possibility that the overturning of an evolutionist and progressivist humanism and a Eurocentric cultural elitism required, as far as avant-garde artists and critics responding to modern ethnography and psychoanalysis were concerned, an aggressive assertion of the savagery that was being repressed philosophically even as it was manifesting itself politically in Western Europe with increasing regularity. From this standpoint, it is not surprising that they would seize on the feminine as a figure for the antithesis not of the *masculine*, but, inverting a traditional truism, of the *civilised*, or that which an idealist humanist Europe was claiming for itself and denying to others. In that case, such representations would not express the male surrealist's fear of women's otherness, but would rather critique the Eurocentric humanist's fear of his own fundamental savagery.

Chadwick distinguishes between, on the one hand, male surrealists who identified woman with nature in order to secure for themselves a "magical or symbolic other", and, on the other, women surrealists who "identified their own psychic reality with the barren or fruitful earth" (1985: 142). She thus assumes, like many critics currently writing on surrealist figurations of women, that the surrealist foregrounding of feminine difference served primarily to reassure male artists' sense of their own masculine authority. She seems to confirm this when she writes, "the image of woman that emerges from Surrealist poetry is a being controlled by, rather than in control of, her childlike vision and magical powers" (181). Though I cannot indulge here in a discussion of so-called orthodox surrealist representations of feminity and their relation to those of the dissident surrealists, my reading of the latter as using the concept of woman to evoke the primal as Western man's ostensible but not actual other should raise the possibility of reading the women of Breton, Masson, Magritte, etc., as symbols not of otherness, but rather of Western man's own natural but culturally repressed state.

At any rate, attempting to interpret dissident surrealist representations of the feminine without detailed reference to the early twentieth-century ethnographic and primitivist dialogues in which they were explicitly participating will more likely than not produce a reading that evaluates those representations in terms more properly ours than theirs. Obviously, the surrealist use of female figures to explore not the socio-politics of gender difference but rather presumed essential yet latent features of the human does little to explore, much less affirm, either sexual or cultural difference in itself. At the same time, dissident surrealist critiques of European cultural elitism constituted powerful indictments in their time of capitalist and imperialist social hierarchies and, more specifically, showed some of the limits of the idealist humanism that served often to justify those hierarchies.

Of course, the dissident surrealists had means of attacking Western idealist hierarchies besides their exploitation and subtle manipulation of conventional gender categories. Karl Blossfeldt's photographs of plants resembling architectural forms, published in *Documents* to accompany Bataille's essay "The Language of Flowers", and Brassaï's photographs of architectural details resembling natural forms in *Minotaure*, may be read as avant-garde efforts to obscure boundaries generally taken for granted between eminently familiar structures, as Dawn Ades's brief discussion of them in "Photography and the Surrealist Text" makes clear (1985: 179).[12] With *Suspended Ball* and *Man and Woman* we saw the collapse of conventional demarcations of the sexes, and, in surrealist constructions of the praying mantis, we saw the collapse of erotic pleasure and violence on the one hand, and of natural impulse and automatism on the other. Taken together, Blossfeldt's and Brassaï's series make dubious, as *Mannequin* and *Woman with her Throat Cut* do in very different ways, the conceptual division between animate and inanimate. This collapse of distinction, too, facilitates the discovery of structures that are at once occluded and commonly extant. Blossfeldt's photographs and what seems to be Brassaï's response to them identify resemblances among structures that have been produced instinctively, automatically, not willfully, and that therefore challenge notions of individual autonomy and cultural exceptionalism assumed by the Eurocentric humanist to be markers of civilisation and ideal humanity.

Particularly suggestive in this context is the Paris Metro detail that Brassaï's camera revealed to resemble a praying mantis. With this photograph Brassaï envisions, as Giacometti does in these same early years of the 1930s, a world of inscrutable identities, and erotic violence that is ineluctable precisely because it is fundamental. The photograph associates modern technology, customarily considered in the West as a proof of human intellectual complexity and progress, with an insect, and what is more, an insect seen perhaps more than any other as both anthropomorphic and savage. Like his series of *Graffiti*, initiated in the same year he published his metallic mantis, Brassaï's photograph isolates the primitive in modern Paris in order to expose formal resemblances obscured by conventional practices of classifying and representing everyday phenomena. Ubac's later photographic "fossils" of the stock exchange, the opera, and the Eiffel Tower may be read as functioning similarly, though where Brassaï's works situate the archaic or primitive in Paris, Ubac's situate Paris in the archaic. In this sense they recall the way in which *Spoon Woman* disrupts viewers' reception of familiar forms and thereby destabilises the identity categories usually associated with those forms. Where before it was European gender distinction that was broken down to reveal a more fundamental feminine structure, we now see the distinctions of the modern city, exemplary site of civilisation *par excellence*, folded back into the structures of its apparent opposite.

But such a reading needs to be extended to acknowledge the fact that Bataille's use of Blossfeldt's photographs in *Documents* has nothing directly to do with their potential to evoke architectural forms. Moreover, the five photographs published in *Documents* were part of a much more extensive series which, for the most part, does not reveal resemblances between unrelated phenomena so much as particularities of plants many times magnified and, hence, capable of being scrutinised in isolated sections as if under a microscope. Thus the technical possibilities of photography enable Blossfeldt to convey a new realism impossible prior to the development of his medium. Indeed, this project and Bataille's are closely related. In "The Language of Flowers", Bataille rejects the tendency deeply ingrained in European cultural tradition to conceive of flowers symbolically, or as representing "the human *ideal*", and calls instead for the development of an "interpretation by the objective value of *appearance*" (1970a: 176, 175). In a crucial passage, he reverses what he sees as the usual privileging of the symbolic over the material sphere by defining "the *word*" as that which "permits one to envisage in things only the characteristics that determine a relative situation", while "the *appearance*" is that which "would introduce the decisive values of things" (174). This reversal is entirely in keeping with Bataille's general base materialist commitment to demoting the status of the culturally relative (i.e., philosophical systems, which codify relative values as universal) in relation to psychological and other physical attributes that, for him, testify to a farther-reaching humanness.

Throughout "The Language of Flowers", Bataille attempts to destroy the aura of the flower by identifying various overlooked or hidden features of flowers, base features that fail to conform to the poetic ideal and that, once acknowledged, show this ideal to be a fiction. He emphasises the "hideous" qualities of flowers, the "hairy taint" of their sexual organs, their inevitable regression into "primitive filth" ("*ordure primitive*"), and their universal dependence on "roots that swarm, under the surface of the soil, nauseating and naked like vermin" (176, 177). The argument closely parallels that of "Big Toe" — also illustrated by photographic enlargements, this time of the big toe — in which Bataille attempts to destroy the aura of the human by arguing that the foundation of man's erect posture and of the pretensions to rationality and spirituality that go along with it is, in fact, the ignoble foot and its own groundedness in base matter: "The big toe is the most *human* part of the human body" (Bataille 1970a: 200). Just as "Big Toe" claims that idealism distorts what the human *is*, "The Language of Flowers" claims that idealist metaphors distort what a flower *is*. What Bataille's use of Blossfeldt's photographs (a use consistent with Blossfeldt's overarching project) and a reading based on their evocation of architectural forms have in common is a potential to reveal how limited acculturated modes of defining and perceiving "raw phenomena" are when confronted with characteristics inexplicable by the terms already established for those phenomena.

Thus what is more properly modernist than poststructuralist in Bataille's work and the art his cultural critiques helped to generate is that they render suspect a culturally divisive and progressivist humanism not by deconstructing the category of the human, but rather by disrupting it to uncover its primal underside. This primal underside is the base matter of latent and mysterious attributes that self-professedly "civilised" Europeans are accustomed to overlooking, but that they share in varying degrees with peoples whose psychological and moral development they pride themselves on having long surpassed. Bois writes of Bataille that "it is humanism above all that he is after, and thus all systems (he loves revolution for the revolt, not for the utopia of its realisation)" (Bois and Krauss 1997: 17). But it is essential to address the relationship between Bataille's anti-humanism and his method of undermining humanism through insistent references to the human and the primitive. Failing to address this issue can lead to a confusion of Bataille's iconoclasm with that of, say, Derrida, who hardly appears to share Bataille's faith in the possibility of getting outside representation "to the unexchangeable heterogeneity of reality, to an irreducible kernel of resistance to transposition, to substitution, a reality intractably resistant to metaphor", as Denis Hollier (1997: 131) has described Bataille's aim, that is to say, to the "raw phenomena" as such.

In such essays as "The Language of Flowers" and "Big Toe", Bataille differentiates between cultural/symbolic constructions of matter and matter itself. His many references to primal, irrational, and collectively shared impulses, and to practices or states of being generated by such impulses, assert latent or potential resemblance in a world of apparently natural and necessary conceptual and social hierarchy. In order to subvert this hierarchical mode of understanding and organising reality, Bataille seeks to uncover "a reality intractably resistant to metaphor" by clearing away idealist uses of metaphor that preclude "direct interpretation" of the physical reality of such phenomena as flowers and human beings. Representation, or "the word", is for Bataille a displacement produced and naturalised by culture. It is precisely the ostensible naturalness of representation that he attempts to destroy by opposing representation to the base matter it has displaced. However, beyond promoting awareness that such representation is subsequent to base matter, and beyond trying to disprove idealist representations specifically, Bataille himself is hardly averse to the deployment of metaphor (recall his roots "like vermin"). Metaphor can be a useful tool so long as the analogist makes clear that the relationship between metaphor and the matter it displaces is relative, "merely" culturally produced rather than essential (for the distinction does exist for Bataille and is important to him). Hence his often quoted conclusion to *Informe*:

> All of philosophy has no other goal: it is a question of giving a frock coat to what is, a mathematical frock coat. By contrast, to affirm that the universe resembles nothing and is only formless amounts to saying that the universe is something like a spider or spit. (1970a: 217)

In other words, when philosophers classify "what is", i.e., base matter, they cover it up with a "frock coat", a certain definition that quantifies it, hides aspects of it, and to some extent confines its movement. But as long as we affirm that all such definitions are just metaphors of sorts, just substitutions for "what is", then we are free to formulate any metaphor we like, even ones both conventionally absurd and mutually exclusive, like "the universe is like a spider" and "the universe is like spit".

When Bataille, in a footnote to "The Use Value of D.A.F. de Sade", appeals to the authority of the renowned evolutionary ethnographer James Frazer on the subject of "the identical nature, from the psychological point of view, of God and excrement", he is relying on a quotation consistent with his own casual reference to an outdated "primitive" conception of human life at the end of the same essay. Bataille quotes Frazer as saying:

> These different categories of persons differ a great deal in our eyes with regard to character and condition; of some we would say that they are sacred, of others that they are dirty or impure. For the savage, there is none of this, for his mind is still too coarse to conceive distinctly of what a sacred being is, and what an impure being is. (1970b: 59)

Bataille's emphasis is not the same as Frazer's, certainly. Bataille quotes Frazer not to promote a progressivist view of human development but, on the contrary, to expose the artificiality of the attainments of civilisation by foregrounding how, in our originary psychological state, we have yet to learn the culturally produced hierarchies of high and low, sacred and base; in our originary state, they amount to the same thing. Still, though he shifts Frazer's emphasis, Bataille nevertheless retains Frazer's basic faith in a linear progression of stages of development. In so doing, Bataille operates at a significant remove from Clifford's more self-critical anthropology in "On Ethnographic Surrealism".[13]

The implications of Bataille's attempts to recode the primal as that which remains definitive even of "civilised man" need to be acknowledged more specifically than they have been in contemporary celebrations of his subversive critiques of language. In "No More Play", Krauss compares Bataille's term "alteration", which signifies both evolution and devolution, to the Latin terms *altus* and *sacer*, "double-directed, primal concepts that interested Freud". She continues:

> The primal, or originary, is therefore irresolvably diffuse — fractured by an irremediable doubleness at the root of things that was [...]dear to Bataille. [...] [I]t is this play of the contradictory that allows one to think the truth that Bataille never tired of demonstrating: that violence has historically been lodged at the heart of the sacred; that to be genuine, the very thought of the creative must simultaneously be an experience of death; and that it is impossible

for any moment of true intensity to exist apart from a cruelty that is equally extreme. (1985b: 54)

In refraining from putting his fascination with these "primal concepts" into its intellectual-historical context, Krauss implies that it amounts to a critique of discursive convention comparable to those of poststructuralist criticism. But Bataille's repeated assertions of his closely related notions of the primal, the primitive (as in *Documents*) and the collective (as in the Collège de Sociologie) casts doubt on this. Given the frequency with which these themes emerge in *Documents* and elsewhere it may well be that what captivates him about the "doubleness at the root of things" and, more specifically, at the root of language, is that this doubleness points back to a time or state when the distinctions and divisions of language and history, i.e. the superficial stuff of culture as opposed to the base matter of the human, did not yet exist. This would explain why Bataille distinguishes so sharply between "word" and "appearance" in "The Language of Flowers".

Though select passages and concepts of Bataille are, undoubtedly, richly suggestive in light of currently prevailing theoretical trends, it should be noted that his trust in Frazer and Freud on the subject of the primal, like his many attempts to delve into the nature of collective ritual and what he took to be the base instincts at their heart, are no more anomalous to his work on the whole at this time than they are easily reconciled with the epistemological assumptions of poststructuralists eager to claim an affinity with Bataille. When he finds in different archaic periods evidence of a recurrent impulse to draw humans as deformed, he is re-reading what he takes to be artistic instincts, a project far from the poststructuralist one of rendering problematic the very notion of essential instincts ("Primitive Art" in 1970a: 251). For him, the impulse to alter and deform is fundamentally shared, sadistic impulses are shared, and we can identify them by observing children's artistic impulses as well as the artistic productions of primitive peoples. The fact that, as the decade progressed, Bataille moved increasingly away from the exploration of art's psychological and communal impact to communal experimentation via his Collège de Sociologie and the more mysterious collective contemporaneous with it, Acéphale, is understandable given that his interests always lay more in revolutionising ideas of the human than in revolutionising art or aesthetics for their own sake.

That Bataille manipulated the evolutionist oppositions implicit in modern ethnography in such a way as to assert a universally shared human primitiveness, a fundamental complex of base instincts common across cultures, was a jarringly subversive variation on the themes of imperialist humanism, but not the proto-multiculturalist glorification of cultural diversity *as such* that some have implied it to be, nor the proto-deconstructionist skepticism of systems *as such* that others have implied it to be. On the other hand, it is clear enough that, in redefining the (white European male) self as fundamentally similar to (exotic, archaic, or otherwise "primitive") others, Bataille and others in the *Documents* group expressed a highly significant skepticism not just of the colonialist mentality but of the communally formulated and perpetuated nature of knowledge itself, a skepticism anticipatory of poststructuralism's more broad-based skepticism of conventional identity categories, including that of "the human". The reason that it is important not to overlook Bataille's acceptance of some then standard assumptions about the human and the primitive, however, is that in doing so we risk reading him as ourselves and focusing on those aspects that confirm our reading. Such passages as his conclusion to "The Use Value of D.A.F. de Sade" and his contributions to ethnographic and primitivist discourses have tended to be downplayed most likely because they do not cohere easily with current critical agendas, while other passages, like his *Informe* entry to the "Critical Dictionary", appear, at least when read in isolation, fairly compatible with them.

The conclusion to "The Use Value of D.A.F. de Sade" seems puzzling and exceptional within Bataille's project only when that project is approached from the outset in terms of what it has in common with us. To interpret it thus is to minimize the degree to which Bataille and a number of the artists whose work he appears to have influenced took for granted certain ideas about the human, the primal, and the primitive common to ethnographic and, more broadly, modernist discourses of their time. Avant-garde responses to these discourses did vary considerably, and should not be assumed always to work in the same ways and toward the same ends, but neither should discussion of them be avoided just because they appear foreign to the frameworks in which we seek to fit them.

Certainly Bataille's theory of the *informe* as that which operates to declassify the ideological forms of a dominant bourgeois idealism should be recognised in all its theoretical power and complexity by poststructuralists whose debates it has facilitated. But to read his definition of the *informe* in poststructuralist terms and then to interpret Giacometti's primitivist art and writings primarily in connection with that, or to read *Documents*'s juxtaposition of seemingly radically different cultures in multiculturalist terms, without attending to *why* Bataille shared with so many artists and critics of the period a pronounced interest in sadism, or eroticism, or ancient and exotic ritual practices, is to neglect a significant amount of the material characteristic of *Documents* and later journals that retained *Documents*'s conjunction of avant-garde art and ethnography, notably *Minotaure*. What Bataille shared with a number of modernists and ethnographers of these years was a commitment to disputing a then traditional progressivist humanist conception of primitive impulses and practices as wholly separate from the civilised ones of educated Western European bourgeois, and to suggesting instead that the identities by which these Europeans "knew" and defined themselves were representations whose persuasive force depended on the repression of more fundamental structures and impulses that human beings shared across cultures. Once we accept that Bataille shared a great many of his assumptions about the human and the primitive with his contemporaries and even with his predecessors, we can begin to examine more precisely, first, in what ways his assumptions differed significantly from what were then mainstream ones in avant-garde and scientific circles, and, second, what his abiding love affair with the possibility of a new, base humanism might mean, whether for his work, for the dissident surrealists, or, not least of all, for the critical theorists who have since claimed him as their precursor and ally.

Notes

[1] Metraux 1963: 677.

[2] From "The Use Value of D.A.F. de Sade" (Bataille 1970b: 66). All emphases are Bataille's except where otherwise noted.

[3] The first three issues were subtitled "Doctrines-Archéologie-Beaux Arts-Ethnographie".

[4] All translations are mine except where otherwise noted.

[5] Bataille writes, "I doubt the possibility of reaching the few people for whom this letter is no doubt intended, over the heads of my present comrades. For—my resolution is all the more intransigent as it is absurd to defend—it would have been necessary to deal not with individuals like those I already know, but only with men (and above all with masses) who are comparatively decomposed, made amorphous and even expelled violently outside of every form. But, it is likely that such men do not yet exist (and the masses certainly do not exist)" (1970b: 54-55).

[6] By "primitivist discourses" I refer both to ethnological and ethnographic representations of "the primitive" as well as to art-historical categories prominent at the time, such as *style nègre*, "soft primitivism", and "hard primitivism".

[7] Krauss uses these phrases in her subsequent discussion of *Suspended Ball*: "this collapse of distinction [...] this obliteration of difference, is for logic what the perversions are for eroticism: it is transgressive", 63.

[8] The phrase is Krauss's (1985b: 58).

[9] In his discussion of the Collège de Sociologie, for instance, a project whose critical agenda he closely associates with the earlier *Documents*, Clifford fairly describes Bataille and fellow Collège founders Leiris and Roger Caillois as "preoccupied with those ritual moments when experiences outside the normal flow of existence can find collective expression" (141). The very words Clifford uses to characterize this tendency rest on a dichotomy between a world of convention, that is, a world of surfaces subject to sociological analysis, and a world of experience that is outside the normal and resistant to known definitions and categories but nonetheless determinant. Bataille reaffirms this view years later when he writes:

> The sacred cannot be limited to the remote experience of ancients or primitives [....] The world we live in is, in its depths, still impregnated with the sacred" ("War and the Philosophy of the Sacred" in 1988: 49).

But Bataille's attempt to universalise human instinct implicit in this dichotomy (and also implicit in his appeal for a *pratique nègre* in the service of worldwide revolution) is almost entirely obscured in Clifford's construction of Bataille as a ludic warrior of radical philosophical and cultural contingency.

[10] Xavière Gauthier has discussed at length surrealist literary representations of woman as nature (1971: 98-158). Whitney Chadwick has supported Gauthier's reading and extended it to surrealist visual art, emphasising the ways that women surrealists intervened in the trend (1985: 141-80).

[11] By Suleiman, see especially "A Double Margin: Women Writers and the Avant-Garde in France" and "Transgression and the Avant-Garde: Bataille's *Histoire de l'œil*" in Suleiman 1990: 11-32 and 72-87, as well as Suleiman 1994 and her contribution to Chadwick 1998. See also Chadwick 1998, and Caws's contribution to Suleiman 1985.

[12] My interpretation of the thematic connections between these two series and of their links to Brassaï's *Graffiti* and Ubac's *Fossils* draws on Ades's lucid discussion of them in Ades 1985: 179.

[13] But then even Clifford is not so consistently "ludic" as he appears. For even while arguing that "the authority arrogated by the humanist too often goes unquestioned", he cautions against abandoning "the humanism that still offers grounds for resistance to oppression and a necessary counsel of tolerance, comprehension, and mercy" (1988: 145). Despite its incongruity with the rhetoric of multiculturalist play that runs throughout "On Ethnographic Surrealism", this assertion of certain ideals that the West has claimed for itself is not far different from his recent determination to "recuperate historical realism" by "updating Auerbach and Lukács", and thereby to try to delineate, in a potentially cross-cultural and transhistorical sense "what counts as history, what are the limits". Clifford introduced this project in his address, "Big Enough Stories: Reflections on Historical Realism", at Columbia University, April 23, 1998.

Bibliography

Ades, Dawn

1985 "Photography and the Surrealist Text". In: Rosalind Krauss and Jane Livingston (eds), *L'Amour fou: Photography and Surrealism*. New York: Abbeville Press, 153-192.

Bataille, Georges

1970a *Œuvres complètes* I. Paris: Gallimard.

1970b *Œuvres complètes* II. Paris: Gallimard.

1988 *Œuvres complètes* XII. Paris, Gallimard.

Bois, Yve-Alain, and Rosalind Krauss
1997 *Formless: A User's Guide*. New York: Zone Books.

Caws, Mary Ann
1986 "Ladies Shot and Painted: Female Embodiment in Surrealist Art". In: Susan Rubin Suleiman (ed.), *The Female Body in Western Culture*. Cambridge, Mass.: Harvard University Press, 262-287.

Chadwick, Whitney
1985 *Women Artists and the Surrealist Movement*. Boston: Little, Brown and Co.

1998 "An Infinite Play of Empty Mirrors: Women, Surrealism, and Self-Representation". In: Whitney Chadwick (ed.), *Mirror Images: Women, Surrealism, and Self-Representation*. Cambridge, Mass.: MIT Press, 2-35.

Clifford, James
1988 "On Ethnographic Surrealism". *The Predicament of Culture*. Cambridge, Mass.: Harvard University Press, 117-151.

Edwards, Brent Hayes
1999 "The Ethnics of Surrealism". *Transition* 78, 84-135.

Foster, Hal
1993 *Compulsive Beauty*. Cambridge, Mass.: MIT Press.

Gauthier, Xavière
1971 Surréalisme et sexualité. Paris: Gallimard.

Hollier, Denis
1997 "The Use Value of the Impossible". *Absent Without Leave: French Literature Under the Threat of War*. Cambridge, Mass.: Harvard University Press, 125-144.

Krauss, Rosalind
1985a "Corpus Delicti". In: R. Krauss and Jane Livingston (eds), *L'Amour fou: Photography and Surrealism*. New York: Abbeville Press, 55-112.

1985b The Originality of the Avant-Garde and Other Modernist Myths. Cambridge, Mass.: MIT Press.

Metraux, Alfred
1963 "Rencontre avec les ethnologues". In: *Critique* 195-196. 677-684.

Suleiman, Susan Rubin
1990 *Subversive Intent: Gender, Politics, and the Avant-Garde.* Cambridge, Mass.: Harvard University Press.

1994 "The Fate of the Surrealist Imagination in the Society of the Spectacle". In: *Risking Who One Is: Encounters with Contemporary Art and Literature.* Cambridge, Mass.: Harvard University Press, 125-139.

1998 "Dialogue and Double Allegiance: Some Contemporary Women Artists and the Historical Avant-Garde". In: Whitney Chadwick (ed.), *Mirror Images: Women, Surrealism, and Self-Representation.* Cambridge, Mass.: MIT Press, 128-154.

INSIDE OUT: PAVEL FILONOV AND THE ANATOMY OF FANTASY.*

JOHN E. BOWLT

The artist Dmitrii Pokrovsky, a disciple of Pavel Nikolaevich Filonov (1883-1941), once recalled that "Pavel Filonov never said anything about the subjects of his paintings" (Pokrovsky undated: 16). Indeed, examination of Filonov's autobiographies, theoretical statements, and diaries provides comparatively little information on the sources and derivations of the artist's images and ideas, a deficiency that places him among the most recondite and enigmatic artists of the Russian avant-garde. Filonov's paintings and drawings, while clearly inspired by certain concepts and movements, do not yield easily to thematic and formal analysis in the way that the works of Kazimir Malevich and Vladimir Tatlin do. Like them, Filonov was affected by similar trends — from Symbolism to Socialist Realism — but his methods of interpretation and refraction constitute a private and difficult language that, when first heeded, seems almost incomprehensible. This is especially true of Filonov's so called Ideology of Analytical Art where terms such as "madeness" and "universal flowering" never receive a concise or clear definition. However, the more we study Filonov's early development as an artist, including his experience of the St. Petersburg Academy of Art, the more we realize that the complex consistency of his theory and practice can be explained — to some extent — by reference to specific areas of expertise such as graphic technique, anatomical drawing, and the science of physiology.

This is not to say that certain pictorial derivations cannot be recognised immediately, e.g. the carriage in *Shrovetide* (1913-14) is borrowed from a traditional wooden toy troika; the repeated forcelines in *Rebirth of an Intellectual* (1913) tell us that the artist knew about Italian futurism; and the florid clothing in *Officers* (1916-17) evokes the *kupecheskaia Rossiia* [merchant Russia] of Boris Kustodiev's paintings. But these analogies are casual and fragmentary, and, by and large, the imagery of Filonov's major paintings such as *Feast of the Kings* (1912 and 1913, and watercolor and oil versions) is as cryptic and as bewildering as the scheme of his personal life. Entire episodes in his biography are unaccounted for: What did Filonov see during his pilgrimage to Jerusalem in 1907?[1] What was the profound experience that, allegedly, transformed his personality in 1909-10?[2] What was the exact itinerary of his Grand Tour in 1912? What was the "medical organisation" for which he painted two heads in 1936 (cf. Filonov 1936: 29)? These and many other questions remained unanswered.

The contemporary historian, therefore, is obliged to assume the difficult role of spokesman for the reticent and misleading Filonov and, against his wishes, to "act behind the artist's back and on the artist's behalf" (Filonov 1923). Fulfilling such a role can produce elegant results, although, in deference to Filonov's genius, we must exercise great caution in our attributions and deductions. There is, for example, the vexed question of Filonov's apparent debt to the German Renaissance, a parallel suggested by a number of critics. That Filonov knew the work of Cranach, Dürer, Grünewald, and Holbein is clear, and his analytical mind appreciated their incisive styles. Their cultivation of line as an unmitigating force that exposes human frailty and deformation — "realistic not to the point of illusion, but realistic to the point of horror" (as the artist Boris Grigoriev would have said: cf. Grigoriev 1922) — must have appealed to Filonov's own worldview, unrelenting in its sobriety. But these assumptions cannot be documented, because Filonov does not discuss German art in his writings, makes only one brief mention of Holbein, and gives no indication of the works of art that he saw in Austria and Germany in 1912 (Filonov 1936: 43).[3]

Even so, a close-textual reading of Filonov's copious writings does provide us with a number of clues that contribute to a clearer understanding of his visual language. Occasionally, he mentions concrete names and events, and certain recurrent words and phrases such as "Analytical Art", "universal flowering", "biological madeness", and "work from the particular [...] to the general" help to reveal those primary confrontations that played a substantial part in the evolution of his artistic style and lift the curtain of mystery shrouding his *oeuvre.* One decisive encounter that Filonov acknowledged with particular emphasis was his discovery of comparative anatomy that "determined the entire future evolution of his work" (Filonov 1983a: 117). Filonov's critics, especially of the 1910s, often commented on this, asserting that his paintings were like "anatomical specimens" (Kuzmin 1982: 262), from "anatomical textbooks" (B.A. 1913), revealing "heads and faces [with] the outer skin missing so that the tendons and bundles of nerves show through"(Breshko-Breshkovsky 1911: 6). But even though such works might have been "more suited to medical students" (Breshko-Breshkovsky 1911: 6), it was thanks to Filonov's excellent knowledge of anatomy that he passed the entrance examination to the Imperial Academy of Arts in St. Petersburg, enrolling in its Higher Art Institute in1908. In turn, the Academy reinforced his technical skill and facility for graphic analysis — in spite of his professed antipathy towards the entire Academy program. For Filonov, most of the teachers there were "artistic garbage" in a "slaughter-house" (Filonov 1983b: 203), and he took every opportunity to voice his irritation with its pedagogical system. On the other hand, the fact that Filonov took the entrance examination three times before passing, that in 1912, with his own means, he assumed the role of *pensionnaire,* duplicating the typical Academy itinerary through Vienna, Naples, Rome, and Paris, and that he dedicated much time and effort to replanning the Academy in the 1920s demonstrates that, for Filonov, the Academy of Arts was not so much a target of abuse as an object of secret affection. There can be no question that Filonov's artistic worldview and, specifically, his Ideology of Analytical Art, were molded by his tenure at the Academy, by his exposure to its teaching methods, and, above all, by his advanced study of anatomy there.

The Higher Art Institute of the Academy of Arts provided a basic training in the fundamentals of perspective, anatomy, and color theory that students were obliged to learn before entering one of the master studios guided by senior professors such as Arkhip Kuindzhi and Il'ia Repin. Filonov attended the Life Class there, learning how to proceed "from a simple form to a more complex one" in accordance with the "analytical principle" (Moleva and Beliutin 1967: 293) and to draw from plaster casts and the nude, until he was expelled in 1910 for "corrupting his colleagues with his paintings" (Filonov 1983a: 122). He was reinstated after a petition and then left of his own accord shortly thereafter. But although Filonov was a student at the Higher Art Institute for less than two years, its imprint on his artistic production was indelible, and even the convoluted works of the 1920s still carry references to the Life Class, e.g. *Nude Male Figure* of 1925 is an Analytical counterpart to one of the early studio nudes.

The courses in the Life Class at the Higher Art Institute, offered by Professors Vasilii Savinsky, Yan Tsionglinky, and Gugo Zaleman, were of an extremely high professional level, and maintained the fine traditions of the great pedadog and draftsman Pavel Chistiakov. He, in turn, had been nurtured on the same strict conventions that had produced Russia's great Academy painters — Karl Briullov, Aleksander Ivanov, and Orest Kiprensky. Savinsky was Chistiakov's "favorite pupil" (cf. Moleva and Beliutin 1967:196), and, like his mentor, demanded that external form correspond to the complexities of the internal structure. The painter Arkadii Rylov recalled that, under Savinsky's tutelage, "I drew nudes, probing all the details of the bones and body with my pencil" (Moleva and Beliutin 1967: 293). Savinsky also insisted on the need for an "integral vision" in figure drawing (Moleva and Beliutin 1967: 297), i.e. on the need to observe all parts of the figure simultaneously, even while drawing a single component such as a hand or a nose. Filonov's basic concept of drawing seems to extend Savinsky's — and Chistiakov's — prerequisites:

> The drawing stands for the most characteristic data and properties of the form or complex or sum of forms in all their articulateness or unity. [...] Depict the object not via its outward, visible form, but via the realization of the inner functions and processes occurring in the object. (Filonov 1983c: 147)

Although by the time Filonov enrolled at the Academy of Arts Chistiakov was less active (he retired in 1911), his principles were maintained there by his many disciples, Savinsky and Tsionglinsky among them. We should remember this fact since it helps to explain the unexpectedly close points of contact between Filonov's and Chistiakov's artistic doctrines, vocabularies, and authoritative attitudes. In fact, a number of Filonov's favorite tenets repeat or invert the aphorisms of Chistiakov, e.g. Filonov's "begin the work, develop it from the particular to the general" (Filonov 1983d: 292) seems to be a deliberate and intractable retort to Chistiakov's "you should draw from the general to the particular" (Chistianov 1953: 120). On the other hand, Filonov's exhortation to his students to pay particular attention to the grouping and arrangement of the model echoes Chistiakov's insistence that "[still-life] groupings should be arranged 'by the mind' and not by the 'eye'" (Chistianov 1953: 154). Both Filonov and Chistiakov also urged their students to paint the "living head" (Chistianov 1953: 138) after exercises from the anatomical atlas and the plaster cast — an assignment that resulted in numerous paintings and drawings by Filonov called *Living Head* and *Living Heads*. Chistiakov, Filonov, Savinsky, and Tsionglinsky were excellent draftsmen, convinced that "if you don't know the anatomy of the human being and are not capable of applying this in practice, then you cannot be a serious historical painter" (Chistianov, cf. Beliutin and Moleva 1953: 322). Just as Filonov complained that the Academy of Arts ignored a scientific approach to art, so Chistiakov, in the 1880s-90s, lamented the fact that the Academy had lost its prestige because it had severed the connection between art and science, between esthetic idea and practical application:

> Just as a noble art cannot exist without science, so its technique must be noble and developed according to the essential sciences that relate directly to it. (Chistianov, cf. Beliutin and Moleva 1953: 456)

For both Chistiakov and Filonov mastering the discipline of drawing was evidence of this organic link between the "noble art" and the "cold calculation" (cf. Glebova 1984: 228)[4] of the exact sciences. For this reason, both men gave preeminence to drawing and bad their pupils study the technical recipes of the Old Masters before contemplating any deviation. "The drawing should be a Colossus", exclaimed Filonov in 1914 (Filonov, Kakabadze et al. 1983: 135) —

although, unlike Chistiakov, he felt that drawing was an organic part of the process of painting.

That Filonov heeded the behests of Chistiakov by way of Savinsky and Tsionglinsky is particularly clear in the context of anatomy. For Filonov, the study of anatomy in its artistic and scientific applications was of primary concern: he was a frequent visitor to the Zoological Museum in St. Petersburg, followed the latest developments in physiology and botany, and studied, obviously with great enthusiasm, the manuals on anatomy for medical and art students. These included Il'ia Buial'sky's *Anatomicheskie zapiski* [Anatomical Notes] (1860), Ehrenberg's and Richel's *Prakticheskii samouchitel iziashchnykh iskusstv* [Practical Self-Instructor of the Fine Arts] (1873), and, above all, Mikhail Tikhonov's cycle of lectures called *Kurs plasticheskoi anatomii* [Course of Plastic Anatomy] (1906) (which Filonov mentions in his autobiographies), as well as translations of Albrecht Dürer's treatises on proportions of the human body, Leonardo's anatomical drawings, and the antique atlases such as Andreas Vesalius' *De Humani Corporis Fabrica* (1543) and Bernard Siegfried Albinus' *Tabulae Sceleti et Musculorum Corporis Humanum* (1747). We can assume that Jean-Antoine Houdon's plaster musculature and the bronze *Supine Body* that Petr Klodt cast from a cadaver specially prepared by Buial'sky for anatomical exposition in 1836 also instructed Filonov (as it did many Academy students). The excellent illustrations that accompanied Tikkhonov's explanations of plastic anatomy (he taught at the Academy in 1901-04) also left a deep impression on Filonov. Such sources reinforced the basic knowledge that Filonov acquired from his own ethnographical and naturalist observations as well as from his lessons with the ethn ographical painter, Lev Dmitriev-Kavkazsky, in1903-08. Indeed, as a student of Dmitriev-Kavkazsky, Filonov attended the anatomy lectures that S.N. Delitsyn — a privat-docent at the St. Petersbrug Medical Academy — gave to the studio and, no doubt, paid particular attention to his teacher's own collection of "animal skins, stuffed birds, paintings, engravings, drawings" (Isakov 1941:9). The descriptions, instructions, and charts that Filonov found in the Buial'sky and Tikhonov textbooks, therefore, enhanced this appreciation of anatomy, convincing him still further that

> from Anatomy Painters and Sculptors should know: Osteology, the outer muscles, the outer veins and the few other parts of the body that are more or less visible beneath the skin, and Artists depict these in their paintings and sculpt them in their statues. (Buial'sky 1860: iii)

Of course, appreciation of these sources did not compel Filonov to support the Academy's practice of distorting anatomical harmony and proportion for the sake of beauty: "The nose should not be too big", we read in Ehrenberg's and Richel's manual, "for this lends the face a coarse and bestial character" (Ehrenberg and Richel 1872: 53). On the contrary, Filonov broke the rules of Classical beauty, elongating the head, widening the eyes and nostrils, and emphasising the articulations, so as to express what he felt was the physiological truth, the "biodynamics [...] emanations, insertions, geneses, color and form processes, in brief, life as a whole" (Filonov 1983e: 170). The point is, then, that Filonov was very familiar with the anatomical lessons of Buial'sky, Chistiakov, and Tikhonov, and reference to their tenets can explain some of his own artistic inclinations. Filonov's early nude studies, for example, paraphrase the Tikhonov diagrams, and his vision of "universal flowering" with its efflorescence and incrustation extends Buialskly's idea that "in Nature there is nothing that is inorganic" (Buial'sky 1860: iii). Filonov's aspiration to depict the "process of becoming" (as he subtitled some of his pictures) also illustrates the popular assumption of the time that the

> living being out of which all our tissues are formed, beginning with our bones and muscles and ending with our brains and nerves, is forever decomposing, requiring a constant renewal of those complex chemical combinations. (Obolensky 1902: xiii)

Filonov's peculiar concentration on the head, the eye, and the nose also derives from the primary assignments offered in the 19th century textbooks:

> In drawing the head (en face), one should designate all the variety of its surfaces; here one should try to draw the neck with all its anatomical component parts, the finger with its characteristic inflexions. [...] The nostrils form part of the lower horizontal surface of the nose in the shape of a triangle. [...] From optics we know

> that the pupil has neither form, nor color and that, strictly speaking, it is an orifice via which we can see the dark interior of the eye. (Ehrenberg and Richel 1872: 53, 55, 57)

Filonov's pyrotechnic masterpiece, *The Head and the Thumb* (1925), can also be regarded as a bold response to Ehrenberg's and Richel's complaint that most draftsmen neglect the fingernail, forgetting that it "is already under the skin and that the skin, therefore, should be slightly puffed and raised" (Ehrenberg and Richel 1872: 57). Similarly, Filonov's remarkable rendering of hands, as in his graphic self-portrait of 1909-10, reminds us of Chistiakov's demand that "a finger be a finger truly possessing fourteen bones in all" and that "behind each line one should feel not surface, but bone" (Chistianov 1953: 146-147). Even Filonov's recurrent motif of nostrils, for example, *Head* (1924) and *Head and the Thumb* (1925), might be taken as a response to Chistiakov's advice to "paint the eyes, the pupils with all your strength, so that they live...Pay more attention to the nostrils and lips, too" (Chistianov 1953: 156). As Nikolai Lozovoi, one of Filonov's pupils in the 1920s, wrote: "I remember feeling very moved when Filonov drew nostrils, a hand, or the joints of the fingers. He drew them lovingly" (Lozovoi undated: 5).[5]

Evdokiia Glebova, one of Filonov's sisters, recalled that "knowledge of anatomy changed his attitude to art abruptly" Glebova 1984: 132). Undoubtedly, awareness of Filonov's deep interest in anatomy helps us to understand the "internality" of his paintings with their "beheaded heads" (Breshko-Breshkovsky 1911: 6), disjointed limbs, and vivisectioned monsters. In turn, this brings us to the related subject of freaks and mutants that Filonov also seems to have investigated. That he did examine medical specimens and physical deformations is clear not only from the comments by contemporary critics who tended to identify his art as a "surgical stunt" (B.B. 1913), but also from the several paintings and drawings that deal with physiological abnormality such as the *Armless Ones* (1913-14), the hairless *Mother* (1916), the amputated noses in *Head* (1924), and the woman with two heads in *Formula of the Bourgeoisie* (1923). The fact that Filonov designed the costumes for the "earless man, the eyeless and legless man, and the headless man" in Vladimir Maiakovsky's *Vladimir Maiakovsky. A Tragedy* of 1913 also seems to illustrate this morbid inclination. Such works could well be pictures of the lame and the crippled whom he met on his pilgrimage to Jerusalem and at the Rumanian front during the Great War or a visual record of the experiments at the Imperial Institute of Experimental Medicine in St. Petersburg. They constitute what Filonov himself described as the "cemetery" of his art (Glebova 1984: 155).

Glebova also recalls that Filonov liked to visit the seamy side of St. Petersburg life with its slums and bars and that he often went to the cinema to see cult movies of the 1910s such as *Green Spider* (1916) and *Guilty without Guilt* (1916) with their themes of lust, violence, and black magic. Filonov's apprenticeship as a dancer to the Korsh, Lentovsky, and Sokolov theaters in Moscow before his move to St. Petersburg in 1896 exposed him to the fantastic world of conjuring tricks and circus acts, involving decapitations, levitations, and chiromancy. No doubt, later on Filonov traced a direct relationship between these weird manifestations of urban culture and the specimens displayed in the Zoological Museum in St. Petersburg. Filonov's autobiographical references to the Museum are not accidental, because this was one of the Academy of Science's major research centers for the natural sciences (others being the Botanical Museum, the Geological Museum, the Mineralogical Museum, and the Museum of Anthropology and Ethnography). The Zoological Museum housed an excellent collection of animal and human skeletons that students from the Academy of Arts studied and copied; it also supervised a special Zoological Laboratory connected in turn with the Physiological Laboratory that Ivan Pavlov directed in 1907 onwards. In any case, that Filonov was very interested in zoology, botany, chemistry, and minerology is clear from the readings that he recommended to his disciples, i.e. the biographies of the chemist Antoine Laurent Lavoisier, the naturalist and physician Carl von Linné, Dmitrii Mendeleev (an honorary member of the Academy of Arts, incidentally), the biologist Ivan Michurin, Louis Pasteur, Pavlov, and the surgeon Nikolai Pirogov as well as Charles Darwin's *Voyage of the Beagle* and the *Origin of the Species* (Filonov 1983d: 294). With their investigations into horticultural and biological transformation, physiological processes and saltatory change in zoological evolution, Michurin and Pavlov, in particular, contributed much to the advances of the Russian natural sciences at the beginning of the century.

The installations in the Museum of Anthropology and Ethnography adjacent to the Zoologcal Museum also supplied Filonov with iconographic sources. By ca. 1900 this Museum already contained primary artifacts, ritualistic instruments and domestic tools from Black Africa, the Pacific Rim, and Siberia, and although it is now virtually impossible to identify particular items that Filonov saw on display and reinterpreted in his paintings, we can assume that the vast holdings did inspire some of the exotic imagery — perhaps the Zulu headdress and belt in *Flight into Egypt* (1918), the "idols" in *Feast of the Kings* (1913), and the "Hawaiian shirts" in *East and West* (1912-13).

However, Filonov's paintings demonstrate a concern not only with the physiological or ethnographical accuracy of a certain bone structure or ceremonial artifact. Rather, they convey the artist's fascination with the monsters and hybrids that he saw in the public and private collections of "very excellent plastic and allegorical depictions taken from the global creation of nature and human life"[6] — especially Peter the Great's *Kunstkammer* also attached to the Academy of Sciences in St. Petersburg. From its establishment in 1714, the *Kunstkammer* gave primary attention to its anatomical, medical and "monster" section — something symptomatic of Peter's personal taste. Peter even issued a decree requesting citizens to bring "unusual stones, human, cattle, fish and bird bones [...] both very great and small" (cf. Staniukovich 1953: 29). As a result, the *Kunstkammer* received all manner of weird and wonderful items — a sword fish, a monstrous ewe which had "two mouths on either side with tongues and two eyes that could see", a "sheep with eight legs; another with three eyes, two torsoes and six legs", "a baby with three legs from Nizhnii Novgorod", "a baby with two heads from Ufa", etc. (Staniukovich 1953: 30) Suffice it to say that, within a short time, the *Kunstkammer* contained one of the richest and most varied collections of monsters and freaks in Europe. Some of the deformed wretches even lived there and were used as public entertainment, a practice that prefigured our inclusion of dwarfs and bearded ladies in modern circuses and funfairs.

Apart from the *Kunstkammer*, there were several private collections of oddities in St. Petersburg that offered cheap thrills under the guise of public education, for example, the so called Exhibition and Museum of Vilgel'm Vinter. This was a conglomeration of zoological and anatomical specimens, wax figures of the famous and infamous, and installations reconstucting the horrors of the Inquisition, the Franco-Prussian War, etc. One of the three sections in the Vinter Museum even contained the "horizontal cross-section of five male torsoes which explain didactically the strength of a bullet penetration fired from a new system, small caliber infantry rifle" (Staniukovich 1953: 30). This group of five specimens illustrated the effect of the bullet on the chest cavity, the ribcage, the shoulder, the heart, etc. Vinter's Museum also boasted an Ethnographical Section with renderings of Sitting Bull, a Zulu, a Nubian, an Eskimo, a real mummy — and also a living Nightmare. Although Filonov does not include the Vinter Museum or even the *Kunstkammer* in the collections that he mentions in his autobiographies, we can assume that he examined the exhibits with particular fervor, especially in the light of his passion for anatomical structures. After all, several of his paintings and drawings contain the kind of monster that was on display such as the the cockerel with two heads in *Girl with a Flower* (1913) and the human pig in *Formula of the Bourgeoisie* (1924-25). Even the very early works such as the self-portrait and *Hero and His Fate* (both of1909-101; present whereabouts unknown), while less "vivisectional", remind us of the grotesque preparations in the *Kunstkammer*: the "deathly putrefied" faces in *Hero and His Fate* (Pokrovsky undated: 22), the "corpses" of *Feast of the Kings*,[7] even the exquisite *Heads* of 1910 evoke the impression of human remains distilled in formaldehyde. Appropriately, enough, Filonov included a self-portrait in the lower left of *Heads* — "tormented and sorrowful as if he had foreseen his life" (Glebova 1984: 133).

Filonov's more than casual acquaintance with the twilight world of outcasts and cripples is demonstrated by his pictorial and verbal references to the victims of the Great War and the Spanish Civil War, to corporal punishment and torture as in *Execution (After 1905)* (1913) and *Colonial Politics* (1925-26), to abortion (Filonov 1983f: 200), and even to laboratory monkeys (Filonov 1983c: 150). Evidentally, Filonov was aware of the "abnormality" of his own art, as he indicated in his retort to people who reproached him for his rejection of Realism: "Why won't you let my monster live, you damn murderer!" (Lozovoi undated: 5) But, of course, Filonov was not alone in his cult of the monstrous and the deformed, especially among the artists of St. Petersburg; and to some extent he was continuing the recent traditions of the Decadents such as Avgust Ball'er, Andrei Dmitriev, and Nikolai Kalmakov, noted for their necrological imagery. Boris Grigor'ev, Vasilii Masiutin and other Northern artists influenced by the German Renaissance also come to mind. As in the case of Filonov, their appreciation of the German and Flemish masters, their fascination with the grotesque, and their invocation of the darker forces of life point to rich avenues of enquiry — to the relationship of late Symbolism to the St. Petersburg avant-garde, to the question of a Russo-Baltic Expressionism, and to the "demonic" heritage of Al'fred Eberling and Mikhail Vrubel'.[8]

But unlike the exotic preparations in the *Kunstkammer* and the Decadent paintings, Filonov's monsters are alive. Filonov seemed to be using his mutants just as a scientist uses laboratory animals, i.e. to diagnose disease, analyze corporeal condition, and investigate the potential for regeneration and metamorphosis. After all, Filonov not only regarded his paintings as living organisms, but also envisaged a world in which the human race would be reborn (cf. *Regeneration of an Intellectual).* The fact that Filonov observed a careful diet, that he slept on an iron bed, and worked 18 hours a day also illustrates his conviction that discipline, calculation, and science contituted the true denominator of art. "We need the scientific method", he wrote, "and this will be the collective method. This will give us Analytical Art" (Filonov undated). Filonov did not hesitate to use his scalpel and strip the skin from the cadaver of traditional art.[9] But in exposing its nerves and tendons, in redesigning its members and articulations, Filonov also fashioned new and fantastic anatomies that suddenly seem very familiar: Filonov's monstrous paintings now symbolize a universal flowering of a different kind that seems to arise from the double forces of ecological disaster and genetic engineering.

Notes

[*] An earlier version of this article was published in German in the catalogue of the exhibition "Filonov und seine Schule" at the Kunsthalle Düsseldorf, 1990.

[1] There is some confusion regarding the date of Filonov's trip to Jerusalem. 1907 seems to be a reliable date since, in his "Autobiographies", Filonov mentions that he made the trip while he was studying in Lev Dmitriev-Kavkzsky's studio, i.e. between 1903 and 1908 (cf. Filonov 1983a: 120). Also see Vera Anikieva 1983: 55.

[2] Petr Buchkin, Filonov's colleague at the Academy of Arts, mentioned that when Filonov first enrolled in the courses he was "cheerful, rosy-cheeked, sociable", but that after the summer vacation he became "unrecognisable, pale, unsmiling" (Buchkin 1963: 50-52).

[3] Filonov's student Nikolai Lozovoi recalled that Cranach, Dürer, and Holbein were among Filonov's favorite artists and that he also held Leonardo Da Vinci in very high regard. I wish to thank Aleksandr Lozovoi, son of the artist, for supplying me with this information.

[4] See also the publication of Nikolai Lozovoi, "Pavel Fionov's Analystical Method", in *Experiment,* Los Angeles, 1995, No. 1, pp. 141-58.

[5] Filonov wrote in his diary entry for 12 June, 1932: "I never draw with enthusiasm, only with cold calculation" (quoted in E. Glebova 1984: 228).

[6] From the front page of the catalog of the Vilgel'm Vinter Museum 1896.

[7] In his description of *Feast of the Kings,* Velimir Khlebnikov referred to a "feast of corpses" (cf. Khlebnikov 1916: 55)

[8] In describing Filonov's contribution to the second "Union of Youth" exhibition in April-May, 1911 (which included Filonov's *Heads,* then untitled), Nikolai Breshko-Breshkovsky stated that "every joint has been understood with an anatomical precision that, involuntarily, makes you think of Vrubel'" (Breshko-Breshkovsky 1911: 121). Both Vrubel and his epigone Eberling achieved their reputation as "Decadents" in part through their respective illustrations to Mikhail Lermontov's poem *Demon,* i.e. M. Lermontov: *Sochineniia,* Moscow: Kushnerev, 1891; and *Demon Lermontova,* St. Petersburg: Golike and Vil'borg, 1910.

[9] Filonov wrote: "Cut the object of your study and its painting as if with a scalpel". See Filonov 1983c: 150) Filonov wrote: "Cut the object of your study and its painting as if with a scalpel" (Filonov 1983c: 150).

Bibliography

Anikieva, Vera

1983 "Filonov". In: Misler and Bowlt 1983: 53-61.

B.A.

1913 "Vystavka kartin 'Soiuza molodezhi' v Peterburge". In: *Ogonek*, no. 48.

Beliutin, Elii, and Nina Moleva

1953 *P.P. Chistiakov. Pis;ma, zapisnye knizhki, vospominaniia 1832-1919,* Moscow: Iskusstvo.

Breshko-Breshkovsky, Nikolai

1911 "Vystavka 'Soiuz molodezhi'". In: *Birzhevye vedomosti.*

Buchkin, Petr

1963 *O tom, chto v pamiati,* Leningrad: Khudozhnik RSFSR.

Buial'sky, Il'ia

1860 *Anatomicheskie zapiski dlia obuchaiushchikhsia zhivopisi i skulpture v Imperatorskoi Akademii khudozhestv,* St. Peterburg: Prokhorov.

Chistiakov, Pavel

1953 "Risunok". In: Moleva and Beliutin 1953: 118-157.

Ehrenberg, K., G. Richel' et al.

1872 *Prakticheskii samouchitel' iziashchnykh iskusstv,* Moscow: Bakhmetev.

Filonov, Pavel

1923 *Osnova prepodavaniia izobrazitel'nykh iskusstv po printsipu chistogo analiza, kak vysshaia shkola tvorchestva, sistema "Mirovoi rastsvet. Vystuplenie.* [Manuscript in Russian State Archive of Literature and Art, Moscow, Call No.: f. 2348, op. 1, ed. khr. 8.]

1936 *Dnevniki.* [Typescript copy in the collection of the Institute of Modern Russian Culture, Los Angeles]

1983a "Autobiographies". In: Misler and Bowlt 1983: 117-123.

1983b "Lecture at a Conference in the Department of Painting at the Academy of Arts". In: Misler and Bowlt 1983: 203-205.

1983c "The Basic Tenets of Analytical Art". In: Misler and Bowlt 1983: 145-152.

1983d "Letter to Baskanchin". In: Misler and Bowlt, 1983: 291-295.

1983e "Declaration of 'Universal Flowering'". In: Misler and Bowlt, 1983: 167-171.

1983f "Presentation at the AKhRR Debate". In: Misler and Bowlt, 1983: 199-205.

Undated "Otvechaite zhe nam, mudretsy-pedagogi". [Unpublished manuscript.] Moscow: Private archive.

Filonov, Pavel, and David Kakabadze et al.

1983 "Made Paintings". In: Misler and Bowlt, 1983: 135.

Glebova, Evdokiia

1984 "Dnevniki Filonova v vospominaniiakh ego sestry Glebovoi" in *SSSR. Vnutrennie protivorechiia,* Benson, Vermont: Chalidze, 1984, No. 10, 129-273.

Grigoriev, Boris

1922 "Liniia". In: Aleksei Tolstoi et al., *Boris Grigoriev. Rasseia.* Berlin: Efron; and Postdam: Müller, unpaginated.

Isakov, Sergei

1941 *M. Avilov,* Leningrad-Moscow: Iskusstvo.

Khlebnikov, Velimir

1916 "Ka" in *Moskovskie mastera,* Moscow: Vermel'.

Kuzmin, Nikolai

1982 *Davno i nedavno,* Moscow: Sovetskii khudozhnik.

Lozovoi, Nikolai

Undated *Analiticheskii metod P.N. Filonova.* [Unpublished manuscript.] Moscow: Private archive.

Misler, NNicoletta, and John Bowlt (eds)

1983 *Pavel Filonov: A Hero and His Fate,* Austin: Silvergirl.

Moleva, Nina, and Elii Beliutin

1953 *P.P. Chistiakov. Teoretik i pedagog,* Moscow: Akademiia khudozhestv.

1967 *Russkaia khudozhestvennaia shkola vtoroi poloviny XIX-nachala XX veka,* Moscow: Iskusstvo.

Obolensky, Lev

1902 *Snovy krasoty i iskusstva,* St. Petersburg: Vaisberg and Gershunin.

Pokrovsky, Dmitrii

Undated *Trevogoi i plamenem.* [Unpublished manuscript]. Moscow: Private archive.

Staniukovich, T.

1953 *Kunstkamera Peterburgskoi Akademii nauk,* Moscow-Leningrad: Akademiia nauk.

Vilgel'm Vinter Museum

1896 *Illiustrirovannyi Katalog vystavki i muzeia Vilgel'ma Vintera,* Vilnius: Zhirmunsky.

DIFFICILES NUAGE: GERTRUDE STEIN, OULIPO AND THE GRAMMAR OF THE AVANT-GARDE

EDWARD LINTZ

There is no room at the inn in Peter Bürger's *Theory of the Avant-Garde* for the neo-avant-garde. He argues that the neo-avant-garde cannot possess even the historical avant-garde's intention to de-institutionalise art and integrate it into the praxis of life, because having transformed that protest against institutionalising art into art itself, the neo-avant-garde can offer only an inauthentic gesture. His dismissal is total:

> The neo-avant-garde institutionalises the *avant-garde as art* and thus negates genuinely avant-gardiste intentions. [...] Neo-avant-gardiste art is autonomous art in the full sense of the term, which means that it negates the avant-gardiste intention of returning art to the praxis of life. (1984: 58)

Bürger supports his thesis that the historical avant-garde attempted to reintegrate art into the "praxis of life" by arguing that the avant-garde attacks artistic autonomy on three levels: 1. purpose; 2. production; and 3. reception. He traces how the avant-garde negates the lack of social purpose in aestheticist art, the "genius" myth of individual artistic production, and, most suggestively, the passivity aestheticist autonomy assigns to the artistic recipient. To prove this third point, he turns to dadaist and surrealist poetry for his primary examples.

In Bürger's theory, the avant-garde poem works to eliminate the gap between active producer and passive recipient by giving the recipient access to its own mode of production. Thus Bürger explains that "it is no accident" that both Tristan Tzara's instructions for the making of a Dadaist poem and André Breton's for the writing of automatic texts have "Rezeptcharakter" (1974:72). Bürger uses the dual meaning of "Rezept" to emphasise that by providing its recipient with a *recipe* to create art, the avant-garde poem thereby produces a *remedy* for the recipient's passivity. Picking up on the praxis in Breton's "*pratiquer la poésie*", Bürger argues that avant-garde poetry should be understood not as artistic production but as part of a "liberating life praxis" (1984: 53). Dadaist and surrealist poetry attacks aestheticism not only on the level of production by refusing to acknowledge the "individual creativity of the artist", but also by providing its recipients with a model for their own future creative activity. By supplying the recipe for its form, the avant-garde removes poetry from aestheticism's elitist sense of autonomy and integrates it into the social, turning the reader into a writer and art into social practice.

Yet Bürger's representation of the neo-avant-garde as inauthentic and institutionalising betrays his own theory of the avant-garde's revolutionzing of aesthetic reception. Rather than returning art to an aestheticist ideal of autonomy, the Paris based group OuLiPo provides a potent example of how the neo-avant-garde actually takes the historical avant-garde's attack on the ideology of autonomy one step further. Founded in 1960, OuLiPo, or *l'Ouvroir de Littérature Potentielle*, successfully expanded the historical avant-garde's redefinition of the role of the artistic recipient by creating the opportunity for the recipient not only to create new works of art but to play the determining role in the production of the avant-garde work itself.

OuLiPo shared the commitment of dada and surrealism to attack aestheticist art on the level of production by undermining the value placed on individual inspiration, beginning by reclaiming fixed form poetry. Aestheticism rejects fixed poetic forms such as anagrams, palindromes, or lipograms — once prized by the Alexandrian poets, the Grands Rhétoriqueurs, and the German Baroque poets — as mere *Difficiles nuage*, trifling pests which spoil the purity of the poet's autonmous inspiration. In his 1983 essay "Rule and Constraint" OuLiPo member Marcel Bénabou defends fixed form poetry against aestheticism's dismissal because it serves as an important means of constraint. Bénabou's essay reflects the founding Oulipian principle that formal constraint must replace autonomous inspiration as the basis of literature. François le Lionnais, the co-founder of OuLiPo along with Raymond Queneau, uses the metaphor of Russian *babuschka* dolls to describe the function of constraint in "LA LIPO", the first manifesto of Oulipian poetics published in 1962:

> Toute oeuvre littéraire se construit à partir [...] d'une série de contraintes et de procédures qui rentrent les unes dans les autres comme des poupées russes. (1987:iv)

In the second manifesto, published in 1973, Le Lionnais emphasises to an even greater extent OuLiPo's insistence that all literary forms derive from principles of constraint, contrasting the literature of constraint with what he derisively terms "la littérature-cri" or "la littérature borborygme" [eructative literature] (1987: ix).

In this spirit, the first edition of *La littérature potentielle* in 1973 showcased the various ways in which constraint and fixed form could act as generative devices. Organised under different categories of constraint, the issue featured under the heading *Utilisation de structures déja existantes*: Georges Perec's "Un roman lipogrammatique", Jean Lescure's "Tautogramme", and Jean Queval's "Cinq sonnets"; under *Manipulations Lexicographiques, Syntaxiques ou Prosodiques*: Lescure's "La méthode S + 7", Jacques Bens's "Inventaires", and Bénabou's "poésie antonymique"; under *Synthoulipismes Lexicographiques ou Prosodiques*: Noël Arnaud's "Poèmes algol", Albert-Marie Schmidt's "La Lamproie (dizain saphique à la lionnaise avec rimes initiales et terminales,)" and François Le Lionnais's "Poèmes-barre"; under *Synthoulipismes périmathématiques:* Queneau's "Cent mille milliards de poèmes", Jacques Roubaud's "ε. Mode d'emploi de ce livre", and Le Lionnais's "Poèmes booléens". Perec achieved OuLiPo's most notorious success with his use of the lipogrammatic method in the novel *La Disparition*, written entirely without the letter "e".

If Perec's lipogrammatic method showed the potential of exclusion as a formal catalyst, then Queneau showed the expansive potential of formal experiment in his sequence of ten isomorphic sonnets, *Cent mille milliards de poèmes*, where each line in a given sonnet is interchangeable with its homologous line in each of the other nine sonnets. Given that a sonnet has fourteen lines, the potential of the set is 10^{14}, *Cent mille milliards*, or one hundred trillion. Thus, by Queneau's rather generous estimation of reading habits, if one reads one sonnet a minute for eight hours a day, 200 days a year, it would take over a million centuries to read all the potential combinations of the sonnets.[1] If that sounds like a tall order for the reader, be glad he didn't choose to write ten homologous sestinas! While Queneau obviously recognises the practical impossibility of any reader achieving every combination, the mere potential of near infinite creation reflects OuLiPo's synthetic ambition to create new poetic forms which transfer the final choice of the literary product to the reader. After the artistic producer's initial selection of elements, all power is turned over to the recipient. The reader must choose how to achieve the "potential" of the literary set by selecting her own combinations. Queneau's potential poetic set shifts the empowerment of the recipient from Tzara's and Breton's recipes instructing the reader how to make their own work — while leaving the dadaist or surrealist poem as an unchangeable entity — to giving the recipient the power to control the reading experience itself.

In an essay discussing the use of mathematics in Queneau's writing, Roubaud, a professor of mathematics who joined OuLiPo in 1966 and published his first book of poems one year later, focuses on the importance of the writer's voluntary submission to constraint. He states:

> Le caractère intentionnel, volontaire, de la contrainte sur lequel il revient à maintes reprises, avec insistence, est indissolublement lié pour lui à ce vif refus de hasard. (1981:56)

This active refusal of chance, and therefore of the bourgeois equation of chance with freedom, compels the producer of art to accept that formal constraint shifts the burden of choice from the producer to the recipient. This insistence that the potential of literature must come from choice and not chance is where Queneau, Roubaud, and the members of OuLiPo break with dada and surrealism. A literature which truly means to avoid autonomous "inspiration" and empower the reader must leave choice not to chance but to the reader.

If the appeal of *Cent mille milliards de poèmes* to a mathematician like Roubaud is obvious, then what was it that attracted him to the poetry of Gertrude Stein, whose writing on the surface would appear diametrically opposed to a synthetic implementation of formal constraint? On one level, one senses that Roubaud feels a certain affinity with Stein because of her treatment at the hands of the French avant-garde, one which ultimately ruined her reputation in France through the 1960's. The evolution of Stein's relationship with the avant-garde is best seen through her involvement with the avant-garde Parisian literary journal *transition*, edited by Eugene Jolas and Elliot Paul. Founded in 1927, *transition* featured the art of prominent avant-garde figures like Picasso, Man Ray, Tanguy, Ernst, de Chirico, Masson, Duchamp, and Picabia; Irish and American writers including Joyce, Riding, Williams, Barnes, and Beckett; and French writers Lautréamont, Gide, Hugnet, Leiris, Eluard, Soupault, Breton and Tzara. From its first issue which printed her "An Elucidation", Stein was the darling of *transition*. The journal featured her work in thirteen of the first twenty-one issues, highlighted by *transition* 14, which contained her photograph and a complete reprint of the largely forgotten *Tender Buttons*, and *transition* 15, which offered a "Complete Bibliography" of her writing.

While *transition* is best known now as the first journal to publish excerpts from Joyce's *Finnegan's Wake* under the title *Work in Progress*, Stein was given equal billing with Joyce in the journal's own advertisements of upcoming issues.[2] Yet after the publication of *The Autobiography of Alice B. Toklas* in 1933, *transition* turned against Stein, publishing a supplemental pamphlet with its February 1935 issue entitled "Testimony against Gertrude Stein." Incensed by her representation of the avant-garde in *The Autobiography*, Eugene Jolas collected "Testimony" against Stein from Braque, Matisse, André Salmon and Tzara. In his introduction to the pamphlet, Jolas attempted to discredit any involvement Stein may have had with the avant-garde, stating that "Her participation in the genesis and development of such movements as Fauvism, Cubism, Dada, Surrealism, Transition etc. was never ideologically intimate" (1935:2). Tzara's attack was more acidly personal, claiming that

> underneath the "baby" style, which is pleasant enough when it is a question of simpering at the interstices of envy, it is easy to discern

> such a really coarse spirit, accustomed to the artifices of the lowest literary prostitution, that I cannot believe it necessary for me to insist on the presence of a clinical case of megalomania. (1935:13)[3]

This unmerited blackballing by the French avant-garde was one of the main factors which led Roubaud to promote Stein's writing in *Vingt poètes américains*, the 1980 anthology he edited with Michel Deguy introducing new American poetry to a French audience.[4] But it is in his article "Gertrude Stein Grammaticus", a key element of the 1983 special issue of the French journal *In 'hui* devoted to Gertrude Stein, that Roubaud best reveals the quality of Stein's writing that links her to OuLiPo's use of formal constraint to connect producer and recipient. One senses that Roubaud could offer no higher compliment to a writer than his description of Stein as "essentiellement grammaticale" (1983:47). His analysis of grammar's function in Stein's writing leads him to compare Stein and Gerard Manley Hopkins on the poetic object:

> l'intérieure de l'objet est son *inscape*, et la poésie le saisit par son accent propre, son *instress,* son insistance à être, qui, pour Gertrude est mise à jour par la poésie dans *l'amour du noun*, en supposant que le *noun* dit, désigne *l'inscape* des choses.

Inscape, Hopkins's term for the quality of an observed object which makes it unique to the perceiver, suggests one important way in which poetry can energize the recipient, creating a structure where the perceiver's experience of the poetic object becomes absolutely unique. In Stein's writing it is love for the noun which brings out the inscape of things, leading Roubaud to what he terms a "par-agertrudian axiom": "en poésie, *l'inscape* d'un objet est atteint à travers son *nom* (le *noun*), ou ces nuages de mots qui entourent le nom et sont soudés ensemble par la grammaire." Roubaud's metaphor follows Bohr's model of the atom: Stein places her noun at the nucleus of the poem, surrounded by "clusters of words" welded together by grammar. In an October 1999 interview, Roubaud reaffirmed this atomic metaphor, referring to substantives as the "noyau centrale", or central nucleus of a poem (1999). If the noun is a nucleus, then grammar is the electromagnetic force which binds the orbiting electrons to the nucleus and holds the atom together.

The work of grammar thus presents a solidarity with the reader's labor, for *souder* is the job of the *ouvrier*. In place of aestheticism's autonomous art object, the *chef d'oeuvre*, the Oulipian poem results from "ouvrer", the working of its material. By reconnecting writing to its artisanal roots, grammar replaces the genius's solipsistic creation with the socially oriented labor of the craftsman. In place of aestheticism's dismissal of fixed form writing as trifling "nugae", grammatical constraint creates the poetic solidarity of the "nuage des mots."

What is truly ahead of its time in Stein's writing is that her exploration of grammar sits in direct opposition to the principles of the historical avant-garde. While Tzara, for one, in his 1922 "Lecture on Dada" proclaimed that "Dada tries to find out what words mean before using them from the point of view not of grammar but of representation", Stein turned to grammar as the focus of her literary work (1981: 248). From her own description of the pleasure she receives from diagramming sentences in her lecture "Poetry and Grammar" to her analysis of grammar in works such as "Arthur a Grammar", "A Grammarian", and "More Grammar for a Sentence", Stein places grammar at the forefront of her literary efforts in the late 1920's and 1930's. In the Fall 1928 *transition* 14 Stein gives her most direct explanation of the anti-bourgeois motivation behind her turn to grammar. In a footnote accompanying the reprint of *Tender Buttons* Stein explains: "[*Tender Buttons*] was my first conscious struggle with the problem of correlating sight, sound and sense, and eliminating rhythm; some of the solutions in it seem to me still alright, now I am trying grammar and eliminating sight and sound" (1928: 13n). The elimination of sight in particular suggests that Stein abdicates the sense most intimately tied to the bourgeois subject's position as privileged observer, the sense which grants the subject the ability to speak from a position of autonomy. By giving up sight for grammar Stein accepts the one constraint that creates the universal bond that unites every user of language.

If Stein is virtually alone in the 1920s and 1930s in exploring the literary potential of grammar (with the notable exception of Wittgenstein), her focus anticipated some of the most important structuralist and narratological inquiries into language, including Greimas's attempt to define the semiotic project as the construction of a general grammar, Todorov's critique of rhetoric for historically privileging the paradigmatic over the syntagmatic, and Genette's work on the assimilation of rhetorical transformations to syntactical, grammatic patterns.[5] But the most important advocate of grammar in this period, and the most direct influence on Roubaud, was the linguist Noam Chomsky, whose 1966 *Topics in the theory of generative grammar* came in the same year as Roubaud joined OuLiPo, and whose 1972 *Studies on semantics in generative grammar* arrived the same year Roubaud and Deguy conceived their anthology of new American poetry.[6] In the interview, Roubaud discussed how his reading of Chomsky's syntactic structures helped lead to his interest in Stein:

> As a mathematician, I became interested in Chomsky's syntactic structures and was one of the founders of a review dedicated to his linguistics. Chomsky's emphasis that language is made not just of words but of sentences changed my conception of language significantly. This shift in thinking from words to sentences, and Chomsky's focus on grammar as a generative agent helped foster my interest in syntax. It became evident to me that Gertrude Stein had a new vision of how syntax could function in literature.

By showing that all humans share a "universal mental grammar", Chomsky's new theory of linguistics helped establish that Stein's and OuLiPo's focus on grammar truly represented the most fundamental connection between producer and repicient. As Bürger applauds Benjamin's discovery of the "*Formbestimmheit* der Kunst", (1974: 40) Benjamin's realization that not just society but art could be determined by form, Chomsky's discovery insists on the formal determination of language by grammar. That Stein and OuLiPo recognised the potential of language's structural universality as a generative device for poetry and a means to unite writer and reader suggests the genuinely "avant-garde" nature of their achievement. But perhaps the best expression of the solidarity grammar creates between producer and recipient comes in the final line of the first section of "Arthur a Grammar", when Stein declares triumphantly to herself and to her readers that "Grammar is in our power" (1975:13).

Notes

[1] Warren Motte gives a good reading of Queneau's experiment, and an excellent selection of OuLiPo's theoretical works in *Oulipo: A Primer of Potential Literature*, ed. Warren Motte, (Lincoln, NE: University of Nebraska Press, 1986), 2-4; *passim*.

[2] The back page of *transition* 2 (Paris, May 1927) features the following two announcements:

> Miss Stein's "As My Wife Has a Cow, A Love Story" will appear in the next number of *transition*.
> The complete text of Mr. James Joyce's work, the first two installments of which have already been published in *transition*, will be printed consecutively from month to month.

[3] Other dadaists and surrealists remained fiercely loyal to Stein, however, including Marcel Duchamp, who translated one of the *Stanzas in Meditation* in the preface to the catalog of a 1932 exhibit of Francis Picabia's drawings. Picabia himself wrote a flattering article on Stein published in the *Nouvelle Revue Française* and sent her a handwritten copy in a long letter on February 12, 1937, one of the nearly one hundred he sent her continuing until 1946. Georges Hugnet, another dedicated correspondent who translated *Dix Portraits*, wrote the poem "Le Berceau de Gertrude Stein", later set to music by Virgil Thomson. Duchamp's translation was reprinted in the journal *Orbes* as "Stance 69 des Stance de Méditation", (Paris, Hiver 1932-33), 64-7. The stanza is actually number LXXI in Part V of *Stanzas in Meditation*. See Douglas Messerli's 1994 edition of*Stanzas in Meditation* (Los Angeles: Sun & Moon Press). "Le Berceau de Gertrude Stein ou Le mystère de la rue de Fleurus: 8 poems by Georges Hugnet : adapted for voice and piano by Virgil Thomson", (1928; New York: Southern, 1979).

[4] *Vingt poètes américains* was conceived in 1972 by Deguy and Roubaud. The bilingual text begins with selections from Stein's *Stanzas in Meditation*.

[5] Marjorie Perloff gives the best account of the shared affinity for grammar between Stein and Wittgenstein in her chapter "Grammar in Use", *Wittgenstein's Ladder: Poetic Language and the Strangeness of the Ordinary* (Chicago: Univ. of Chicago Press, 1996), 83-112.

[6] Chomsky's major linguistic works of this period include: *Syntactic structures* (The Hague; New York: Mouton, 1957); *Aspects of the theory of syntax* (Cambridge, MA: M.I.T. Press, 1965); *Topics in the theory of*

generative grammar (The Hague: Mouton, 1966); *Language and mind* (New York: Harcourt, Brace & World, 1968); *Studies on semantics in generative grammar* (The Hague: Mouton, 1972).

Bibliography

Bürger, Peter

1974 *Theorie der Avantgarde*. Frankfurt am Main: Suhrkamp Verlag.

1984 *Theory of the Avant-Garde*. Trans. by Michael Shaw. Minneapolis: University of Minnesota Press.

Deguy, Michel and Roubaud, Jacques ed.

1980 *Vingt poètes américain*, Paris: NRF.

Jolas, Eugene

1935 "Testimony against Gertrude Stein." In Supplement to *transition* 23.

Le Lionnais, François

1987 "LA LIPO." In *La Bibliothèque Oulipienne*, Volume II Paris: Éditions Seghers: i-vi.

Roubaud, Jacques

1978 "Gertrude Stein, Gertrude Stein et Gertrude Stein" *Critique*, No. 379, 1095-1106.

1981 "La mathématique dans la méthode de Raymond Queneau", *Atlas de littérature potentielle* Paris: Gallimard, 42-72.

1983 "Gertrude Stein Grammaticus." In *Gertrude Stein, encore* Amiens: Trois Cailloux, 45-59.

1999 Interview with the author, 17 October 1999.

Stein, Gertrude

1928 transition 14.

1975 *How to Write* New York: Dover.

Tzara, Tristan

1924 "Lecture on Dada". In: Robert Motherwell (ed.), *The Dada Painters and Poets*. Cambridge, Mass.: Harvard University Press, 1981, 246-251.

III.

AVANT-GARDE IN CONTEXT

THE SELECTION OF AVANT-GARDE POETRY FOR ANTHOLOGIES

KLAUS BEEKMAN

In the Low Countries (i.e. the Netherlands and Belgium), the anthology is one of the better-selling types of literary text. This can be seen if one looks at the number of editions and reprints of anthologies. For example, between 1970 and 1979, 328 Dutch anthologies were published (Conderaerts 1985: 838). *New Sounds* (*Nieuwe geluiden*) — an anthology of poetry first published by Dirk Coster in 1924 — was reprinted five times. *Mirror of Modern Dutch Poetry* (*Spiegel van de moderne Nederlandse poëzie*) — an anthology compiled by Hans Warren — reached its sixth edition in 1992. The eight edition of *Dutch Poetry of the* 19th *and* 20th *Century in 1000 and Some More Poems* (*De Nederlandse poëzie van de negentiende en twintigste eeuw in duizend en enige gedichten*) — an anthology compiled by Gerrit Komrij in 1979 — appeared as early as 1987. The editions of *New Slate-Pencils, Clean Slates* (*Nieuwe griffels schone leien*) — a selection of poetry by the Dutch and Belgian avant-garde — can even be called best-sellers: between 1954 and 1957, 37,500 copies were sold. The number of anthologies sold is, anyhow, remarkably high, especially considering that poetry is hard to sell.

Anthologies come in various types. Some are arranged according to era, generation, genre or sub-genre, while others are arranged according to theme, area, a specific aim or target group, or a combination of these criteria. Here, I focus on anthologies that have a survey character, the so-called literary-historical anthologies. In particular, I am interested in anthologies that purport to give a historical survey of the poetry of the Netherlands and (Flemish-speaking) Belgium.

What arguments are advanced for the selection of avant-garde poems, particularly poems written by expressionists? By the anthologists' own account, the most important selection criterion when compiling anthologies that have a survey character is the extent to which poems can be called representative of a period or literary movement *and* of the oeuvre of a poet. The determination of the representative character of a poem seems to be a rather uncomplicated affair. Victor E. van Vriesland, for example, calls his anthology *Mirror of Dutch Poetry (1900-1940)* (*Spiegel van de Nederlandse poëzie (1900-1940)* (3[e] ed. 1965) representative, "because trying to represent individual expressions, as well as literary movements, as far as they were the expression of the uninterrupted, continuous development of a continuous poetic movement and had taken the shape of a specific period". In other words, poems manifest themselves as representative of a specific period, as well as of the oeuvre of a poet. However, I will argue that this is a fallacy.

Anthologies which purport to give a representative survey of literature, I will argue, have an institutional character. Just like literary critics and other representatives of literary institutions operating in the literary field (e.g. literary critics), anthologists defend a specific conception of literature. To a large extent, such a conception determines their selection of texts. However, the choice of avant-garde poems for an anthology — especially those by expressionistic poets — is not based solely on an individual conception of literature, but is partly the result of a continuous struggle or competition in the literary field, a competition between all kinds of cultural institutions and between individuals who represent those institutions, as the French cultural sociologist Pierre Bourdieu puts it. In this struggle, where conceptions of literature are defended, the combatants make decisions on a strategic basis. This also applies to anthologists. Strategic factors steer their choices.

An anthologist tries to create a distinct profile for himself by choosing other poems for his anthology than those chosen by his predecessor, who purported to have compiled the same sort of anthology. An anthologist can distinguish himself by choosing other poems from the same poet and presenting these as representative of his oeuvre, or by changing the number of poems by several poets who belong to the same group (in our case, Dutch and Flemish expressionists). I will explore this in a discussion of Dutch anthologies of poetry that have a survey character.

The greater the distance from the interbellum period, the fewer problems an anthologist has in gathering the same expressionist poems as his predecessor. The urge to create a distinct profile of himself with the help of expressionist poems then decreases. At that particular moment, an anthologist obviously has other means with which to create a distinct profile for himself.

What is surprising is that in the 1970s, anthologists generally selected an expressionist's poems from the interbellum period, even if the poet had published more poems after World War II than before it. How can we account for this?

1. Selection according to type, quality and representativeness

Literary-historical anthologies, I have argued, have an institutional character. This assertion requires an explanation. What is meant by 'institution'? In one of the leading studies in the field of the historical avant-garde (*Theorie der Avantgarde*, 1974), Peter Bürger uses the conception of 'institution'. In his study it even functions as a key notion. According to Peter Bürger, the historical avant-garde must be considered an attack on the status of art in bourgeois society: Dada — the most radical movement within the European avant-garde — criticises not just former literary movements, but the '*institution of art*', as it has been developed in bourgeois society; in other words, art as it was made until the beginning of the twentieth century on the basis of the principle that a work of art is autonomous, forms a unity and is characterized by a personal signature. According to Peter Bürger, a literary institution is a set of norms that reacts immediately to another set of norms. He forgets, however, that in the literary field 'real' institutions are active. These 'real' institutions affect, to a large extent, the attribution of value to texts. I will use the conception of 'institution' in another sense. I agree with H. Verdaasdonk and Kees van Rees (two empirical literary sociologists from the Netherlands) that one may use the conception of 'institution' only if 'real' institutions are at issue. 'Real' institutions are forms of organisation situated between producers and consumers of literature. Publishing houses and bookshops deal with the material production and distribution of literature, sections of art councils give their advice, and all kinds of literary critics (e.g. journalists, essayists and academics) provide symbolic production, i.e. they assign some kind of value to texts (Van Rees in *Institution & Innovation*, 1994, Klaus Beekman (ed.); Van Rees / Dorleijn 1994). There is a case for putting the activities of anthologists within this institution of literary criticism, in view of the fact that the representatives of this institution see it as their task to distinguish texts according to type and quality (see Verdaasdonk 1987) and to assign to them symbolic value, whether intentional or unintentional.

To decide whether texts are suitable for a compilation, anthologists classify them according to type and quality. For example, for the compilation of *New Sounds* (*Nieuwe geluiden*, 1924), the anthologist Dirk Coster first had to decide whether a text belonged to the class of 'poetry', and then whether it could be labelled as 'new' or 'modern'. Here, Coster suggested (as others have done), intersubjective arguments can be advanced. Even when making a choice based on quality, anthologists seem to be convinced that they do not have to appeal to subjective criteria: they simply refer to the qualitative features of a selected text. For example, in his preface to *River Basin: an Anthology from the Poetry of the Post-War Generation of Poets* (3rd impr. 1958) (*Stroomgebied. Een bloemlezing uit de poëzie van de na-oorlogse dichtergeneratie*) Ad den Besten writes that he compiled according to what forced 'itself' upon him as 'valuable or promising' (p. 5). As I said before, anthologists are supposed to make a selection based on representativeness without involving their personal value judgement, because poems will have taken on the shape of a specific 'period of time', as Van Vriesland puts it. No long story is required to argue that personal value judgements are at stake when classifying texts. A clear indication of this are the discussions about the selection criteria anthologists have used. The Dutch author and critic Du Perron (1955, p. 14), for example, had his doubts about the classification Dirk Coster used for the compilation of his anthology *New Sounds*: "For Mr Coster, 'new' seems to be: not a better synonym for 'modern', but more related to recently published: the *latest* (not to mention too late)" (idem, p. 15). The reaction of Ter Braak, a literary colleague of Du Perron, to the anthologies *New sounds* (1924) and *Prism* (*Prisma*, 1930) shows that he considered also the criterion 'representativeness' to be charged with a value judgement. His most important criticism of both anthologies is that, as he puts it, the anthologists suggest "that their choice is *the* representative one, the only true one, seen from both points of view" (Ter Braak 1930, p. 350).

2. The function of conceptions of literature

As with all approaches to literature, anthologies are created on the basis of criteria and value judgements embedded in a conception of literature. Each anthologist tries, implicitly or explicitly, to have his conception of literature based on which he created the anthology accepted by others. Thus, there is a strategic aspect to the compilation of an anthology: the anthologist uses his compilation to establish a position for himself in the literary field. The well-known Dutch critic Cyrille Offermans (1993: 829-830) made an appropriate remark when he said that an anthology of experimental Dutch prose — *The Other Prose* (*Ander Proza*, 1975), compiled by the experimental author Sybren Polet — was "a result of as well as a contribution to" the frontogenesis of critics and experimental writers in the 1970s. The famous Dutch author and critic Simon Vestdijk (1960, p. 164) was also aware of the strategic aspect of anthologies: in the anthology *New Slate-Pencils, Clean Slates*, the post-war experimental poets looked for "back support in the form of precursors", i.e. from such historical avant-garde poets as Kurt Schwitters and Theo van Doesburg.

By emphasising the reproductive or representative side of anthologies, one easily forgets that anthologies also have a productive side. Anthologies that have a survey character do not just reflect a specific state within the literary field: they also contribute to changing the existing image of literature in that field. In other words, they help to create a certain image. In this, the compilation of an anthology does not differ from any other approach to literature in which symbolic value is attributed to texts.

When Dirk Coster argues that in *New Sounds* he wants to "separate the most powerful in life or the most promising of our poetry from the monotonous stream of poetry that flows on from year to year", this does not mean that he automatically accepts all experiments with deviating form. This reveals his attitude to the expressionist poems of the Flemish poet Paul van Ostaijen. Coster selected expressionist poetry by Van Ostaijen for his anthology, but in the introduction he emphasises that Van Ostaijen's poetry is bettered by the expressionist verses of Wies Moens — another, less famous Flemish poet — whose work is more 'charged with life' than that of Van Ostaijen. (Although Coster adjusted his view on Van Ostaijen in later editions of *New Sounds*, this was especially because he tuned his conception of Van Ostaijen to the positive ideas held about Van Ostaijen by others, as Dutch professor of literary science Gillis Dorleijn (1996) has proved in a convincing way.)

When Coster selected poems by the Flemish expressionist Van Ostaijen for his anthology with the comment that the expressionist poetry of Wies Moens is more "charged with life" than the poetry of Van Ostaijen, this tells us something about the conception of literature at the basis of Coster's selection. Coster appreciated expressionist poetry that has a humanist character and regarded it more highly than expressionist poetry with a purely experimental, i.e. formal character. Every anthology, even if it purports to give a neutral survey, will have been created on the basis of a specific conception of literature.

3. Anthologies as means to create a distinct profile for oneself

The selection of poems for an anthology is determined by, among other things, the competition in the literary field. An anthologist tries to distinguish himself from other anthologists by selecting other poems from the same poet and by presenting them as representative of the poet's oeuvre, or by changing the number of selected poems. I will demonstrate this on the basis of selected poems by three expressionist poets: the Dutch poets Herman van den Bergh and H. Marsman, and the Flemish poet Paul van Ostaijen. I will concentrate especially on Herman van den Bergh.

Table 1 shows when the above-mentioned poets published their expressionist volumes of poetry. It also shows that in the same period some anthologies that have a survey character were published, namely *New Sounds* — which was compiled by Dirk Coster and reprinted four times in the interbellum period — and *Prism*, which was compiled by D.A.M. Binnendijk, published in 1930 and was not reprinted.

The number of poems Coster and Binnendijk selected from the volumes of poetry by Van den Bergh, Marsman and Van Ostaijen is shown in Table 2. What can we see from Table 2? As to Coster, it is noteworthy that in the several editions of *New Sounds* he increased the number of poems by Marsman. The number of Marsman's poems towers above the average number of selected poems. The number of poems by Van Ostaijen and Van den Bergh Coster does not change a lot, as we can see.

Binnendijk, too, selected more poems by Marsman than by Van Ostaijen and Van den Bergh. But Binnendijk was clearer in developing a hierarchy between the three expressionist poets than Coster was. Binnendijk selected more poems by Van Ostaijen than Coster did. The reason for this could be the different conceptions of literature on which Coster and Binnendijk based their selection. Coster preferred, as we have seen, humanitary expressionists. Binnendijk, on the other hand, preferred expressionist poems that are a sign of 'power of form' (*vormkracht*), as he put it in the preface to his anthology *Prism* (Oversteegen 1969, p. 261 ff.)

There is yet another point on which Binnendijk distinguished himself from Coster. This can be seen from Table 3, which shows which poems by Herman van den Bergh were selected by Coster and Binnendijk, respectively, and from which volumes they come. What is noteworthy in Table 3 is that for his selection Coster concentrated on *The Arch* ('*De Boog*'), a volume of poetry Van den Bergh published in 1917. For this volume, Van den Bergh selected such poems as 'The Flame' ('*De Vlam*') and 'Sabbath' ('*Sabbat*'), poems he had earlier published in the avant-garde journal *The Tide* (*Het Getij*), for which he had worked as a member of the editorial staff for some years (Kurpershoek-Scherft 1956). For the third edition of *New Sounds*, Coster also selected a poem from *The Mirror* (*De Spiegel*), a volume Van den Bergh had published in 1925.

Binnendijk, on the other hand, took poems only from *The Mirror* and did not select even one that Coster had selected. Binnendijk obviously considered other poems to be representative of the oeuvre of the expressionist Van den Bergh than the ones Coster did. However, Binnendijk does not give arguments for this. Indeed, he could not do so, because the conception of literature he refers to and the terms at issue (e.g. 'power of form') have a very broad meaning. Besides, one must not rule out the possibility that the choice Binnendijk made can be traced back to an attempt to distinguish himself from his predecessor. He was not alone in this. The way other anthologists selected poems by Van den Bergh confirms the proposition that the desire for distinction was involved here. I will show this by analysing the anthology *Poets of this Time*.

Poets of this Time (*Dichters van dezen tijd*) is an anthology that has a survey character. Over the years, it has been compiled by several anthologists, who have presented different poets and poems. The first to the ninth editions were edited by Van Hall, and the tenth to the twelfth by Prinsen; Greshoff was the editor of the thirteenth edition, Binnendijk of the fourteenth to the nineteenth editions, and Rodenko of the twentieth and twenty-first editions. Judging by the number of editions that have appeared, one can speak of a very successful anthology. I did not take into consideration earlier editions of this anthology because I am interested in the way expressionist poets and poems were selected for an anthology that has a survey character, and that happened for the first time in the 1920s. I want to show that the opposition between Dirk Coster (1924) and D.A.M. Binnendijk (1930) with respect to the selection of such expressionists as Van den Bergh, Marsman and Van Ostaijen can be traced back to a different conception of literature, with the help of which Binnendijk and Coster tried to create a distinct profile for themselves. This urge for stressing the distinctive features was present not only in the interbellum but also in the post-war period, as the editions of *Poets of this Time* — which were published between 1939 and 1964 — will show (Tables 4 and 5).

A quantitative analysis of several editions of *Poets of this Time* (Table 4) shows that Binnendijk kept the number of poems by Van Ostaijen as low as his predecessor Greshoff had, but that he increased the number of poems by Van den Bergh in gradual stages, and greatly increased the number of Marsman's poems. Binnendijk's successor, Rodenko, for his part created a distinct profile for himself by keeping the number of poems by Van den Bergh constant, increasing the number of poems by Van Ostaijen and reducing the number by Marsman.

The anthologists distinguish themselves from each other in yet another way. When we ask which poems by Herman van den Bergh they selected, it turns out that they all chose different ones, and that each defended his choice by referring to the supposed representative character of the chosen poems. For his anthology *Prism*, Binnendijk did not select the same poems by Van den Bergh as Coster did (see Table 2). The anthology *Poets of this Time* is similar in this: none of the three anthologists of *Poets of this Time* selected the same poems by Herman van den Bergh (see Table 5).

There are also similarities between the different anthologies. For example, all three anthologists of *Poets of this Time* (Greshoff, Binnendijk and Rodenko) selected poems from the two volumes of poetry Van den Bergh had published in the interbellum period, i.e. *The Arch* (1917) and *The Mirror* (1925). That Coster and Binnendijk made their selection from these volumes for *New Sounds* and *Prism* is not surprising in view of when their anthologies were published, i.e. in 1924 and 1930, respectively. But Van den Bergh published more volumes of poetry after World War II than before it. According to specialists in the literary field, these later volumes do not differ from the earlier work as to the quality of the poems. The literary historian Professor Dr G. Stuiveling (1961, p. 202), for example, writes in his *Outline of Dutch Literature* (*Schets van de Nederlandse letterkunde*): "After having been silent for thirty years as a poet, Herman van den Bergh announced new work in his edition of his *Collected Poems* [1954] (*Verzamelde gedichten*). The volumes *The Scar of Odysseus* [1956] (*Het litteken van Odysseus*), *Chances of a Wreck* [1957] (*Kansen op een wrak*) and *On Good Terms with the Enemy* [1958] (*Verstandhouding met de vijand*) demonstrated that his personality and talent had been deepened and that his new, but still undiminished expressionist style was also capable of expressing these deeper emotions in a striking way." Notice that Stuiveling argues that Van den Bergh was still using an expressionist style, not that he had written poetry which can be labelled 'expressionistic'.

In later compilations, anthologists invariably selected poems from the first two volumes of poetry by Van den Bergh (see Tables 6 and 7). For the anthologies of Gerrit Komrij and Hans Warren that have a survey character — *Mirror of Modern Dutch Poetry* (*Spiegel van de moderne Nederlandse poëzie*) and *Dutch Poetry of the 19th*

and 20th Centuries in 1000 and Some More Poems (*De Nederlandse poëzie van de 19^{e} en 20ste eeuw in 1000 en enige gedichten*), both of which were first published in 1979 — only poems from *The Arch* and *The Mirror* were selected. Besides, it is remarkable that Komrij and Warren selected the same poems Coster had selected for his *New Sounds*. Apparently, in 1979 anthologists no longer felt the urge to create a distinct profile for themselves with the help of a specific selection of expressionist poets and poems.

That so many poems by the expressionists Marsman and Van Ostaijen and so few by Van den Bergh were selected for anthologies has nothing to do with textual qualities. I cannot produce evidence to indicate that differences in quality are at stake here. The difference in selection can be traced back to external factors, for example to the fact that only a few articles have been written about the oeuvre of Van den Bergh, while in the 1970s extensive publications were devoted to Marsman and Van Ostaijen: G. Borgers compiled the documentary *Paul van Ostaijen* (*Paul van Ostaijen. Een documentatie*, 1971) and Hannemieke Postma obtained her doctorate with a thesis on Marsman's *Verses* (*Marsmans 'Verzen'*, 1977).

Selection does not take place only on the basis of an ideology or a personal conception of literature. The Dutch academic Van Rees (1985) showed that literary critics base their judgement of poetry not only on the poems themselves, but also on the judgements of other, influential critics. In selecting poems for anthologies that have a survey character according to type and quality, contextual factors also play an important role. I shall illustrate this on the basis of the poems by Herman van den Bergh selected by anthologists over the years. A research group at the University of Amsterdam in 1994 found that while the number of poems by Marsman, Nijhoff and Van Ostaijen remains unchanged or increases in later anthologies (i.e. from the 1970s), the number of poems by Van den Bergh decreases a little. This decrease is remarkable, because Van den Bergh — who died in 1967 — published five volumes of poetry after World War II and only two during the interbellum period. Also, we found that of the twenty-three poems by Van den Bergh selected for anthologies, ten were from the volume *The Arch* — which contains twenty-three poems — and six were from *The Mirror*, which contains seventeen. In other words, sixteen of the twenty-three selected poems (approximately 70%) are from the first two volumes of poetry. Therefore, most of the selected poems are from Van den Bergh's so-called expressionist period.

How can one account for this selection? Van den Berg's post-war poetry could have been of lesser quality. Some anthologists who claim to have made a selection on the basis of quality suggest this, but no-one can prove it. The generally respected anthologist Paul Rodenko is one of the few anthologists who did select Van den Bergh's post-war poems, for *Poets of this Time* (1964).

It could also be due to the so-called plagiarism affair. Van den Bergh had presented poems he had translated as poems of his own, and in the 1960s this led to a stream of articles accusing him of plagiarism. These articles could have had a negative effect on anthologists. However, no correlation can be found between the moment Van den Bergh's plagiarism became known and the selection of his poems in anthologies.

It seems quite likely that a proposition put forward by the empirical sociologist H. Verdaasdonk (1985) applies to our problem. Verdaasdonk examined the relation between classification according to type and that according to quality, and proposed the thesis that texts which can be fitted into a literary movement or literary genre are more highly regarded than those for which this is not possible. He founded this thesis on the basis of the oeuvres of F. Bordewijk and S. Vestdijk, who are labelled as authors from the 'interbellum period'. The result of his statistical research was that both authors are presented in school books especially with fragments from novels and short stories from the interbellum period, although Bordewijk and Vestdijk published more novels and short stories after World War II than before it. This also applies to Van den Bergh: anthologists turned out to be interested especially in those poems he published in the interbellum period and which were labelled 'expressionistic'.

4. Reputations of anthologies and anthologists

According to the Flemish academic Conderaerts (1985, p. 392v), anthologies that have a survey character matter greatly when it comes to the formation of the literary canon. Conderaerts even supposes that an author "who is not selected (anymore) for an anthology, will not live on". This could explain the fierce character of the discussions about anthologies. To a large extent, it is this fierceness which makes the reputation of an anthology. The question is whether an anthology can draw the attention of other institutions, i.e. the attention of their authorised representatives. The academic Mosheuvel (1970, p. 77) argues that the reason *Prism* still receives a lot of attention even though it was printed only once, is connected with the fact that Menno ter Braak — one of the most important Dutch critics ever — reacted to it in a fierce way and expounded his conception of literature on the basis of just this one anthology. Thus, the judgement of *Prism* by academics and literary historians has been greatly influenced by the authority of the journalist Ter Braak.

Anthologies compiled by authoritative literary authors and critics (e.g. Dirk Coster, Paul Rodenko and Gerrit Komrij) seem to have a good chance of acquiring a reputation, especially if they contain an informative and/or provocative preface. The Dutch critic M. Nijhoff (1982, p. 192), for example, considered Coster's introduction to his anthology *New Sounds* to be important, because it included a history of poetry and an animated argument, which encourages awareness and judgement. If authoritative critics have given their opinion on an anthology that has a survey character and literary historians have calibrated the anthology, its reputation will have been more or less established.

Conclusion

I argued that anthologies that have a survey character also have an institutional character. Just like literary critics and other representatives of literary institutions, anthologists defend the conception of literature on which they base their selection. Dirk Coster defended a humanistic conception of literature, and Binnendijk referred to a formal criterion. A selection always takes place with strategic intentions: an anthologist tries to create a distinct profile for himself. By choosing other poems by the expressionist Van den Bergh than the ones his colleagues chose and presenting them as representative, and by changing the number of chosen poems by Marsman, Van den Bergh and Van Ostaijen, Binnendijk distinguished himself from Coster, Rodenko distinguished himself from Binnendijk, and so on.

But not only individual interests play a role: contextual factors also play an important role in the selection of poems. Poems that earlier were labelled 'expressionistic' have a greater chance of being selected for an anthology than poems that were published later and do not have such a label.

The questions I posed are quite different from those raised by Peter Bürger in *Theorie der Avantgarde*. I was not looking for essential characteristics of the historical avant-garde; I am interested in the way literary institutions transfer the historical avant-garde into our times, for example, by way of anthologies.

Bibliography

Berge, H.C. ten

1978 "Notities bij een bloemlezing". In *Raster*, no. 7, 151-156.

Bordewijk, F.

1991 "Amsterdam die grote stad… A. den Besten, *Stroomgebied*". In: *Verzameld werk*, deel 13, Amsterdam, 223-227.

Braak, Menno ter

Undated "Prisma of Dogma?" In: *Verzameld Werk*, dl. 1: 348-355.

1978 "Een tijdgenoot onder tijdgenoten. I en II". In *De Propria Cures*-artikelen, 's-Gravenhage, 151-155; 320-324.

Conderaerts, E.

1984 "Ik zie de lezer niet: de poëziebloemlezingen tussen 1970 en 1979". In: *Ons Erfdeel*, vol. 28, no. 3, 387-397.

Coster, Dirk

1970 *Nieuwe Geluiden. Een keuze uit de Nederlandse poëzie tussen de beide wereldoorlogen.* 6e dr. In *Verzamelde werken.* Leiden. Tekstverzorging Piet Oomes.

Dorleijn, Gillis J.

1996 "'Daargins kent men u door Coster!' Paul van Ostaijen in het Nederlandse literaire veld". In: P. Peeters / E. Spinoy (eds.), *Het vouwbeen van de lezer. Over literatuuropvattingen.* Leuven, 51-70.

Jager, Gert de
1992 *Argumenten voor canonisering. De Vijftigers in de dag- en weekbladkritiek 1949-1959.* Dissertatie Rijksuniversiteit Utrecht.

Kuitert, Lisa
1993 "De bloemen van Bohn. Doel en samenstelling van een negentiende-eeuwse bloemlezing". In: *Haarlemse kringen. Vijftien verkenningen naar het literair-culturele leven in een negentiende-eeuwse stad.* Onder red. van W. van den Berg et al. (eds), Hilversum, 77-92.

Marja, A.
1963 "Koos Den Besten De Besten?" In: *Poëzieproeve*, 88-95.

Mosheuvel, L.
1970 "Over de historische context van *Prisma*". In: *Studia Neerlandica*, nr. 3, 77-94.

Nijhoff, Martinus
1982 "Nieuwe Geluiden". In: *Verzameld Werk II. Kritisch en verhalend proza.* Amsterdam, 191-201.

Offermans, Cyrille
1994 "1978: Sybren Polet geeft de bloemlezing *Ander Proza* uit". In: *Nederlandse literatuur, een geschiedenis.* Hoofdred. M.A. Schenkeveld-Van der Dussen. Groningen, 829-834.

Oversteegen, J.J.
1969 "Schisma: de Prisma-polemiek". In: *Vorm of vent. Opvattingen over de aard van het literaire werk in de Nederlandse kritiek tussen de twee wereldoorlogen.* Amsterdam, 261-284.

Perron, E. du
1955 "Dirk Costers Nieuwe Geluiden". In: Verzameld Werk II. Cahiers van een lezer. De smalle mens. Amsterdam, 12-18.

Rees, Cees van
1984 "Consensusvorming in de literatuurkritiek". In *De regels van de smaak.* Robert Anker et al., Amsterdam, 59-85.

Rees, C.J. van / G.J. Dorleijn
1992 "Literatuuropvattingen in het literaire veld: over de integratie van twee benaderingen". In: *Spektator*, vol. 23, 91-114.

Verdaasdonk, H.
1984 "Literatuursociologie". In: R.T. Segers (ed.), *Vormen van literatuurwetenschap. Moderne richtingen en hun mogelijkheden voor tekstinterpretatie*. Groningen, 115-136.

Vestdijk, Simon
1960 *Voor en na de explosie. Opstellen over poëzie*. Den Haag.

Vliet, Eddy van
1989 "Bloemlezingen". In: Literatuur in Nederland en Vlaanderen. Samengesteld door Marcel Janssens et al. Speciaal nr. van *Dietsche Warande en Belfort*: 134, nr. 6, 774-777.

Zuiderent, Ad
1990 "Wat bedoelt de bloemlezer?" In: *Voortgang, Jaarboek voor de Neerlandistiek*, no. 11, 23-40.

1993 "Bloemlezen en bakens verzetten". In: *Nederlandse literatuur, een geschiedenis*. M. A. Schenkeveld-Van der Dussen et al. (eds), 841-846.

Tables

Table 1: Expressionists in anthologies that have a survey character

Volume of expressionists	*Anthology*	*Poet / anthologist*
1916 *Music-Hall*		Paul van Ostaijen
1917 *De boog*		Herman van den Bergh
1918 *Het Sienjaal*		Paul van Ostaijen
1921 *Bezette Stad*		Paul van Ostaijen
1923 *Verzen*		H. Marsman
1924	*Nieuwe geluiden* (1st impr.)	Dirk Coster
1925 *De spiegel*		Herman van den Bergh
1925	*Nieuwe geluiden* (2nd impr.)	Dirk Coster
1927	*Nieuwe geluiden* (3rd impr.)	Dirk Coster
1927 *Paradise regained*		H. Marsman
1930	*Prisma*	D.A.M. Binnendijk
1932	*Nieuwe geluiden* (4th impr.)	Dirk Coster

Table 2: Poems by Van den Bergh, Marsman and Van Ostaijen in Coster and in Binnendijk

	Coster 1924	*Coster 1925*	*Coster 1927*	*Binnendijk 1930*
H. van den Berg	3	3	3	3
H. Marsmann	2	8	10	6
P. van Ostaijen	3	2	3	4
Average number	3.4	3.9	3.8	2.4

Table 3: H. van den Bergh in anthologies of Coster and of Binnendijk in the interbellum period

Poem	*Volume*	*C. 1924*	*C. 1925*	*C. 1927*	*B. 1930*
Sabbat	*The Arch* (1917)	+	+	+	
En sourdine	*The Arch* (1917)	+			
Nocturne	*The Arch* (1917)	+	+	+	
Het dorp	*The Mirror* (1925)		+	+	
Vialayre	*The Mirror* (1925)				+
Achter de stilte	*The Mirror* (1925)				+
De blinde karner	*The Mirror* (1925)				+

Table 4: H. van den Bergh, H. Marsman and P. van Ostaijen in *Poets of this Time*

Anthologist	*Year*	*Impr.*	*H.v.d. Bergh*	*H. Marsman*	P. v. Ostaijen
J. Greshoff	1939	13	2	5	2
D. Binnendijk	1941	14	3	14	2
D. Binnendijk	1948	16	3	14	2
D. Binnendijk	1949	17	4	14	2
D. Binnendijk	1954	19	4	14	2
P. Rodenko	1960	20	4	10	6
P. Rodenko	1964	21	4	9	6

Table 5: H. van den Bergh in Poets of this Time

Poem	*Volume*	*Greshoff*	*Binnendijk*	***Binnendijk***	*Rodenko*
		1939	1941 / 48	1949 / 54	1960 / 64
Bergland	*The Mirror*	+			
De kleine tuin	*The Arch*	+			
Tegen de avond	*The Arch*		+	+	
Nocturne	*The Arch*		+	+	
Achter de stilte	*The Arch*		+	+	
De blinde karner	*The Arch*			+	
Faustus	*The Arch*				+
Mare d'Afrika	*The Scar of Odysseus*				+
Een jonge Griek zong	*On Good Terms*				+
Hotel Het Ruime Sop	*On Good Terms*				+

Table 6: H. van den Bergh in Coster, in Komrij and in Warren

Poems		*Coster '24*	*Coster '25*	*Komrij '79*	*Warren '79*
Sabbat	(*The Arch*)	+	+	+	
En sourdine	(*The Arch*)	+			+
Nocturne	(*The Arch*)	+	+	+	
Bergland	(*The Mirror*)		+		+

Table 7: H. van den Bergh, H. Marsman and P. van Ostaijen in 1st editions of anthologies

	Coster 1924	Binnendijk 1930	Warren 1979	Komrij 1979
H.v.d. Bergh	3	3	3	2
H. Marsman	2	6	10	10
P. v. Ostaijen	3	4	10	10

AVANT-GARDE PRODUCTIONS AND PSYCHOANALYTIC THEORY. THE STORY OF AN ENCOUNTER.[1]

KATHARINE SWARBRICK

Interpreters of Peter Bürger's *Theory of the Avant-Garde* see the focus of its impact as determined by the specific, critical perspective the author gives on the historical development of artistic practice. Jochen Schulte-Sasse, in his forward to the 1984 edition of Bürger's book, argues that Bürger shows with particular clarity the way in which the production of works of art is conditioned at every stage of their historical evolution by the institutionalised framework which art itself generates. For Bürger, what allows the art historian and critic to perceive art in this way, is an avant-garde praxis which throws institutionalised art forms into relief by attacking them directly (1984: xxxiv-xxxix).

In order to emphasise this oppositional perspective between the institution and the avant-garde, Bürger seeks to give a definitive presentation of the former in terms of its closure. The self-reflexive ideology of the increasingly autonomous institution of bourgeois art is posited as the monument against which the avant-garde artist operates his or her assault. Correspondingly, the artist must act from a position which remains unambiguously external to the ideology of the institution; and thus for Bürger the closure of art must be challenged by life itself, whose various manifestations are associated with the subject's engagement with the material world, direct social practice and intervention, or the experience of the senses. In artistic terms the fragmentation of the closure of the work of art is presented as being achieved through techniques of *collage* and *montage*; and through analyses of the function of the fragment, the focus of avant-garde effort is encapsulated in the formulaic notion of the reintegration of art into life (1984: 73-82). The effect of Bürger's argument tends to fix the concepts art and life in a binary whose oppositional concision, while illuminating the emergence of avant-garde praxis for some commentators, has acquired, in the opinion of others, the status of an unchallenged given which needs itself to be analysed.

The art-life opposition postulated by Bürger enters intriguing debates as the interpretation of artistic practise engages with surrounding theories from the disciplines of linguistics and psychoanalysis. In structuralist and post-structuralist contexts there emerges the theoretical difficulty of maintaining positions external to a web of discourses which sweep up life as well as art, and preclude a locus for experience outside their mediation.[2] On the other hand, psychoanalysis, that is to say theories which work with the concept of the unconscious as developed by Freud, postulates new subjective positions from which closed ideological systems, whether conceptualised or lived out, can be challenged. In fact psychoanalysis goes much further if we consider the overall implications of the discovery of unconscious subjectivity as precluding the possibility of closed systems of thought and ideological practice because these systems, subtended by unconscious operations, break down at the precise moment they are brought into an encounter with the effects of the Freudian unconscious. Thus when Freud approaches the question of aesthetics in the gothic tales of E.T.A.Hoffman for example, he reads its motivation as arising not from the autonomous developments of literary practice but from a gaping hole at its centre where castration anxiety pierces (1955a: 217-52). When his successor, French psychoanalyst, Jacques Lacan, presents his analysis of painting, he posits its perspectival laws as oriented around a vanishing point signalling the invisible force of unconscious structures, which demarcate the limits of the possibility of representation (1977: 79-119).

Psychoanalytic theory thus from its own perspective supports the views of critics who do not endorse the concept of the closure of aesthetic practice. For psychoanalysis, artistic and unconscious material are profoundly bound up with each other. Likewise

Freudian theory can make significant contributions to theories concerning the relation between avant-garde practice and the idea of life in its opposition to art, by offering the possibility of a profound re-evaluation of the distinction between art and life, which is itself necessitated by Freud's problematization of the distinction between life and death which subtends it.[3] The contribution to ways of understanding avant-garde theory and practice which follows, takes as its starting point, a recontextualisation of the historical avant-garde within a framework of ideas where, due to the Freudian revolution, major challenges to apparently self-evident distinctions between art and life, life and death, are already underway.

The language in which the historical avant-garde talks about its practice and aims is solidly interwoven with psychoanalytic theory from the outset. This link is expressed and consolidated by the significance attributed to Freudian theory by Andre Breton in his prose writing on the nature of surrealism. Although historical accounts of the exchanges between Breton and Freud characterize these communications as a celebrated *dialogue de sourds*, Breton nevertheless demonstrates a core of intuition concerning the relevance of psychoanalysis for avant-garde production which has had enduring impact. The psychoanalytic canon acknowledges this in the clinically oriented publication, *L'Apport Freudian. Eléments pour une encyclopédie de la psychanalyse*. Here in a contribution entitled "Psychanalyse et peinture", Andoche Praudel (1993: 560) focuses his discussion on Duchamp, Max Ernst and Dali, as artists who exemplify the avant-garde's understanding of the Freudian revolution through productions which formally evoke the radical cut, *coupure*, inaugurated by Freud, between the conscious and unconscious operations of the mind. Praudel focuses his analysis on the artists' exploration of mental states propitiating the instantaneous, dream-like emergence of images, linked in irrational, delirious associations. In other words, he restates the well-known analogy between avant-garde painting and the operations of what Freud, through his analysis of dream life, will chart as the primary processes of the unconscious.[4]

In the writings of Breton, the indications that he, too, is exploring the potential of the primary processes are present in his attention to the oneiric spontaneity of automatic writing, and, more significantly for the discussion which follows, in his early experiments with *le hasard objectif*. The significance of chance and associated concepts such as the *rencontre capitale*, *le trouvaille* and *le trouble* form part of a detailed study of Breton's work in *Profane illumination* by Margaret Cohen (1993: 120-216). Chapter Five of Cohen's book focuses on two texts from Breton's Parisian Prose Trilogy, *Les Vases communicants* (1981) and *L'Amour fou* (1982), where, she argues, Breton seeks to articulate psychoanalysis and Marxism. What follows is essentially a summary of aspects of Cohen's discussion, to which I am indebted, of Breton's exploration of these issues. In an attempt to problematize the interaction between the material world and the world of the psyche, Breton presents not merely the determination of subjectivity by material forces, but a complex encounter in which the forces of the objective world make a mark of a particular resonance on the psyche. This encounter, variously described as the *rencontre*, *le trouvaille*, *le hasard objectif*, and *le trouble*, has an effect related to the wish and retains an erotic potential which characterizes it as a happy occurrence which offers glimpses of utopian revolution (Cohen 1993: 151). It is likewise a privileged moment in its capacity to bring to light a hidden dimension which lies beyond habitual perception, beyond reality as it is accepted in everyday consensus. Conversely, in a complexification of the notions of outside and inside, the surrealist project presents this encounter as a moment at which unconscious forces which themselves remain invisible, unleash traces on the visible world. As an artistic representation of the impact of these forces, surrealist art thus works with tactile, indexical, anfractuous substance on which traces, whose cause is invisible, imprint themselves (Cohen 1993: 133).

Moving away now from Cohen's discussion, I would like to suggest that Breton's evocation of a reiterated, compulsive quest for an object both real, and beyond reality, both external to the subject and yet integral to intense expressions of subjectivity, presents analogies with a Freudian concept more specific than that of the primary processes — the structure of the drive. In its inception the concept of the drive is associated with the organic functioning of the body; with the manner in which the living organism requires to interact with the material world to satiate its needs and to keep psychic and somatic amounts of tension reduced tolerable levels of constancy. However by 1920, Freud's observation that the repetitive tendency of the drive in numerous cases, returns the subject to incidences of intolerable unpleasure leads him to postulate the existence of the death drive — a vicissitude of the drive which takes the subject beyond the pleasure principle. In a compulsive return to traumatic occurrences and the excessive levels of tension which accompany them, Freud's subject demonstrates its inveterate capacity for self-destruction. From the introduction of the concept of the death drive Freudian theory suggests both an opposition between the life drives which support self-preservation, and the death drives, and the idea that the death drive actually epitomizes the repetitive function of the drives generally .

If Freud's observation of trauma plays a crucial role in his charting of the death wish, the impact of trauma is highly significant in Breton's presentation of the surrealist encounter whose effects are similar to the traumatic breaching of the defences of consciousness described by Freud (1963: 275). Breton's surrealist dreams strongly suggest that avant-garde art like psychoanalytic science, at a certain historical inter-war moment, involves itself explicitly with an emerging theory of human mentality centred on the notion of the death drive.

The elaboration of the death drive is taken further by Jacques Lacan, a figure who consolidates the links between the avant-garde and psychoanalysis at many levels. The extent to which surrealism influences Lacan's work, and the personal interest of Lacan in artists and productions of the avant-garde, is well documented.[5] Later, Lacan comes to figure prominently in critical analyses of the work of the neo-avant-garde, suggesting that if it is possible to find a definition of the avant-garde which can demonstrate its continuity beyond the historical moment which gives it it's definition in the theory of Peter Bürger, then Lacan's development of Freudian theory may provide the means to do it.

In his 1964 seminar, *The Four Fundamental Concepts of Psychoanalysis*, Lacan, presenting the drive as one of the major concepts of psychoanalytic theory, demonstrates that from the outset the very structure of the Freudian drive renders problematic it's association with a self-preservative instinct or an adaptive role in the relation of the subject to its environment. Lacan proceeds by emphasising the disjunction proposed by Freud between four components of the drive — its source, pressure, aim and object. The source of the drive arises in the erogenous zones of the body, but these areas are specifically differentiated from the surface of the body in that they are structured around a cut or a rim or a hole whose erogenous function goes beyond its biological role; the pressure of the drive is constant and thus impossible to satisfy; the aim of the drive follows a trajectory which turns repeatedly around its object and returns to its source in an autoerotic curve; while the drive object itself is radically contingent in relation to its source (Lacan 1977: 163-184).

Crucial to Lacan's presentation is his emphasis of the drive not as libidinal energy, but as a chain of signifiers, each related to the others in a manner which makes it impossible for them to break their self-referential circuit and grasp the object which is their target. Hence the movement of the drive is fated to turn around a void demarcating the impossibility of the object in relation to the reach of the drive signifier. This reformulation of the drive as signifying material turning around a voided centre radically distances the drive's association with the maintenance of biological life, as Lacan's analysis replots the sexual drives to place them, in general terms, under the aegis of the death drive. And if one were required to visualise this radical heterogeneity of signifying elements, whose disjunction emphasises the inscription of a cut into corporeal substance, and whose dynamism enacts the movement of a tear which repeatedly detaches the object from the erogenous zones of the body surface, then one could do no better than to conjure up the image of a surrealist *montage.* As Lacan remarks in *The Four Fundamental Concepts of Psychoanalysis*, "Let me say that if there is anything resembling a drive it is a montage" (1977: 169).

It is useful elaborate further the way in which the lost object, to which Lacan will give the name object (a), is presented in Lacanian theory in order to explore the explicit link Lacan makes retrospectively between the artistic work of the avant-garde and the perspectives opened by the structural relations between the Lacanian drive and the object (a). From a corporeal perspective, the object is tied to the erogenous zone of the body which seeks to enjoy it. The breast and faeces exemplify the object (a) as body part, while it's structural relation to the erogenous cut or hole underlines it's destiny with regard to the body, as a detachable object. This notion of detachability determines those forms of the object which relate it to what is thrown away — rubbish, excrement, the urinary flow —

whilst the idea that the object falls, epitomizes its status as a lost object whose disappearance permanently compromises the unity of the body. Thus the invisibility of the voice and the gaze come to represent the object as well as the notion of the nothing — the void or hole around which the drive structure turns endlessly.[6]

Structurally, this lost, invisible body part forms a residue which is expelled from visual and symbolic systems of representation and associates itself with an ineffable third dimension which Lacan terms the *Real*.[7] It is, however, important to understand the object (a) in its function as constructive support of the symbolic systems to which it is lost: its disappearance triggers the operations of meaning which seek endlessly to recapture it. Expelled, but ensconced as the target of the drive, it constitutes the ultimate longing of subjective desire — the being of the unconscious subject.[8] In this role, as cause of subjective desire, the object (a) brings the unconscious subject into (lost) being; while as the most intimate and the most excluded point of the psychical structure, it encapsulates the paradox of an excluded inside, or of an internal object that returns from the outside. But as a body part which can no longer be lodged within the body as a signifying construction, the object (a) is assimilated with death. Its recuperation would entail the disintegration of the body and the signifying operations which give rise to meaning.

Cohen has explored in detail the way in which the Lacanian *Real* as an alterior dimension, a threshold which haunts the field of perception and meaning as its limit and the possibility of its collapse, is Lacan's rigorous, intrapsychic formalisation of an encounter in which material and psychical forces meet and merge. She describes how Breton, in the impact he ascribes to the *rencontre*, renders with intuitive prescience, an analogous encounter in the field of surrealist experiment (Cohen 1993: 153). The significant point to note in the context of rereading Bürger's account of the relation between the avant-garde project and life, is that the *rencontre* is not of the order of life or experience, the arena of its attempt being intrapsychic; it is an evocation of the immanence of the object (a) as residue of the *Real*. But this *Real* is far from reality, and far from life in the sense of its distinction of its distinction from art. One might say that surrealism, viewed through the optic of psychoanalysis, attempts a reintegration of art, not into life but into death.

It is interesting to look more closely at the relation of the object (a) to the signifying material which evokes it in order to demonstrate the explanatory force it can have when it comes to analysing the privileged forms which feature repeatedly in avant-garde productions. The drive structure foregrounds above all, the anfractuous dynamism of the signifier, the face of the signifier turned towards the *Real*; it presents a radical heterogeneity of elements, the disjunction between which emphasises the inscription of the cut into corporeal substance, or the movement of a tear detaching some part of the image which features thereafter as an absent presence in the picture. It focuses attention on the explicit or implicit dominance of the erogenous body in the work of the historical avant-garde: the body as a textured mobile made up differentiated, erotogenic zones whose heterogeneous surfaces display in a privileged manner, the point at which signifying material meets cuts into the flesh. This presentation of the body is particularly foregrounded by the cubists, epitomized by Braque, for example, in a *papier collé* such as *Woman with a guitar* (1913 or 14), where the image is fractured around an emphatic, primary, diagonal cut. The shifting distance between surfaces evokes the libidinal movement of a tear, the emergence of a line which marks the disappearance of the object. The telescoping of planes which can be emphasised through this technique of fragmentation demonstrates how the foregrounding of the erotogenic cut achieves an evocation of the object (a), in a juxtaposition of nearness and distance which conveys the inaccessible proximity of its location in terms of the subject. Hannah Höch's *Dadandy* (1920) could be cited as an rich illustration of this technique.

The methods of *collage* and *papier collé* in themselves emphasise the idea of an incorporation into the image of extraneous pieces of matter which again evoke the object (a) and underline particularly the detachable potential of the incorporated bits. The presentation of the ready-made can be envisaged in its entirety as an incorporation of the extraneous object in the framework of art. In the case of Duchamp, the ready-made object, beneath the apparent randomness of its selection, suggests in an overdetermined manner varied ways of evoking the relation between the signifying body and the object (a). Hence the *Fountain* (1917) or *Bicycle wheel* (1913) present as their most salient features the structure of the rim or edge — the defining feature of the erogenous zone — skirting the contours of an occluded centre. The *Bottle Dryer* (1914) displays its rib-cage series of rims around the cylindrical lining of a central hole — a nothing which marks the place of the object (a). And Duchamp's frequent foregrounding of a body part emphasised as detachable from the rest of the body is explicit in a work such as "With my tongue in my cheek", or alluded to in the ready-made *In advance of a broken arm* (1915).[9]

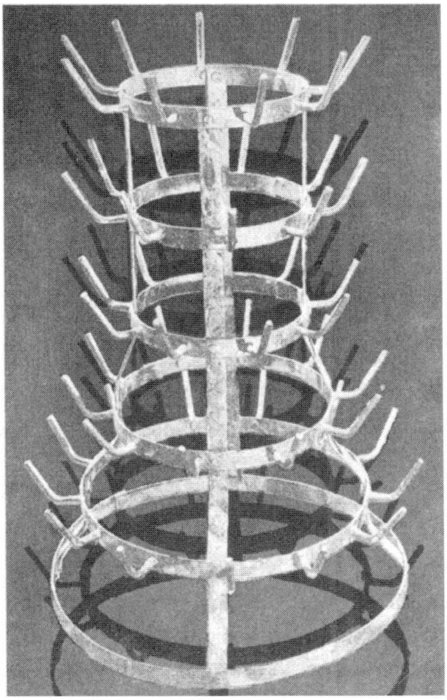

18 Marcel Duchamp: *Bottle Dryer*. 1914

From this perspective a strong continuity between the historical avant-garde and the neo-avant-garde can be envisaged by demonstrating the ways in which neo-avant-garde work orients its images around an object homologous to the Lacanian object (a). Scraps waste, refuse and rubbish, excrement and urine feature in much neo-avant-garde production; seriality of objects in Minimalist contributions conveys the endless, self-replicating resurgence of the object in response to the constant pressure of the drive; and a problematic representation of outside and inside visualises the challenge of intimating in signifying material, the excluded inside — the object as *extime*. For example, Frank Stella's *Darabjerd I* (1967), presenting a spherical shape sliced by a central fissure, suggests a cutting movement in which the enclosed centre of the sphere falls away as an outside edge.

Lacanian theory, notably Lacan's increasingly explicit theorisation in the fifties and sixties of the dimension of the *Real* to which the object is related, begins to have considerable impact around that time, and is taken up explicitly in critical appraisals of the neo-avant-garde. The significance of Lacan's work to certain studies of neo-avant-garde productions, can be exemplified by citing Hal Foster who traces the development of artist Cindy Sherman with concrete reference to the Lacanian diagram of visuality as it appears in the *Four Fundamental Concepts of Psychoanalysis* (1977, 106). Foster describes the subject of Sherman's work as, "caught in the gaze [...] invaded by the gaze [...] obliterated by the gaze" as it "moves across the three main positions of the Lacanian diagram" (1996, 149).

The broader implications of the interpretations above radically distance the avant-garde from ideas which have defined it as the negation of institutionalised aesthetic principles, or the reintegration of art into life. Instead it becomes a way of envisaging art in which potential artistic material explodes into ubiquitous possibilities under the impact of a vision which sees the purpose of artistic practice as the production of multi-perspectival configurations which evoke the qualities of a dimension beyond the representational possibilities of art; a dimension associated with death. Lacan's perspective on the significance of artistic practice, if we consider for example his well-known analysis of Holbein's *Ambassadors* (1977, 88-89) suggests this orientation of artistic practice as a universal possibility whose potential exists from the beginnings of artistic practice. But a Lacanian interpretation of the distance between earlier forms of art and avant-garde innovation would suggest that in the case of the former, however different the structural technique employed to achieve it, the intimation of the object (a) is circumscribed in terms of its subversive function; it remains veiled behind or within recognisable, representational forms. From the advent of cubism, however, with its specific emphasis on fragmentation and *coupure*, a post-Freudian climate contributes to the emergence of unveiled analogies between art and the death drives, and from cubism onward as far as the neo-avant-garde, these analogies become more and more obvious.

Art criticism has interpreted the distinctions between avant-garde movements from cubism onwards in various ways. For Bürger, the differences between cubism and the historical avant-garde as he defines it are radical, and serve to separate the latter from what immediately precedes it. In the *montage* canvasses of Picasso, Bürger argues, "the reality fragments remain largely subordinate to aesthetic composition" whereas the photo montages of Heartfield are "not primarily aesthetic objects" (1984: 74-75). The individual parts of the avant-garde work, for Bürger, "`emancipate' themselves from a superordinate whole" (1984: 80) . When we reach the neo-avant-garde, the encroachment of the *Real* is expressed in images which are often explicitly deaestheticised. My question is this: does this working between the psychoanalytic drive structure and the avant-garde production have anything to say about precisely this sort of distinction?

For Freudo-lacanian theory the operation of aestheticisation, which psychoanalysis call sublimation, is linked to the vissicitudes of the drives in terms of their relation to the object. Here the object can be repressed, sublimated or put into play in such a way that the trajectory of the drive refinds it, and hits its target (Lacan 1977: 182-84). In this last instance we might say that the object is simply left as it is. The idea of leaving the object as it is has its analogy in avant-garde criticism when it comments on the impact of the ready-made or the photomontage and emphasises the avant-garde technique of essentially desublimating the painting by the insertion of fragments of reality which have not been worked over aesthetically. For the neo-avant-garde the nature of the object is highlighted as traumatic, toxic, increasingly and unbearably disruptive of the image.[10]

The pattern which emerges from the observations above suggests that from the development of avant-garde art from cubism demonstrates its ongoing resistance to endemic effects of desensitization whose outcome would be to neutralise the subversive potential of artistic expressions of the death drive. Once put into play in the field of art, the object (a) is obliged to challenge the possibility of its reintegration as a loss into the signifying material which evokes it. In doing so it increasingly presents its most irrecuperable and inert aspect — its identity with death. Neo-avant-garde productions are characterized by this identity of the object in a particularly striking way.

Such an argument dovetails with debates that present neo-avant-garde art as a reflection of conflicts which develop at the level of a culture and society caught up in the rents and tears occasioned by the failure of more traditional symbolic networks and the invasion of technological progress into the most intimate areas of life. These conflicts turn incurably around a traumatic core into which the *Real* floods (Hal Foster 1996: 218-26). In the context of such debates, the neo-avant-garde acquires a symptomatic status which condemns it to "apocalyptic" (Hal Foster 1996: 25) expressions of subjective impasses which are impossible to resolve. However, there remains a more positive, more proactive interpretation of the neo-avant-garde's determination to keep the radically disturbing quality of the *Real* in the picture. Inasmuch as the *Real* is beyond designation, and emerges in representational systems as a lack, it presents insurmountable inconsistencies which subvert the field of ideological closure by pointing to a limit at which knowledge stops and certainty ends. The encroachment of science and technology, the mythical power of the new medias, from photography onward, to vivisect reality to the extent that everything can be shown, are challenged by the structural limit suggested by the Lacanian *Real*. The evident political extension to this argument involves the situation of the object (a) in a location beyond pleasure which renders it impossible to exchange, quantify or commodify; the recognition of its nature marks a frontier at which the means-end rationality of bourgeois capitalism, comes to a halt. So, one could argue, it is precisely the production of effects of the Lacanian object (a) in the work of the historical avant-garde and what succeeds it, that gives the movement its cutting edge when it comes to unmasking the ideological myths surrounding the autonomous origin and production of the "work of art", and, by extension, gives it its power to undermine the closure of the institution in general. For the object focuses the effect of unconscious operations which underlie the production of all meaning, and thus subvert the fictional power of ideological discourse to present a fully conscious and complete mastery of its own self-evident myths. These operations testify to an unconscious subjectivity which comes into being as the espousal of a loss whose disappearance is nothing other than the breach in the closed sphere of the discourse of domination.

In conclusion, like the work of many critics who have argued against Peter Bürger's negative appraisal of the lasting subversive impact of the avant-garde, this contribution allows us to reconsider the view that the avant-garde failed in its attack on the institution and that the neo-avant-garde is condemned to repeat this failure indefinitely. Psychoanalytic theory has proved useful in various ways to debates which reinterpret positively the continuing achievement of avant-garde productions. What it is important above all to highlight, are structural relations between the two fields which emphasise the infinite potential of avant-garde practice to subvert institutionalised ideologies, in as far as it can encompass and express within this practice a recognition of the nature of the object (a).[11] Our understanding of the success of the avant-garde likewise depends on a recognition of the manner in which avant-garde practice, at this level, is engaged, in ways analogous to psychoanalytic theory in a profound re-evaluation of the interaction between life and death for speaking subjects. The activities of avant-garde artists in the field of art depend for their impact on the privileged locus their productions give the unconscious acknowledgement of death as both limit and source of signifying possibilities.

Notes

[1] This contribution was first given as a seminar paper at the annual meeting of the American Comparative Literature Association, Yale University, in February 2000. I wish to acknowledge the generous support of the University of Edinburgh Development Trust whose Small Project Grant Scheme enabled me to attend this event.

[2] See Schulte-Sasse for a detailed discussion of this issue in Theory of the Avant-Garde, xxix-xxxii.

[3] The developing discussion on the problematization of life and death in psychoanalysis refers at all stages to Freud's contribution of 1920, "Be-

yond the Pleasure principle" in which he introduces the concept of the death drive. For Freud's discussion of the drives in general see the 1915 text ,"Instincts and their Vicissitudes". I wish to draw the readers' attention to the fact that the Strachey translation of the *Complete Psychological Works* renders the Freudian term "trieb" by the term "instinct". Lacanian interpreters of Freud favour the term "drive".

[4] For Freud's discussion of the dream-life of the unconscious, as well as the broad distinctions he lays out between the conscious and unconscious the reader is recommended to consult in particular *The Interpretation of Dreams* and "The Ego and the Id".

[5] See, for example, David Macey, *Lacan in contexts.*

[6] The Lacanian concept of the object (a) evolves gradually over many of Lacan's seminars, taking early shape in *Le Séminaire IV* of 1956, and its final form in *Le Séminaire X* of 1962. Lacan gives a succinct account of its nature and function in *The Four Fundamental Concepts of Psychoanalysis*, 179-181, and a full list of the forms of the object (a) in the *Ecrits*, 817.

[7] The elaboration of the order of the *Real*, associated with the evolution of the object (a), exists in its embryonic state as early as 1953. Here Lacan introduces three interrelated psychical dimensions, *Imaginary*, *Symbolic* and *Real*, in a lecture to the *Société Française de Psychanalyse*. The *Real* figures initially as an enigmatic register which escapes the other dimensions in that it can be neither named nor visualised. The full conceptualisation of the *Real* will not emerge until *Lacan's Séminaire XXII* of 1975.

[8] See *The Four Fundamental Concepts of Psychoanalysis*, 195, where Lacan, elaborating the relation of the subject to the oral object of the breast makes the following statement: "Thus we see clearly enough, at this level, the nature of the subject's claim to something that is separated from him, but belongs to him and which he needs to complete himself". For a much fuller analysis of the struuctural relations between subject and object see Lacan's text, "Subversion du sujet et dialectique du désir" in the *Ecrits*, 793-827.

[9] For a detailed psychoanalytic reading of Duchamp's choice of the ready-made, which takes biographical material and the personal evolution of the artist into consideration see, Lieven Jonckheere's article "Marcel Duchamp and the Lacanian analyst".

[10] I am basing this interpretation of neo-avant-garde work on the presentation by Hal Foster in his book, *The Return of the Real*, and I am making particular reference again to chapter 5, 127-168.

[11] Further to these general statements concerning the value of psychoanalytic criticism for avant-garde productions, it is clear that detailed psychoanalytic theory could also be brought to bear profitably on current debates regarding definitions of what constitutes an avant-garde work, as well as the degree of success achieved by individual productions in terms of the avant-garde project which constitutes their objective.

Bibliography

Breton, André

1981 *Les Vases communicants*. Paris: Gallimard.

1982 *L'Amour fou*. Paris: Gallimard.

Bürger, Peter

1984 *Theory of the Avant-Garde*. Minneapolis: University of Minnesota Press.

Cohen, Margaret

1993 *Profane Illumination. Walter Benjamin and the Paris of Surrealist Revolution*. Berkeley: University of California Press.

Foster, Hal

1996 *The Return of the Real*. Cambridge, Mass.: MIT Press.

Freud, Sigmund

1953-74 *The Standard Edition of the Complete Psychological Works*. London: The Hogarth Press and the Institute of Psychoanalysis.

1953 *The Interpretation of Dreams*. In: Freud, *S.E.* 4 and 5.

1955a "The Uncanny". In: Freud, *S.E.* 17, 217-52.

1955b "Beyond the Pleasure principle". In: Freud, *S.E.* 18, 1-64.

1957 "Instincts and their Vicissitudes". In: Freud, *S.E.* 14, 109-40.

1961 "The ego and the Id". Freud, *S.E.* 19, 1-66.

1963 *Introductory lectures on Psychoanalysis*. *S.E.* 16.

Jonckheere, Lieven

1999 "Marcel Duchamp and the Lacanian Psychoanalyst". From: "'*La Mariée mise à nue par ses célibataires,*

> into the unifying framework of theoretical categories, and is therefore doomed to failure. (Buchloh 1984: 19)

Any detailed engagement with the range of practices that have been designated as part of the historic avant-garde would find such an argument persuasive. It is after all hard to imagine a unifying theory that might subsume the very real differences that existed between, say, surrealism and constructivism, let alone the differences that existed within and between the various factions of the Soviet avant-garde. It might seem strange then that rather than abandoning the job of theorising artistic avant-gardism, Foster sets out to re-theorise avant-gardism by reversing a crucial component of Bürger's argument. Bürger argues that the historical avant-garde (the classic art movements of the 1910s and 1920s — dada, surrealism, constructivism) allowed the institutional condition of art to be recognised *as such* and consequently denounced. He also argues that the neo-avant-garde (neo-dada, pop, conceptualism, etc.), following in the footsteps of this *failed* attempt to destroy or overcome the institutional condition of art, "institutionalises the *avant-garde as art* and thus negates genuinely avant-gardiste intentions" (Bürger 1984: 58). For Foster on the other hand it is the neo-avant-garde (in the guise of Michael Asher, Silvia Kolbowski, Fred Wilson, Hans Haacke, etc.) that provides the most stringent critique of "the old charlatanry of the bohemian artist as well as the new institutionality of the avant-garde" (1996: 11).

I mention Foster's critical response to Bürger's work to make clear how his perspective differs from the one I want to pursue here. Foster's critique is a powerful one and his twin arguments (the refusal of *a* theory of the avant-garde, and the privileging of neo-avant-gardism) although inconsistent, makes for a compelling response to Bürger's work. But the critical moves that Foster make (in relation to Bürger's work) need to be recognised. Firstly, whereas for Bürger the institutional circumstances of bourgeois art are tied to the social function that autonomous art performs, for Foster the idea of the institution of art has become hardened into the literal institutions of art (the museum, the gallery, the journal, etc.). So, whereas for Bürger the institution of art exists as a "complex of modes of conduct (purposeless creation and disinterested pleasure)" (Bürger and Bürger 1992: 6) for Foster it is the "museum above all else" (Foster 1996: 20) that constitutes the institution of art. Secondly (and more importantly for this essay) the investigation of an avant-garde relationship with the "praxis of life" has been dropped. Most of Foster's examples are from gallery artists working specifically both in and against the conditions of museum culture. It would be hard to make any substantial claims that the highly professional practices of the artists privileged by Foster and Buchloh could be seen as overcoming the distinction between art and life so as to forge a new life praxis. This is clearly not their intention.

Life praxis or more simply *everyday life* will be the uneasy conceptual theme of this essay. To insist on the importance of everyday life for both avant-gardism and the investigation of avant-gardism allows for an assessment of both the limitations and productivity of Bürger's thesis. Everyday life is, I want to argue, an ambiguous but central category for the historical avant-garde and one that can be productively viewed through the dialectical theorising of everyday life in the work of Henri Lefebvre. The English phenomenon of Mass-Observation, which can be seen as a form of practical surrealism, will provide a case-study for examining this ambiguity and for exemplifying a theory of avant-gardism in *general*, a theory that will not be restricted by the disciplinary boundaries set by the category *art*.

Bürger's characterisation of the intention of the historic avant-garde is simply "the sublation of art in the praxis of life" (1984: 51). In glossing this Bürger insists that "sublation" should not be understood as the obliteration of art and the victory of life: "art was not to be simply destroyed, but transferred to the praxis of life where it would be preserved, albeit in a changed form" (1984: 49). For Bürger, avant-gardism (or rather "genuine" avant-gardism) would require both the transformation of art in the name of life and the transformation of life (seen as constrained by capitalist forces and bourgeois values) in the name of art. Avant-gardism then is the name that Bürger gives to a certain frustration with the institutional conditions of art combined with the revolutionary desire to transform everyday life. Such a use of the term accords with much earlier associations of *avant-garde* with both political and cultural vanguardism as it emerged in the writing of French utopian socialist Henri de Saint-Simon in the 1830s (Nochlin 1991: 1–18). Within Bürger's terms, Marx's famous declaration that "the philosophers have only *interpreted* the world in various ways; the point, however, is to *change* it" becomes an instance of *exemplary* avant-gardism combining as it does a frustration with the disciplinary conditions of philosophy alongside a call for the transformation of society.

Bürger is, of course, directly connecting with this tradition in his account of the avant-garde. While his explicit project is to develop a sociology of art, the materials he mobilises are all centred on a particular critique of modern society. Drawing on aspects of the work of Herbert Marcuse and Jürgen Habermas, Bürger provides a one-dimensional (an undialectical) account of modern life. For him the modern (Western) everyday is simply life dominated and reducible to instrumental reason: "they [the historic avant-garde] assent to the aestheticists' rejection of the world and its means-ends rationality" (Bürger 1984: 49). Bürger joins the ranks of philosophers and theorists for whom the everyday is singularly and negatively associated with the inauthentic. The importance of this characterisation of everyday life is crucial for Bürger's argument about the (seemingly inevitable) failure of the historical avant-garde. Everyday life as governed by means-ends rationality not only wins-out against the transformatory practices of the avant-garde, it succeeds in making *accomplices* of the avant-garde. Modern life may not evidence the revolutionary transformation of daily life ("a new life praxis from a basis in art" (Bürger 1984: 49)), but what it does evidence is the conservative absorption (recuperation) of avant-gardism in daily life by instrumental reason. Or as Bürger puts it: in the period since the historic avant-garde "the culture industry has brought about the false elimination of the distance between art and life" (Bürger 1984: 50). Coca-Cola and Levi jeans have (falsely) reconnected art and life.

For Bürger the success of avant-gardism is necessarily dependant on an artistic revolution being accompanied by a social revolution. And this social revolution must be accomplished in the name of art. Avant-gardist movements in Europe and the Soviet Union would need to be judged (according to Bürger's criteria) on their success in transforming and aestheticising everyday life. Yet, as Bürger notes, a "revolutionary" transformation of everyday life is a central feature of modern life, but it is a revolution in the name of capitalism and the commodity. What is more, this revolution seems to accomplish a certain aestheticisation of everyday life (the wide availability of designer goods, the growing importance of life-styles, etc.). Advertising might provide the exemplary instance of this process, and Bürger's argument can be heard echoed in the work of Thomas Crow who has noted that the avant-garde has often served as an unwilling (and unknowing) "research and development arm of the culture industry" (Crow 1996: 35). Crow goes on to use the example of surrealism to secure his point:

> [Surrealism] had discovered in the sedimentary layers of an earlier, capitalist Paris something like the material unconscious of the city, the residue of forgotten repressions. But in retrieving marginal forms of consumption, in making the latent text manifest, they provided modern advertising with one of its most powerful visual tools: that now familiar terrain in which commodities behave autonomously and create an alluring dreamscape of their own. (Crow 1996: 36)

As we will see, such a critique of surrealism was also a part of an internal (surrealist) critique and central to the formation of Mass-Observation.

What Bürger recognises (although only in passing) is an aestheticisation of everyday life in the twentieth-century that was to powerfully determine any simple transformatory project on behalf of the everyday. What Bürger misses, and what makes his thesis less than adequate for an account of avant-gardism, is the sense of ambivalence with which the avant-garde figured modern everyday life. Within the various avant-gardist formations everyday life registered a contradiction: it was something to be decried and denounced, yet it was also the possibility of salvation. If everyday life was impoverished and repressive it was also home to practices that escaped both the dominance of instrumental reason and the institution of bourgeois of art. This ambivalence needs to be at the centre of any account of avant-gardism as it allows avant-garde formations to be seen as complex responses to the revolutionary (capitalist) forces at work in the twentieth-century. Because avant-gardism is often neither a celebration nor a condemnation of everyday life, it sits awkwardly in its historical moment. But this awkwardness, this ambivalence, is what gives avant-garde formations their particular historical vividness. It is this ambivalence that Bürger misses in his account of avant-gardism and leads him to treating avant-gardism as, on the one hand, a naïve utopianism and, on the other, as simply a necessary platform for a more critical sociology of art. It could reasonably be argued that Bürger's sociology is actually less concerned with accounting for avant-gardism and more concerned with mapping the bourgeois institution of art (the avant-garde providing the best vantage point for doing so). By paying closer attention to how everyday life was being envisaged by both avant-garde artists and associated philosophers we can get a more vivid sense of the historicity of the avant-garde as the various formations awkwardly negotiate the complex forces of modernity.

Everyday Life and Avant-Gardism

Perhaps the theorist most useful for analysing the modern everyday in relation to avant-gardism is the philosopher Henri Lefebvre. A one-time associate of the surrealist group, Lefebvre provides the dialectical approach necessary for attending to the ambiguities of everyday life. His continued project of orchestrating a "critique of everyday life" emerges in the 1930s (partly out of a response to some of the inadequacies he sees in surrealism) and continues throughout his life. For Lefebvre, daily life evidences a fundamental alienation that characterises capitalist society. Diagnosing new forms of modern capitalism, he asserts that everyday life "has already been literally colonised by capitalism" (Lefebvre 1988: 80): "The commodity, the market, money, with their implacable logic, seize everyday life. The extension of capitalism goes all the way to the slightest details of ordinary life" (Lefebvre 1988: 79).

Writing in 1958 he would quote from *L'Express* the words of their "special" New York correspondent: "Kitchens are becoming less like kitchens and more like works of art" (Lefebvre 1991: 8). But if everyday life evidences an aestheticising colonisation by commodification it is not *reducible* to this. And this is where theorists of the everyday differ from theorists like Peter Bürger. For the likes of Henri Lefebvre everyday life has to be attended to dialectically: it is the arena for both the extension of *instrumental reason* and the practical critique and evasion of that reason. Everyday life evidences creativity, a carnival spirit, and an inventive and stubborn refusal to be reduced to such means-end rationality. When Lefebvre echoes the credos of avant-gardism — "Let everyday life become a work of art!" (Lefebvre 1971: 204) — the *work* of art was to be found, not in the canon of art history (avant-garde or not) nor in new commodities masquerading as art, but *within* that daily life itself, within the possibilities of creative transformation to be found in the everyday.

Negotiating the conflict between recognising the poverty of everyday life (its dullness, its relentless alienation) and celebrating its actual and potential liberatory aspects becomes a central task for avant-gardism. How this gets played out in particular avant-garde formations has much to do with (national) cultural connotations surrounding the idea of *everyday life*. Cultural historians of Russian and Soviet life insist on the particularity of the Russian word for everyday life — *byt.* Meaning both the daily grind and the lack of any kind of transcendent value, *byt* was, for the avant-gardist, something that needed to be overcome. As far as this goes, Soviet avant-gardism of the twentieth-century must be seen as a continuation of cultural practices that characterise themselves by their distance from ordinary, everyday life. The various forms of romanticism operating across Europe in the nineteenth-century would provide the most vivid exemplification of this tendency. What sounds so familiar when Tatlin writes "Let Us Declare War on Chests of Drawers and Sideboards" is the denouncing of a form of living seen as middle-class, middle-brow and middle-aged (Matich 1996: 59–61). What is distinct, however, about the Soviet avant-garde is the denouncing of *byt*, not in the name of an elite, non-everyday culture, but in the name of *novyi byt* — a new everyday life. If, in the end, this functioned as a general purging of domestic bric-a-brac (animal figurines and such like) this should not stop us recognising the desire of elements within the Soviet avant-garde to revolutionise such daily activities as eating, reading and dreaming (Boym 1994: 29–40). If this desire was stymied in the increasingly bureaucratic society of post-revolutionary Russia, then this is not a failure of the avant-garde as such, but a failure of the revolution. *Novyi byt* was itself institutionalised, pointing, not simply to a transformation of daily life but a normalising of transformation. The job of transformation had become a new "daily grind" — or as Mayakovsky put it in his suicide note: "Love's boat has crashed on philistine reefs (*byt*)" (Elliott 1982: 90).

But if Russian *byt* should be understood as life rendered one-dimensional (and because of that fits most closely with Bürger's thesis),[1] for the French surrealists *la vie quotidienne* was marked by a more insistent ambiguity. On the one hand, everyday life is to be castigated for its relentless monotony and deathly tedium. For instance in *Nadja*, Breton envisages everyday life as the vortex that will obliterate the marvellous: "She was sucked back into the whirlwind of ordinary life continuing around her and eager to force her, among other concessions, to eat, to sleep" (Breton 1960: 114–5).[2] On the other hand it is precisely in the everyday that the marvellous is to be found. Such a contradiction should be seen as a feature of daily life itself, rather than the inconsistency of avant-gardist rhetoric, and it results in a project that is fundamentally precarious. If everyday life is both home to the marvellous and the negation of the marvellous then the job of avant-gardism is premised (in surrealism) on the recovery of an everyday (a marvellous everyday) that must be rescued from everyday life (the repressive everyday of modern bourgeois life). Louis Aragon in the preface to *Paris Peasant* (*Le Paysan de Paris*) represents the precariousness of this project:

> Each day the modern sense of existence becomes subtly altered. A mythology ravels and unravels. It is a knowledge, a science which begets itself and makes away with itself. I am already twenty-six years old, am I still privileged to take part in this miracle? How long shall I retain this sense of the marvellous suffusing everyday existence? I see it fade away in every man who advances into his own life as though along an always smoother road, who advances into the world's habits with an increasing ease, who rids himself progressively of the taste and texture of the unwonted, the unthought of. (Aragon 1987: 24)

Habit is both the deadly enemy of the marvellous and crucially, of course, the very cornerstone of daily life (its daily-ness). To find the marvellous in such unpromising territory requires an energy that already seems to be exhausting the twenty-six year old Aragon.

This precarious and ambiguous figuring of the everyday accords with Henri Lefebvre's much more explicit dialectical account of everyday life. For Lefebvre *everyday life* is a critical conceptualisation of modernity and as we have seen he conceives of the everyday as simultaneously colonised by capitalism while at the same time evidencing symptoms that critique such colonisation. Insistently, Lefebvre's project is an attempt to make sense of a present that is always mutating into something else. Theorising and critiquing *everyday life* becomes a lifelong task due to the continued transformation of social life. Here critique is always trying to catch up with actuality. Reading across Lefebvre's work, from the 1930s up to his death in 1991, allows us to recognise that the dialectical tensions in everyday life are uneven and unequally figured. In the immediate post war period (for instance) the tenacity of a festive everyday is struggling against the mystifications of capitalist relations. By the late 1960s everyday life was to be dominated by what Lefebvre called "the bureaucratic society of controlled consumption" (Lefebvre 1984) and the "terrorism" of commercial culture, with oppositional forms of daily life hidden by a general culture of individualism.[3] For the purposes of this essay the crucial aspect of all this is the stress on the historicity of the everyday. The modern everyday is always in a dialectical tension between the saturating effects of (state and entrepreneurial) capitalism and the residues and fragments of other forms of life. What changes, though, are the conditions under which these tensions are played out. In this way Lefebvre provides a more productive guide to avant-gardism (or those avant-gardes for whom everyday life is a central concern) than Bürger. It is Lefebvre who provides a theory of everyday life most closely aligned to the use of the term by avant-gardism and it is Lefebvre who allows us to insist on the historical particularity of both avant-gardism and everyday life. To see avant-gardism as positing a precarious and ambiguous relationship to everyday life is to see avant-gardism as deeply and awkwardly embroiled in particular historical and geographical junctures. It is also to insist on an account of avant-gardism that persistently clings to the contemporary context.

To recognise surrealist ambiguity as a response to dialectical tensions present in modern everyday life means reading Louis Aragon's struggle with the everyday as a personification of a greater struggle taking place within a social and historical moment. If Aragon struggles to rescue the marvellous from eradication this is because certain forms of everyday life were in the process of being obliterated. The first half of *Paris Peasant* provides a tour through the *Passage de L'Opéra*, stopping off at the hairdresser, the stamp dealer, as well as such avant-garde haunts as the *Bar Cetera* (the bar where various members of the dada group and surrealists would meet). Aragon wants his tour to be part of a "geography of pleasure", which would constitute an antidote to the habit and dull routines of everyday life: "proficiency in this subject [pleasure] would constitute an effective weapon against life's tediums" (Aragon 1987: 57). It is the *Passage de L'Opéra* that provides Aragon with marvellous pleasures, but these pleasures are themselves precarious. Between the writing (1924) and the publishing (1926) of *Paris Peasant*, the passage was destroyed: "sacrificed to the extension of the Boulevard Haussmann" (Geist 1985: 476). A section of Aragon's text includes newspaper cuttings and shopkeeper's notices telling of the struggle of the *Passage* against the corrupt forces of the Boulevard Haussmann Building Society, the town council, and the Galeries Lafayette (one of the largest department stores in Paris) (Aragon 1987: 39–45). Thus Aragon's text is poised to record a form of life on the brink of extinction as it's home is razed in the name of commercial culture.

Examples such as *Nadja* and *Paris Peasant* demonstrate a surrealism that fundamentally locates its project, not in a future revolution, nor in artistic invention, but in contemporary everyday life itself. Surrealism in these examples operates as a form of archaeology that struggles to uncover and preserve the "revolutionary energies" to be found in everyday life. If Bürger fails to adequately account for the particularity of the everyday for avant-gardism, he at least acknowledges its importance. But situating the everyday at the heart of avant-gardism shouldn't just provide a better understanding of the canon of historical avant-gardism it should also extend the kinds of formations that need to be included in a theorising of the avant-garde. An example of such a formation is the English movement Mass-Observation that, if mentioned at all, is usually relegated to the footnotes of histories of the avant-garde. Mass-Observation is an example of surrealism's insistence on contemporary everyday life, accompanied by a critique of the artistic avant-garde's surrendering of its mission (to uncover the marvellous *in* the everyday) in the name of the manufacture of artistic style.

The Project of Mass-Observation

The project of Mass-Observation is announced in two letters to *The New Statesman and Nation* (January 2 and January 30, 1937). The first letter is signed by the poet and journalist Charles Madge and claims that Mass-Observation (although not yet explicitly named) will be an "anthropology at home" that will "deal with elements so repressed that only what is admitted to be a first-class upheaval brings them to the surface" (Madge 1937: 12). The second letter has a much more manifesto-like quality and is jointly signed by Madge, the painter and filmmaker Humphrey Jennings and the itinerant anthropologist and ornithologist Tom Harrisson. Both letters invite people to participate in the project and within two months about 1,000 people are enlisted to contribute their observations to a Mass-Observation.

Both Madge and Jennings had significant roles in circulating surrealist ideas in England in the 1930s and in defending what they saw as the radical potential of surrealism. Humphrey Jennings' critical promotion of surrealism includes a warning that is surprisingly similar to Thomas Crow's position. In 1936 Jennings writes: "Our 'advanced' poster designers and 'emancipated' business men — what a gift surrealism is to them when it is presented in the auras of 'necessity', 'culture' and 'truth' with which Read and Sykes Davies invest it" (Jackson 1993: 220). Defending the project of surrealism against Herbert Read's understanding that it reveals "the universal truths of romanticism", Jennings insists that surrealism must not be thought of as a production within the institution of art: "to be *already* a 'painter', a 'writer', an 'artist', a 'surrealist', what a handicap" (Jackson 1993: 221). Insisting on the ordinariness of surrealism he writes: "'Coincidences' have the infinite freedom of appearing anywhere, anytime, to anyone: in broad daylight to those whom we most despise in places we have most loathed: not even to us at all: probably least to petty seekers after mystery and poetry on deserted sea-shores and in misty junk-shops" (Jackson 1993: 220). The everyday-ness of the surrealist project is insisted upon: it is in everyday life that the surreal exists, not in the practices of an increasingly professionalised surrealism.

Charles Madge also insists upon the everydayness of the surrealist project. Writing in 1934 Madge bemoans the aestheticising

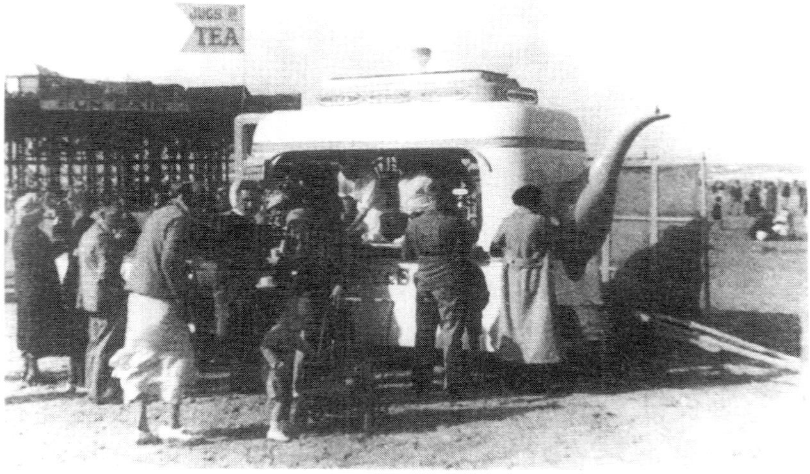

19 Julian Trevelyan: *Blackpool*. 1937

tendency evident in responses to surrealism and argues that this is caused by a failure to recognise the radical interdisciplinarity (or anti-disciplinarity) of the project. Quoting George Hugnet he insists that "surrealism is not a literary school" but "a laboratory of studies, of experimentation, that rejects all inclinations of individualism". He goes on to write, "this should act as a warning to readers who are too apt [...to] treat surrealist poetry separately from the other activities of the surrealist laboratory" (Madge 1934: 13).

That Madge and Jennings should hand in their "artistic license" and join up with an anthropologist to mobilise a vast group of people (sometimes as many as 3,000) to record their observations so as to produce a "weather-map of popular feeling" (Mass-Observation 1937: 30) should not be seen as a renunciation of avant-garde intentions. Rather it should be seen as the outcome of a practice that sees everyday life as central to the project of avant-gardism, and one that uses a dialectical understanding of everyday life to critique tendencies within the practice, circulation and promotion of surrealism. In their letter of January 30, 1937 and in their pamphlet published later that year, Madge, Jennings and Harrisson imagine a huge heuristic enterprise of "fact collecting". As an interdisciplinary enterprise: "Mass-Observation develops out of anthropology, psychology and the sciences which study man", but it also works to transform all disciplinary specialism: a disciplinary framework "will be developed, modified and supplemented until it becomes unrecognisable" (Mass-Observation 1937: 58). Mass-Observation corresponds with Bürger's thesis about the avant-garde's frustration with disciplinarity, though here Mass-Observation expand the critique of disciplinarity (or institutional autonomy) to cover all the fields of (specialised) intellectual work. So, on the one hand Mass-Observation imagines a multi-disciplinarity that will be transformed into an anti-disciplinarity. On the other it is everyday life itself that will provide not just the material conditions for such a transformation, but the very field of practice. Central to the project is the mass of observers: "the observation by everyone of everyone, including themselves" (Mass-Observation 1937: 10). And this is where Mass-Observation seems less like a vast positivist social science project, and more like a social movement dedicated to uncovering the surreal in the heart of the everyday and in the process transforming everyday life.

Observers were asked to describe their nightmares, to give account of their superstitions and the part coincidences play in their life. The second *New Statesman* letter provided a systematically unsystematic list of areas for observation:

> Behaviour of people at war memorials.
> Shouts and gestures of motorists.
> The aspidistra cult.
> Anthropology of football pools.
> Bathroom behaviour.
> Beards, armpits, eyebrows.
> Anti-Semitism.
> Distribution, diffusion and significance of the dirty joke.
> Funerals and undertakers.
> Female taboos about eating.
> The private lives of midwives (Harrisson, Jennings, Madge, 1937: 155).

While this could pass for a list of topics to be addressed by a series of Cultural Studies essays the intention was to trigger investigation of the unregistered aspects of social life.[4] The point of doing so is explained in the letter:

> It [Mass-Observation] does not set out in quest of truth or facts for their own sake, or for the sake of an intellectual minority, but aims at exposing them in simple terms to all observers, so that their environment may be understood, and thus constantly transformed. (Harrisson, Jennings, Madge, 1937: 155)

This attempt to constantly transform the everyday is not understandable within the terms of Bürger's thesis: this is not the revolutionary overthrowing of ordinary life that was imagined by the architects of *novyi byt*. What is being imagined are a number of changes in relation to consciousness, knowledge and the materiality of the social.

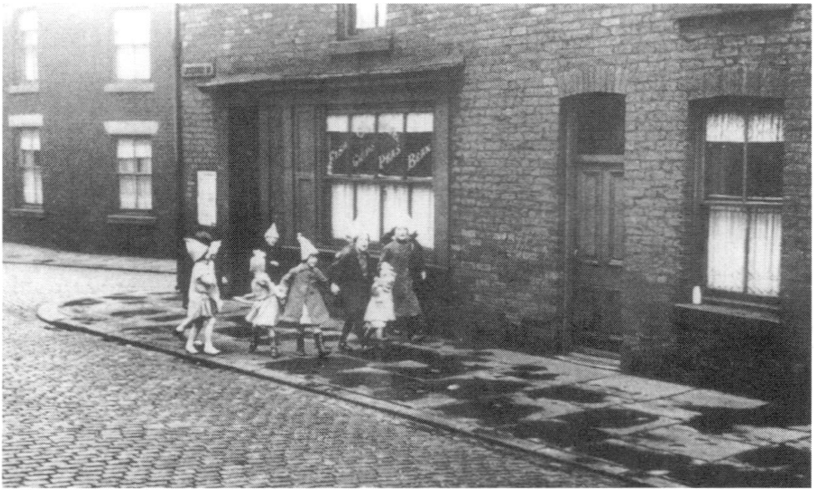

20 Humphrey Spender: *Children in Paper Hats, Bolton*. 1937

By privileging the mundane and ordinary, Mass-Observation suggested a different form of attention for both looking at everyday life and taking part in it. This desire to attend to those aspects of everyday life that are either taken for granted or fall below the horizon of visibility is an act of transformation in itself (to register the unregistered cannot help but transform it). The idea of a Mass-Observation had the potential to alter the conditions under which knowledge was produced. It could effect a radical alternative to the authority of the specialist. In anthropological terms it transformed native informants (potentially everyone) into participant observers (everyone could become their own ethnographer). It is this aspect of Mass-Observation that produces a surrealism both *of* the everyday and *in* the everyday. Here the ordinary, the trivial, that which falls below the horizon of visibility is rescued and given significance. Here too was the possibility of a very ordinary transformation of daily life: by scrutinising the mundane, the mundane takes on a new significance. A "housewife" writes:

> I read in *News Chronicle* articles about the work [of Mass-Observation], and especially the account by an ordinary housewife of her day. Mass-Observation, it was something new, something to talk about; the things I do in the house are monotonous, but on the 12th [the day when observers on the national panel recorded their whole day], they are different somehow, letting the dog out, getting up, making the dinner, it makes them important when they have to be remembered and recorded. (Mass-Observation 1938: 70)

What is significantly different between the practice of Mass-Observation and the work of someone like Louis Aragon is this attempt both to mobilise a body of people in the name of the everyday, and also to generate a culture that can (potentially at least) generate the marvellous in everyday life (rather than memorialise its passing).

The historicity of this moment of avant-gardism is complex. I have been arguing that the privileging of the everyday by avant-garde formations evidences complex and awkward negotiations of particular moments of modernity. I have also been arguing that the precarious and ambiguous figuring of the everyday in avant-gardism is intricately related to an actual everyday that is also precarious and ambiguous (and therefore needs to be understood dialectically). For Mass-Observation two cultural contexts need to be emphasised: the increasing penetration of everyday life by mass-media forms (particularly newspapers and radio) and the example of National Socialist mobilisation of the everyday (through youth movements, ritual, etc.) in Germany. There is not the space here to give the kind of detailed accounts that these contexts require, but it is possible to recognise the ambiguity that is produced in the face of them. For example, mass-media forms saturate daily life (and exemplify a modern sense of daily-ness, for instance the *daily* news) at the same time as continually representing the supposed views of the ordinary person ("the man in the street"). Yet, for Mass-Observation, an enormous gulf separates such representation from the experiences and understanding of the world in everyday life. In various Mass-Observation publications newspaper by-lines are continually juxtaposed with recordings of ordinary people on the same topics. These exhibit a range of responses, from indifference to outrage, and yet rarely seem to correspond to mass-media representation. Here Mass-Observation positions the everyday as an alternative but hidden actuality to that which the mass-media make visible. Everyday life, for Mass-Observation, evidences a whole range of actualities, not the least of which is an incessant creativity in the face of the colonising effects of mass-media forms. Yet the everyday is figured ambiguously and the effects of the mass-media and other forms of cultural domination result in "millions of people who passed their lives as the obedient automata of a system" (Mass-Observation 1937: 9). In the end Mass-Observation are contradictorily dedicated to recovering an everyday that is not only hidden but for the most part dormant: "[Mass-Observation] will counteract the tendency so universal in modern life to perform all our actions through sheer habit, with as little consciousness of our surroundings as though we were walking in our sleep" (Mass-Observation 1937: 29).

Mass-Observation articulates the general precariousness and ambiguity of avant-gardism in relation to the everyday. Its subsequent history would need to be understood partly in relation to these characteristics and partly in relation to a range of historical contingencies. Within three years of emerging, Mass-Observation had become part of the "war effort" attached to the Home Intelligence department of the Ministry of Information (which lead to the resignation of Charles Madge — Humphrey Jennings having already left over differences with Tom Harrisson). After the war Mass-Observation becomes Mass-Observation Ltd., one of the first market research companies to operate anywhere in the world. From a practical surrealism of the everyday, Mass-Observation becomes an uncomfortable arm of government and a willing accomplice in the project of colonising daily life by commodities. But to see this history as a necessary outcome of avant-gardism in the way that Bürger's historiography might suggest would be as blind as not recognising the precariousness of the project in the first place.

Conclusion

Writing 20 years ago and with Bürger very much in mind, the critic Andreas Huyssen wrote that "Today the best hopes of the historical avant-garde may not be embodied in art works at all, but in decentred movements which work towards the transformation of everyday life" (Huyssen 1986: 15). No doubt he had in mind such "decentred movements" as feminism with its desire to see the political in the private, or new social movements centred around identities. Huyssen's willingness to consider non-art projects as avant-garde demonstrates an understanding of the potential of Bürger's work for much more than a description of an already constituted object: the artistic avant-garde. But this is an understanding that is neither shared by Bürger nor by the majority of his critics. The complaint that Bürger's thesis is not adequate for attending to avant-gardism is continually premised on an understanding that avant-gardism exists as an already established set of practices and practitioners. In opting for a "restricted economy" of avant-gardism (the *account* is restricted to the institution of art) Bürger's work is open to the critiques mounted against him. However, a theory of avant-gardism that would take the everyday as the central arena for the imagined sublation of all specialised activity (art, philosophy, politics, etc.) in the name of a dialectically understood everyday life would provide a starting point for a "general economy" of avant-gardism. For this Bürger's thesis would need to be substantially re-worked. It would need, for instance, to historicise the general conditions of specialisation across social life and not limit this to an account of art. It would also need to provide a fully dialectical account of everyday life, and for this I would argue that Henri Lefebvre's work could not be ignored.

It may be that aspects of so-called neo-avant-gardism would provide fruitful material for developing this general economy of avant-gardism. For instance the ethnographic aspect of Warhol's early Factory years (the first films, the book *A: A Novel*, etc.) or the ethnographic work of people like Krzysztof Wodiczko and Martha Rosler. It may be that, as Huyssen suggests, it would be new social movements that exhibit the most productive aspects of avant-gardism. A comparative study of sub-culture theory and theories of avant-gardism would, I think, also be useful, especially given the overlap between the two.[5] Clearly there is a huge amount of material that could provide the basis for producing a general economy of avant-gardism. Were a general economy of avant-gardism to be developed, I like to think that Mass-Observation would be a productively "awkward moment" in its history.

Notes

[1] A study of the Proletkult movement would show a different figuring of everyday life in relation to social revolution. The question of how Proletkult stands in relation to avant-gardism would be pertinent to further discussion of Bürger's thesis.

[2] The gendering of everyday life is crucial here. For Breton, Nadja in her "mad" state represents the marvellous in the everyday, and yet Nadja in her "domestic" state represents the crushing weight of tedium in everyday life. Both the mad and the domestic are figured as feminine, but both relate to different (though related) femininities.

[3] It is worth noting that the phrase "the bureaucratic society of controlled consumption" seems as adequate a description of the situation in socialist countries as it does in and non-socialist ones in the post war era. It is also worth noting that Lefebvre was expelled from the French Communist Party (*Parti Communiste Français*) in 1957.

[4] While the intellectual roots of Cultural Studies is continually open to question, the Australian writer Meaghan Morris is one of a growing minority to claim a heritage for Cultural Studies in "the Western European surrealist tradition of analysing everyday life" (Morris 1997: 40).

[5] For instance in Dick Hedbige's classic study of subculture (Hebdige 1979) the terms and analogies used to describe aspects of a subculture are taken from artistic avant-gardism (especially dada and surrealism). On the other hand historians of avant-gardism including Thomas Crow have used the study of subcultures to account for avant-garde formations (Crow 1996:19-21).

Bibliography

Aragon, Louis
1987 *Paris Peasant*. London: Picador.

Breton, André
1960 *Nadja*. New York: Grove Press.

Boym, Svetlana
1994 *Common Places: Mythologies of Everyday Life in Russia*. Cambridge, Mass.: Harvard University Press.

Buchloh, Benjamin
1984 "Theorizing the Avant-Garde". *Art in America*, 19-21.

Bürger, Peter
1984 *Theory of the Avant-Garde*. Manchester: Manchester University Press.

Bürger, Peter, and Christa Bürger
1992 *The Institutions of Art*. Lincoln: University of Nebraska Press.

Crow, Thomas
1996 "Modernism and Mass Culture in the Visual Arts". In: *Modern Art in the Common Culture*. New Haven and London: Yale University Press.

Foster, Hal
1996 *The Return of the Real*. Cambridge, Mass.: MIT Press.

Geist, Johann Friedrich
1985 *Arcades: The History of a Building Type*. Cambridge, Mass.: MIT Press.

Harrisson, Tom, Humphrey Jennings and Charles Madge
1937 "Anthropology at Home". In: *The New Statesman and Nation*, 155.

Hebdige, Dick
1979 *Subculture: The Meaning of Style*. London: Methuen, 1979.

Huyssen, Andreas
1986 *After the Great Divide: Modernism, Mass Culture and Postmodernism*. Basingstoke: Macmillan.

Jackson, Kevin, ed.
1993 *The Humphrey Jennings Film Reader.* Manchester: Carcanet Press.

Lefebvre, Henri
1971 *Everyday Life in the Modern World.* New Brunswick: Transaction Publishers.

1988 "Towards a Leftist Cultural Politics: Remarks Occasioned by the Centenary of Marx's Death". In: Cary Nelson and Lawrence Grossberg (eds), *Marxism and the Interpretation of Culture.* Urbana: University of Illinois Press, 75-88.

1991 *Critique of Everyday Life. Volume One: Introduction.* London: Verso.

Madge, Charles
1934 "The Meaning of Surrealism". *New Verse*, 10, 13-15.

1937 "Anthropology at Home". In: *The New Statesman and Nation*, 12.

Mass-Observation
1937 *Mass-Observation.* London: Fredrick Muller.

1938 *First Year's Work 1937-38.* London: Lindsay Drummond.

Matich, Olga
1996 "Remaking the Bed: Utopia in Daily Life". In: John E. Bowlt and Olga Matich (eds), *Laboratory of Dreams: The Russian Avant-Garde and Cultural Experiment.* Stanford: Stanford University Press, 59-78.

Morris, Meaghan
1997 "A Question of Cultural Studies". In: Angela McRobbie (ed.), *Back to Reality? Social Experience and Cultural Studies.* Manchester: Manchester University Press, 36-57.

Nochlin, Linda
1991 *The Politics of Vision: Essays on Nineteenth-Century Art and Society.* London: Thames and Hudson.

List of Illustrations

Abstracts

I

On Photography and Painting. Prolegomena to a New Theory of the Avant-Garde.

Dietrich Scheunemann

This essay aims to establish a new theoretical approach to the avant-garde, to the wealth of its innovations and the diversity of its manifestations. The underlying assumption of the essay is that not one unified intention, i.e. the intention of reintegrating art into the practice of life (Bürger), but a common challenge caused the avant-gardist storm in the arts world, the challenge which the new technical media, in particular photography and film, posed to traditional art forms and the traditional understanding of art. The wealth and diversity of new art forms and new artistic techniques which the avant-garde created, including cubist collage and dadaist photomontage, Duchamp's ready-mades and Tzara's and Breton's poems composed out of newspaper snippets, represent nothing other than the range of responses to this challenge and various modes of reflecting upon the place which artistic production can hold in an age in which industrialisation and technological processes rapidly gain ground in all other realms of life.

Dada and the Constitution of Culture: (Re-) Conceptualising the Avant-Garde

Stephen C. Foster

The avant-garde is badly over-realised as a counter-culture reality and equally under-realised as an institutionally based majority culture concept. The avant-garde typically spoke for majority culture and, with few exceptions, served and applied its process of culture making. These exceptions, embodied best in the implications of Berlin Dada, tried to intercept culture at the horizon of its "defining technologies", that is, intercept culture at the point of the avant-garde's creation by larger culture. The essay concentrates on the conflict between the culturally "appointed" avant-garde (the property of majority culture) and certain individuals' attempts to achieve, in operational fact, what was implied in larger culture's "reigning" concept of the avant-garde. The authentic avant-garde aspired precisely to the *defining technologies*, and not the *application technologies*, possessed by the majority culture.

Crucial Moments, Crucial Points: Walter Benjamin and the Recognition of Modernity in the Light of the Avant-Garde

Bernd Kiefer

In his *Theory of the Avant-Garde* Peter Bürger presents Walter Benjamin as a prominent theorist of the avant-garde. He discusses Benjamin's notions of the vanishing of the „aura“ of art through the advances of technological reproduction, the new foundation of art in politics, and his theory of allegory as a theory of the avant-garde work of art. However, for Benjamin the avant-garde, especially surrealism, was important for different reasons. For him the avant-garde movements not only explored new ways of expanding the bounderies of art, but also new ways of living in modern times. They investigated the bursting of the old life structures, the confrontation of the human body and technology and the possibility of a new kind of humanism in a world without centre. Benjamin's *opus magnum*, the *Arcades Project*, is his attempt to give this experience of modernity a form.

II.

Apollinaire and Cubist Innovation. Resetting the Frontiers, Changing the Paradigm

Ian Revie

"Apollinaire and Cubist Innovation" sets out to show how the early invention of certain motifs in the poetry of Apollinaire were central to the connections made between his verse and developments in the work of Picasso and other key painters of the avant-garde. It takes issue therefore with the starting point set by Bürger for the avant-garde and extends this argument by pointing up the problems which occur if the term is mapped onto those which have become the common currency of contemporary discourse — modernism and postmodernism — in order to re-emphasise the primacy of the avant-garde.

Cubist Painting, Automatic Writing and the Poetry of Gertrude Stein

Dietrich Scheunemann

This essay investigates the impact which both cubist painting and psycho-technical experiments in *automatic writing* exerted on the literary style of Gertrude Stein. The essay identifies the exploration of the aesthetic properties of the artistic material as the productive basis on which these influences converge. It emphasises the role of *sound* in Stein's poetic workshop and situates this particular focus within the development of avant-gardist literary style as well as the history of media.

Screeching Voices: Avant-Garde Manifestos in the Cabaret

Martin Puchner

This paper argues that the avant-garde manifesto must be analysed in terms of its theatricality. Born from the shouting matches of avant-garde cabarets and infused with a long history of expressing political dissent, the manifesto is a novel form of speech characterised by ostentatious posing, exaggerated declarations, and an aggressive tone. The manifesto proved to be more effective than even the most outrageous artworks in demonstrating and enacting the avant-garde's challenge to the status quo and its break with the autonomous sphere of art. For this reason, it became the avant-garde's primary form of expression, transforming the other art genres into what one could call manifesto art.

Painterly Concepts and Filmic Objects: The Interaction of Expression and Reproduction in Early Avant-Garde Film.

David Macrae

The aim of this paper is to analyse the phenomenon of early avant-garde film, and to consider the issues it raises in the particular areas which Peter Bürger has referred to as “the negation of the autonomy of art” and the problematic of the categorisation of avant-gardist *works*. The focus of this methodology will be upon the concept of the constructive interactions between expression and reproduction as factors which reveal crucial evidence about the perceptual effects of early avant-garde artistic processes of creation and reception.

The World “Outside of Fiction”: Georges Bataille and Surrealist Sculpture

Mara de Gennaro

This article discusses Georges Bataille’s concepts of “base matter” and “the primitive” and the impact that these concepts had on visual artists associated in varying degrees with surrealism. Artists considered include Giacometti, Ubac, Brassaï, and Blossfeldt. The ethnographic and modernist aspects of Bataille, often downplayed in current poststructuralist interpretations of his work in the late 1920s and ‘30s, constitute the principal focus of this essay.

Inside Out: Pavel Filonov and the Anatomy of Fantasy.

John E. Bowlt

The focus of this article is on the relationship of the art of Pavel Nikolaevich Filonov (1883-1941) to the canons of anatomical drawing as taught in the St. Petersburg Academy of Fine Arts and other professional schools. An impeccable draftsman, Filonov placed the traditions of the anatomical class at the basis of his system of *Universal Flowering* and *Analytical Art* whereby the artist painted or drew creatures, plants and things from many viewpoints and perspectives to produce a world in which interior structures intertwined and interfused within a single, integrated organism. Filonov's exposure to ethnographical painting, anthropological collections, and the carnage of the First World War reinforced his strong interest in anatomy, somatic structure, and the continuous cycle of life and death.

Difficiles Nuage: Gertrude Stein, OuLiPo and the Grammar of the Avant-Garde

Edward Linz

In this essay I focus on the French neo-avant-garde movement OuLiPo to critique Peter Bürger's dismissal of the neo-avant-garde as "inauthentic". Taking Bürger's category of the "Rezeptcharakter" of avant-garde art as a starting point, I argue that the neo-avant-garde completes the unfinished project of negating the autonomy of the work of art by giving control to the artistic recipient as producer of the artwork itself. The main argument focuses on how OuLiPo member Jacques Roubaud takes Gertrude Stein's use of grammatical constraint to explore the potential of grammar to unite aesthetic producer and recipient.

III.

The Selection of Avant-Garde Poetry for Anthologies

Klaus Beekman

Research into avant-garde literature usually takes place within the same paradigm, i.e. from the structural to the ideological approach of, for example, Peter Bürger. Research within this paradigm is primarily interested in image-building by assigning properties and qualities to the literature discussed.

The institutional approach, on the other hand, does not use a conception of literature to build an image of literature, but examines the conceptions of literature employed in various approaches to literature. This type of research permits the function of institutions in the literary field to be clarified. Literary criticism is one of these institutions, anthologies another.

Editors of anthologies use a specific conception of literature when collecting and selecting texts. Such a selection always involves strategic decisions, based on a personal conception of literature as well as contextual factors. I will explore these aspects in a discussion of Dutch anthologies of expressionist poetry.

Avant-garde Productions and Psychoanalytic Theory. The Story of an Encounter.

Katherine Swarbrick

This contribution highlights historical and conceptual links between the phenomenon of the avant-garde and psychoanalysis. It explores selected techniques in avant-garde art by using the psychoanalytic theory of the drive. Its objective is a reassessment of Peter Bürger's interpretation of the avant-garde's relation to art and life, and a demonstration of the significant implications which a psychoanalytic perspective holds for ongoing debates in the field of avant-garde studies.

Awkward Moments: Avant-Gardism and the Dialectics of Everyday Life

Ben Highmore

Responses to Bürger's thesis that the avant-garde aims "to reconnect art and life" have been dominated by critical attention to the field and category *art*. In this contribution it is *life* — *everyday life* in particular — that is privileged. From this perspective Bürger's thesis is both too limited in its scope — attempts to overcome 'autonomy' are evident in other fields besides art — and too inattentive to the ambiguous figuring of *everyday life* in avant-garde culture. Mass-observation provides a useful context for rethinking avant-gardism. Emerging out of the practices of anthropology and surrealism it established an ethnographic approach to *everyday life* that had the dual purpose of registering and transforming the everyday.

Filonov's exposure to ethnographical painting, anthropological collections, and the carnage of the First World War reinforced his strong interest in anatomy, somatic structure, and the continuous cycle of life and death.

Difficiles Nuage: Gertrude Stein, OuLiPo and the Grammar of the Avant-Garde

Edward Linz

In this essay I focus on the French neo-avant-garde movement OuLiPo to critique Peter Bürger's dismissal of the neo-avant-garde as "inauthentic". Taking Bürger's category of the "Rezeptcharakter" of avant-garde art as a starting point, I argue that the neo-avant-garde completes the unfinished project of negating the autonomy of the work of art by giving control to the artistic recipient as producer of the artwork itself. The main argument focuses on how OuLiPo member Jacques Roubaud takes Gertrude Stein's use of grammatical constraint to explore the potential of grammar to unite aesthetic producer and recipient.

III.

The Selection of Avant-Garde Poetry for Anthologies

Klaus Beekman

Research into avant-garde literature usually takes place within the same paradigm, i.e. from the structural to the ideological approach of, for example, Peter Bürger. Research within this paradigm is primarily interested in image-building by assigning properties and qualities to the literature discussed.

The institutional approach, on the other hand, does not use a conception of literature to build an image of literature, but examines the conceptions of literature employed in various approaches to literature. This type of research permits the function of institutions in the literary field to be clarified. Literary criticism is one of these institutions, anthologies another.

Editors of anthologies use a specific conception of literature when collecting and selecting texts. Such a selection always involves strategic decisions, based on a personal conception of literature as well as contextual factors. I will explore these aspects in a discussion of Dutch anthologies of expressionist poetry.

Avant-garde Productions and Psychoanalytic Theory. The Story of an Encounter.

Katherine Swarbrick

This contribution highlights historical and conceptual links between the phenomenon of the avant-garde and psychoanalysis. It explores selected techniques in avant-garde art by using the psychoanalytic theory of the drive. Its objective is a reassessment of Peter Bürger's interpretation of the avant-garde's relation to art and life, and a demonstration of the significant implications which a psychoanalytic perspective holds for ongoing debates in the field of avant-garde studies.

Awkward Moments: Avant-Gardism and the Dialectics of Everyday Life

Ben Highmore

Responses to Bürger's thesis that the avant-garde aims "to reconnect art and life" have been dominated by critical attention to the field and category *art*. In this contribution it is *life* — *everyday life* in particular — that is privileged. From this perspective Bürger's thesis is both too limited in its scope — attempts to overcome 'autonomy' are evident in other fields besides art — and too inattentive to the ambiguous figuring of *everyday life* in avant-garde culture. Mass-observation provides a useful context for rethinking avant-gardism. Emerging out of the practices of anthropology and surrealism it established an ethnographic approach to *everyday life* that had the dual purpose of registering and transforming the everyday.